CHILDREN'S ISSUES, LAWS AND PROGRAMS

CHILDREN AND YOUTH TRANSITIONS FROM FOSTER CARE

CHILDREN'S ISSUES, LAWS AND PROGRAMS

Additional books in this series can be found on Nova's website under the Series tab.

Additional E-books in this series can be found on Nova's website under the E-books tab.

SOCIAL ISSUES, JUSTICE AND STATUS

Additional books in this series can be found on Nova's website under the Series tab.

Additional E-books in this series can be found on Nova's website under the E-books tab.

CHILDREN'S ISSUES, LAWS AND PROGRAMS

CHILDREN AND YOUTH TRANSITIONS FROM FOSTER CARE

JOSEPH A. FERRARI
EDITOR

Nova Science Publishers, Inc.
New York

For permission to use material from this book please contact us:
Telephone 631-231-7269; Fax 631-231-8175
Web Site: http://www.novapublishers.com

LIBRARY OF CONGRESS CATALOGING-IN-PUBLICATION DATA

Children and youth transitions from foster care / editor, Joseph A. Ferrari.
p. cm.
Includes index.
ISBN 978-1-61209-705-3 (hbk.)
1. Ex-foster children--United States. 2. Foster home care--United States.
3. Youth--United States--Social conditions. I. Ferrari, Joseph A.
HV863.C45 2011
362.73'30973--dc22

2011001306

Published by Nova Science Publishers, Inc. † New York

CONTENTS

PREFACE

This new book provides an overview of the federal foster care system and provisions in federal foster care law that are intended to help prepare youth for adulthood.

Chapter 1- While most young people have access to emotional and financial support systems throughout their early adult years, older youth in foster care and those who are emancipated from care often face obstacles to developing independent living skills and building supports that ease the transition to adulthood. Older foster youth who return to their parents or guardians may continue to experience poor family dynamics or a lack of emotional and financial supports, and studies have shown that recently emancipated foster youth fare poorly relative to their counterparts in the general population on several outcome measures.

Chapter 2- Recent research has demonstrated that compared to their peers, current and former foster youth are more likely to experience negative outcomes in adulthood. This research, along with the efforts of policymakers and child welfare advocates, has brought greater attention to the challenges facing youth transitioning from foster care. In response, Congress has sought to improve existing services and provide additional supports for this population. Most recently, the 110th Congress passed, and President George W. Bush enacted, the Fostering Connections to Success and Increasing Adoptions Act of 2008 (P.L. 110-351), which is arguably one of the most significant laws passed in recent history that expands services and supports for older youth in care. This reports presents issues around implementation of P.L. 110-351. It also describes other issues affecting older youth as they transition from foster care into adulthood.

Chapter 3- While most young people have access to financial and emotional support systems throughout their early adult years, former foster care youth often lack assistance in developing independent living skills to ease the transition to adulthood. Recognizing the difficulties faced by older youth exiting foster care, Congress passed the Chafee Foster Care Independence Act (P.L. 106-169) to expand the population of youth eligible to receive independent living services and to give states greater flexibility in designing their independent living programs. Under P.L. 106-169, Congress doubled the mandatory funding available to states for independent living services from $70 million to $140 million. In 2002, Congress passed legislation (P.L. 107-133) to authorize discretionary funding to eligible current and former foster care youth for education and training vouchers worth up to $5,000 annually per youth. The Chafee Foster Care Independence Program (CFCIP) and voucher component are administered by the U.S. Department of Health and Human Services (HHS). Seven pending bills (H.R. 2188, H.R. 3409, H.R. 4208, H.R. 4133, S. 1512, and S. 1956/H.R. 4688) propose to amend the program. This report briefly describes the CFCIP and will be updated.

Chapter 4- A youth's departure from home marks the beginning of adulthood and a new stage in a young adult's life. This critical juncture and the surrounding years, often referred to as the transition to adulthood, is increasingly recognized as a distinct developmental stage between adolescence and adulthood. Youth who reach this stage and are living in foster care are often at a significant disadvantage. In 2005, over 24,000 youths found themselves in this circumstance. They "aged out" of the foster care system and entered into the world of adulthood relatively alone.

Chapter 5- The Fostering Connections to Success and Increasing Adoptions Act of 2008 (H.R. 6893) is an omnibus child welfare bill designed to ensure greater permanence and improve the well-being of children served by public child welfare agencies. The legislation received strong support in Congress and, beyond revising and extending the Adoption Incentives program, responds to a range of issues and concerns that have been raised (some for more than a decade) by public child welfare administrators; youth, adoption, tribal, and child welfare advocates; and by children and youth who have been (or still are) in foster care. The bill passed the House of Representatives, by voice vote (under suspension of the rules), on September 17, 2008, and the Senate, by unanimous consent, on September 22, 2008. It was signed into law by the President on October 7, 2008 (P.L. 110-351).

In: Children and Youth Transitions from Foster Care
Editor: Joseph A. Ferrari
ISBN: 978-1-61209-705-3

Chapter 1

YOUTH TRANSITIONING FROM FOSTER CARE: BACKGROUND AND FEDERAL PROGRAMS

Adrienne L. Fernandes-Alcantara

SUMMARY

While most young people have access to emotional and financial support systems throughout their early adult years, older youth in foster care and those who are emancipated from care often face obstacles to developing independent living skills and building supports that ease the transition to adulthood. Older foster youth who return to their parents or guardians may continue to experience poor family dynamics or a lack of emotional and financial supports, and studies have shown that recently emancipated foster youth fare poorly relative to their counterparts in the general population on several outcome measures.

Recognizing the difficulties faced by older youth in care and youth emancipating from foster care, Congress created a new Independent Living initiative (P.L. 99-272) in 1986 to assist certain older foster youth as they enter adulthood. The legislation authorized mandatory funding to states under a new Section 477 of the Social Security Act. In 1999, P.L. 106-169 rewrote Section 477 to create the John H. Chafee Foster Care Independence Program (CFCIP) and doubled the total annual funds available to states from $70 million to $140 million. The law also expanded the population of youth eligible to receive independent living services—with no lower age limit—and gave states greater flexibility in designing independent living programs. Independent living services can refer to assistance in obtaining a high school diploma and training in daily living skills, among other services.

The CFCIP has been amended three times. In 2002, the Promoting Safe and Stable Amendments of 2001 (P.L. 107-133) authorized discretionary funding for states to provide education and training vouchers (ETV) to youth who age out of foster care and youth adopted from care at age 16 or older. For FY2010, Congress appropriated $45.4 million to the ETV program. The CFCIP was amended again in 2008 by the Fostering Connections to Success and Increasing Adoptions Act of 2008 (P.L. 110-351). The act expanded eligibility for the program by adding as an additional program purpose that youth who are in foster care on their

16th birthday but who subsequently leave care for adoption or kinship guardianship are eligible for CFCIP service. The law also extended the ETV program to youth who leave care at age 16 or older for kinship guardianship; made tribal entities eligible to apply directly for CFCIP and ETV funds directly from the federal government; and authorized additional supports and services outside of the CFCIP to older youth in care, including providing states the option, beginning in FY2011, to extend Title IV-E foster care to youth ages 18 to 21. In 2010, the program was amended for a third time by the Patient Protection and Affordable Care Act (P.L. 111-148, PPACA), which requires states to educate youth aging out about the importance of a health care power of attorney.

Along with the CFCIP, federal child welfare law and other federal programs are intended to help older foster youth and recent alumni make the transition to adulthood. The Title IV-E foster care program has protections in place to ensure that older youth in care have a written case plan that addresses the programs and services that will assist in this transition. Further the law that established the CFCIP created a new optional Medicaid eligibility pathway for "independent foster care adolescents;" this pathway is often called the "Chafee option." Beginning in 2014, eligible young people who emancipate from foster care will be covered under a mandatory Medicaid pathway until age 26, as required under PPACA. Federal law also authorizes funding for states to provide other types of assistance. Most recently, the Higher Education Opportunity (P.L. 110-315), signed into law on August 14, 2008, amended the Higher Education Act to authorize services specifically for youth in foster care or recently emancipated youth, including education and housing services. This report will be updated as warranted.

A significant number of youth spend at least some time in foster care during their teenage years. On the last day of FY2008, approximately 157,000 youth ages 13 through 17 comprised more than one-third of the foster care caseload nationally.[1] Most teenagers left foster care and were reunified with their parents or primary caretakers, adopted, or placed with relatives. However, 29,516 youth aged out, or were emancipated, when they reached the age of majority in their states, usually at age 18.[2] This figure has increased in recent years, from about 26,500 in FY2006 and 24,500 in FY2005.[3]

Youth who spend their teenage years in foster care and those who are likely to age out of care face challenges as they move to early adulthood. While in care, they may forego opportunities to develop strong support networks and independent living skills that their counterparts in the general population might more naturally acquire. Even older foster youth who return to their parents or guardians can still face obstacles, such as poor family dynamics or a lack of emotional and financial supports, that hinder their ability to achieve their goals as young adults. Perhaps the strongest evidence that youth who have spent at least some years in care during adolescence have not adequately made the transition to young adulthood is their poor outcomes across a number of domains. During their early adult years, these youth are much more likely than their peers to forego higher education, describe their general health as fair or poor, become homeless, and rely on public supports.

The federal government has recognized that older youth in care and those aging out are vulnerable to negative outcomes and may ultimately return to the care of the state as adults, either through the public welfare, criminal justice, or other support systems. In 1986, Congress passed legislation to assist certain older youth in care under a new Independent Living program, enacted as part of P.L. 99-272. The legislation authorized mandatory funding to states under Section 477 of the Social Security Act and was made permanent in 1993 as part of P.L. 103-66. In 1999, the Foster Care Independence Act (P.L. 106-169) rewrote Section 477 to create the permanently authorized John H. Chafee Foster Care Independence Program (CFCIP) and doubled the annual funds available to states from $70 million to $140 million. The law also expanded the population of youth eligible to receive independent living services, including youth who have left care through age 21, and gave states greater flexibility in designing independent living programs.

Independent living programs are intended to assist youth prepare for adulthood, and may include assistance in obtaining a high school diploma, career exploration, training in daily living skills, training in budgeting and financial management skills, and preventive health activities, among other services. Further, the act required states to provide services to tribal youth on the same basis as other youth in the state. The act also encouraged youth in foster care to participate directly in designing their own activities that prepare them for independent living and further stated that youth "accept personal responsibility for living up to their part of the program." Other related provisions in P.L. 106-169 enable states to use up to 30% of their CFCIP funds for housing on current and former foster youth ages 18 to 21, and to extend health care to these youth through a new Medicaid pathway known as the "Chafee option."

The CFCIP has been amended three times. In FY2002, the Safe and Stable Families Amendments of 2001 (P.L. 107-133) authorized discretionary funding to states to provide vouchers for eligible youth through a new Education and Training Voucher (ETV) program. Youth were made eligible for the vouchers if they age out of foster care or are adopted from care at age 16 or older (up to age 21 or age 23, depending on when they received the voucher). For FY2010, Congress appropriated $45.4 million to the ETV program. The CFCIP was amended a second time in 2008 by the Fostering Connections to Success and Increasing Adoptions Act of 2008 (P.L. 110-351, Fostering Connections).[4] The act expanded eligibility for the CFCIP by adding as an additional program purpose that youth who are in foster care on their 16th birthday but who subsequently leave care for adoption or kinship guardianship are eligible for CFCIP service. The law also extended the ETV program to youth who leave care at age 16 or older for kinship guardianship, and made tribal entities eligible to apply directly for CFCIP and ETV funds directly from the federal government. Finally, the CFCIF was amended in 2010 by the Patient Protection and Affordable Care Act (P.L. 111-148, PPACA), the health care reform law, to require states to ensure that eligible youth are educated about the importance of designating an individual to make health care treatment decisions for them.

Along with the CFCIP, federal child welfare law and other federal programs are intended to help current and former youth in foster care make the transition to adulthood. The federal foster care program has protections in place to ensure that older youth in care have a written case plan that addresses the programs and services they need in making the transition. Further, federal law authorizes funding for states and local jurisdictions to provide workforce support and housing to older foster youth and youth emancipating from care. P.L. 110-351 and P.L. 111-148 authorized additional supports and services to older youth in care outside of the CFCIP. P.L. 110-351 provides states the option, beginning in FY2011, to extend Title IV-E foster care to youth ages 18 to 21. P.L. 111-148 requires states, as of January 2014, to provide Medicaid coverage to eligible young people who age out of foster care.

This report begins with a discussion of the characteristics of youth who have had contact with the child welfare system, including those who entered care, as well as those who exited care via emancipation. The report then provides an overview of the federal foster care system, including the Chafee Foster Care Independence program, and provisions in federal foster care law that are intended to help prepare youth for adulthood. The report goes on to discuss other federal support—through other programs—for youth aging out of care in the areas of education, health care, employment, and housing. The report seeks to understand how states vary in their approaches to serving older youth in care and those who are recently emancipated. A small number of states are known to extend foster care to youth ages 18 to 21 (and beyond in some cases) and less than half of states provide Medicaid coverage to former foster youth beyond age 18 through the Chafee pathway option. The report also intends to demonstrate that, despite negative outcomes for the group on average, many former foster youth are engaged in decisions about the services they receive and they display resiliency.

Appendix A provides a summary of outcome statistics for youth who were in foster care, compared to youth in the general population; and Appendix B provides funding tables for the Chafee Foster Care Independence program, including information about funds returned to the Federal Treasury.

WHO ARE OLDER YOUTH IN FOSTER CARE AND YOUTH AGING OUT OF CARE?

Children and adolescents age 17 and younger can enter state child welfare systems due to abuse, neglect, or for some other reason, such as the death of a parent or child behavioral problems. Some children remain in their own homes and receive family support services, while others are placed in out-of-home settings, usually in a foster home, relative placement, or institution (e.g., residential treatment facility, maternity group home). This section provides demographic and other information on youth who have had contact with the child welfare system, but did not necessarily enter care, as well as the characteristics of only those youth who entered in care. In addition, the outcomes experienced by young people who left care via emancipation is discussed.

Characteristics of Youth Who Have Had Contact with the Child Welfare System

The National Survey of Child and Adolescent Well-Being (NSCAW), a national random sample study of maltreated children or those at risk of maltreatment, was authorized by legislation (the Personal Responsibility and Work Opportunities Reconciliation Act of 1996, P.L. 104-193) to reform welfare.[5] NSCAW is gathering information associated with 5,501 children from public child welfare agencies in 92 localities across the nation. It is the first national longitudinal study of its kind and the first to relate child well-being to family characteristics, experience with the child welfare system, community environment, and other factors. The study has gathered this information at five intervals since an investigation of maltreatment was closed, even for those children who did not enter out-of-home foster care. For the fifth interval, information was collected by age cohort. One of these cohorts included 620 youth ages 18 to 21 in the sample who were ages 12 to 15 years old when baseline data were collected.[6] The purpose of collecting data on this age cohort was to learn about the extent of their contact with the child welfare system, how they are developing during their transition to adulthood, and which services they need and/or have received to support this transition. Overall, the study demonstrates that youth who have been the subject of a child welfare investigation, regardless of whether they were removed from their homes, were more likely to have challenges in making the transition to adulthood than their same- age peers, and that many youth in need of certain services were not receiving those services.

Almost a third (31.9%) of the youth in the sample were involved in a child welfare services investigation due to physical abuse. A caregiver's failure to supervise was reported for 29.1% of youth; sexual abuse, for 14.5%; a caregiver's failure to provide, for 9.5%; emotional abuse for 7.2%; moral/legal or educational abuse, for 6.3%; and abandonment, for 1.6% (figures add to 100.1% because of rounding). Slightly more than a quarter of these investigations were substantiated, meaning that child welfare services decided that the allegations of maltreatment were valid, and nearly one out of five (17.2%) of the youth were placed in out-of-home foster care during their adolescence. Nearly 60% (57.6%) of the families with youth in the sample were involved with a previous child welfare investigation. Of those families, two-thirds of the abuse and neglect incidents were substantiated.

At Wave 5, more than half (55.5%) of the youth in the sample were living with a caregiver. The balance of the sample were either married and living with their spouse (9.5%), cohabiting with a boyfriend or girlfriend (17.5%), living alone (11.8%), or living with non-relatives (6.3%). The share of youth living with caretakers is consistent with that of their peers in the general population. And like their peers generally, many of the youth in the study were currently employed full or part time (58.1%). Despite these similarities, youth involved in a child welfare services' investigation (even if they did not enter out-of-home care) tended to face negative outcomes across several domains relative to their peers generally as they made the transition to adulthood.

Across several health indicators, youth in the sample were more likely to report negative outcomes. (The study did not evaluate whether the shares of youth in the sample, compared to shares of youth in the general population, are statistically significant.) For example, about one- fifth (21.6%) of young adult females reported being in fair or poor health, compared to females in the general U.S. population ages 18 and older (12.9%). Further, the sample youth were also far more likely to report being depressed in the year prior to the interview (9.5% compared to 27.5%). While the share of youth in the sample having reported to be sexual active was about the same as it is for the general population ages 20 to 24, a larger proportion of sample youth had been sexual activity at an earlier age. Youth in the sample were almost more likely to be in an intimate relationship involving physical violence. More than one-third (34.3%) of young adult females had been in such a relationship. This is higher than the 22.1% lifetime prevalence for intimate-partner violence among adult females.

In education, young adults in the sample scored, on average, substantially below the normative mean of 100 in all categories of a cognitive test. The proportion w ho scored significantly lower than the mean was 15.0% for applied problems, 25.3% for passage comprehension, 29.7% for word-letter identification, and 43.6% for calculation. The sample youth were also more likely to report living in poverty. About four out of ten (41.8%) of sample youth were living in households with incomes below 100% of the federal poverty level, compared to an estimated 30% of all 18- to-24 years living below the poverty level.

Finally, the study suggests that the needs of youth in the sample are not being met. Many young adults in the study who reported having emotional, behavioral, learning, or attentional problems did not get services to address these problems. For example, among youth with clinically significant mental health scores and considered in need of mental health services, just over one quarter (27.6%) received outpatient mental health services and 13.3% receive inpatient mental health services (some received both services). In addition, only half of youth with symptoms consistent with alcohol or drug dependence were receiving substance abuse services.

Characteristics of Youth in Foster Care

Other studies provide data on youth who were removed from their homes and placed in a foster care setting. The Foster Care Dynamics report, a longitudinal study of children in 11 state child welfare systems from 2000 through 2005, provides detailed information about older youth who have been placed in out-of-home care.[7] The study examined state administrative data to determine the typical trajectory of children across four age categories who first entered foster care during the five-year period: less than age one; one through five; six through 12; and 13 through 17. The study found that teenagers make up a significant share of the foster care population; have shorter median lengths of stay relative to younger children; live in placements other than foster family homes; experience more placements in their first year in care than younger children; and most often exit care through reunification, although running away and reaching the age of majority are exit pathways for about 10% to 24% of these older youth, depending on their age.

From 2000 through 2005, about 350,000 children entered care in the 11 states, of whom 27% were teenagers ages 13 through 17. Youth in the age 13 through 17 category comprised the second largest share of children in care (n=94,965), only after children ages six through 12 (n= 95,676). The incidence rate for entering care for youth ages 13 through 17 was about 2.5 per 1,000 over the five-year period; this is compared to about 9.0 per 1,000 infants under age one; about 2.5 per 1,000 children ages one through five; and about 1.8 per 1,000 children ages six through 12. In three cohort years (2000-2001, 2002-2003, and 2004-2005), fifteen-year-olds comprised the second largest share of children in care by single-year age category (approximately 7%), only after infants under the age of one, who comprised 18% to 20% of the caseload.

Of those youth ages 13 through 17 who entered care from 2000 to 2005, 49% lived in congregate care (e.g, a residential school), 37% in foster family homes, and 13% in kinship care. The remaining two percent lived in an independent living arrangement or other arrangement. Across all age categories, 41% to 43% of children were moved within their first six months in foster care; however, a greater share of teenagers experienced multiple placements within their first six months of entering care. About 18% of youth ages 13 through 17 had two or more placements, compared with 12% to 16% of children in other age categories. Teenagers were also more likely to move to new living arrangements in the six to twelve months after entering care. While older youth in care had a shorter median length of stay than younger children in care, this median length of stay increased over the five-year period. The median lengths of stay for infants decreased from 18.7 months in 2000 to 17.6 months in 2004 (data were not available for 2005), and increased for youth ages 13 through 17 from 6.6 months in 2000 to 7.8 months in 2005.

Generally, teenagers were less likely to be adopted or placed with relatives as they got older and were more likely to run away and exit by reaching the age of majority or some other pathway such as independent living. With the exception of 17-year-olds, about the same share of teenagers were reunified as children ages three to 12. One-third to 46% of youth ages 13 through 17 exited to reunification. The balance of youth lived in an independent living arrangement or some other arrangement (12.4% to 15.1% for each age 13 through 17), ran away (6.7% to 11.7%), lived with a relative (5.1% to 8.4%), or reached the age of majority (0.9% to 23.9%). About two percent or less of the teenagers were adopted.

Although older youth tend to have shorter spells in foster care, they are more likely to re-enter care after their first exit. About 28% of youth who were discharged at ages 13 through 17 during 2000 to 2002 reentered care within one year, followed by infants, at 26%. Children ages one to five were least likely to reenter care, at 15%.

Outcomes for Young Adults Formerly in Foster Care

Finally, data is available for those youth who were placed in out-of-home care and ultimately exited via emancipation. The data on these youth demonstrate that they have experienced challenges in transitioning to adulthood. This transition for all youth has becoming increasingly complex. During this period, young people cycle between attending school, working, and living independently. Many youth can rely on assistance from their families for financial and emotional supports during the transition. On average, parents give their children an estimated $38,000—or about $2,200 a year—between the ages of 18 and 34 to supplement wages, pay for college tuition, and help with housing costs, among other types of financial assistance.[8] Parents also allow their adult children to live with them[9] and provide their children with non-material assistance, such as help with obtaining a driver's license, guidance on applying to college, advice on finances and establishing a new household, and connections to other caring adults in their communities. For older foster youth and those who have already aged out of care, this assistance is often not in place. Being in care may inherently cause instability because of multiple out-of-home placements, school transfers, and the challenge in maintaining relationships with parents and other kin. Youth may experience further instability if they cannot afford to live on their own or are unable to live with relatives or friends upon emancipation. In most states, youth may not remain in foster care beyond age 18, a time when most young people explore educational and career options. (P.L. 110-351 has authorized states to seek Title IV-E foster care reimbursement for youth ages 18 to 21, at state option, beginning in FY2011.)

Research on the transition for former foster youth is limited and most of the studies on outcomes for these youth face methodological challenges—they tend to be dated; include brief follow-up periods (e.g., no more than a year after exit from care); have low response rates, nonrepresentative samples, and small sample sizes; and do not follow youth prior to exit from foster care.[10] Few studies include comparison groups to gauge how well these youth are transitioning to adulthood, in relation to their peers in the foster care population or general population. However, two studies—the Northwest Foster Care Alumni Study and the Midwest Evaluation of the Adult Functioning of Former Foster Youth—have tracked outcomes for a sample of youth across several domains, either prospectively (following youth in care and as they age out) or retrospectively (examining current outcomes for young adults who were in care at least a few years ago) and comparing these outcomes to other groups of youth, either those who aged out and/or youth in the general population.

Both studies indicate that youth who spent time in foster care during their teenage years tended to have difficulty during the transition to adulthood and beyond. (The studies do not posit that foster care, per se, is associated with the challenges former foster youth face in adulthood. In fact, children tend to have a range of challenges upon entering care.[11]) The Midwest Evaluation has examined the extent to which outcomes in early adulthood are influenced by the individual characteristics of youth or their out-of-home care histories. The study found that still being in care, as opposed to having left care, and having certain other characteristics (i.e., having aspirations to graduate from college, feeling close to at least one family member, and expressing satisfaction with their experience in foster care) more than doubled the odds of working or being in school at age 19.[12]

The two reports exclude youth with developmental disabilities or severe mental illness that precluded them from participating, as well as youth who were incarcerated or in a psychiatric hospital.

Northwest Foster Care Alumni Study

Researchers with the Northwest Foster Care Alumni Study interviewed and reviewed the case files of 479 foster care youth who were in public or private foster care any time from 1988 to 1998 in Oregon or Washington.[13] On average, they interviewed youth who were 24.2 years old, with a range of 20 to 33 years old. The youth tended to be females (60% versus the 48% of females in foster care nationally in FY2006[14]); to have entered care as adolescents (11.1 years versus 8.1 years for children entering care in FY2006; nearly 60% of the youth in the study were age 12 and older at the time they entered care); and to have exited care between the ages of 15 and older (the mean age at exit was 18.5 years versus 9.6 years in FY2008 for foster youth nationwide).[15] Surveyed young adults experienced these outcomes even though most (83.6%) reported having access to "a lot" of child welfare services and supports, and about eight out of ten (81.5%) said that they felt loved while in care. These findings suggest that a confluence of factors, including the reasons they entered care, family dynamics, and access to services and supports before and after care, among many other variables, have likely influenced how well they function as adults.

The study compared the mental health status, educational attainment, and employment and finances for the foster care alumni to those of the general population.

- Mental health: Over 54% of foster care alumni had at least one mental health problem (depression, social phobia, panic disorder, and post-traumatic stress disorder, among others), compared to 22.1% of the general population. [16] About one quarter of the alumni experienced post-traumatic stress disorder (PTSD). This figure is greater than the prevalence of PTSD among Vietnam or Iraq war veterans—about 15%. Alumni tended to have similar recovery rates as their counterparts in the general population for major depression, panic syndrome, and alcohol dependency, but lower rates of recovery for other disorders such as generalized anxiety disorder, PTSD, social phobia, and bulimia.

- Education: While alumni have obtained a high school diploma or passed the general education development (GED) test at the same rates as 25-to-34-yearolds generally (84.5% versus 87.3%), they are much less likely to have a bachelor's degree—1.8% versus 22.5% of all young people.
- Employment and finances: One third of alumni reported living below the poverty line, which is three times the national poverty rate. Further, almost 17% were dependent on Temporary Assistance for Needy Families (TANF), compared to 3% of the general population (although the high rate of participation in Oregon and Washington could have been due, in part, to TANF rules in those states). The alumni employment rate was 80%, while the general employment rate was 95%. Other indicators show that alumni were not financially secure. One third lacked health insurance (versus 18% of the general population) and 22% were homeless at least one day during the year after they left foster care (versus 1% of the general population who were homeless within the last year).

Midwest Evaluation on the Adult Functioning of Former Foster Youth

Few foster care alumni studies are prospective, meaning that they follow youth while in care through the time they leave care and beyond. The Midwest Evaluation is an ongoing study that tracks 600 or more (depending on the data collection wave) current and former foster youth in three states: Illinois, Iowa, and Wisconsin. All of the surveyed youth entered care prior to their 16th birthday.[17] Surveyed youth responded to researcher questions about outcomes in three data collection waves: at wave 1, when they were ages 17 and 18, at which time most were in care; at wave 2 when they were ages 19 and 20, at which time some remained in care; at wave 3, when they were age 21 and no longer in care; and wave 4, when they were ages 23 and 24 and at least a couple of years out of care. Of those who remained in care beyond age 18, all were in Illinois, the only state of the three that retains court jurisdiction of foster youth (with the youth's permission) until age 21.[18]

At wave 1, about half to 70% of youth in care reported receiving any one category of independent living services (educational services, employment/vocational support, budget and financial management support, housing services, health education services, and youth development services).[19] At wave 2, not more than half of the youth in care reported receiving at least one independent living service.[20] At wave 3, receipt of services decreased for youth, regardless of whether they remained in care. No more than approximately one third of the youth reported receiving at least one independent living service.[21]

For youth in the fourth wave, their mean age was 24 years old and just over half (53.5%) were female.[22] Nearly one-quarter had left foster care within the previous two to three years; about 20% had left within the past three to four years; 10% had left within the past four to five years; 30% had left care in the past five to six years; and 17% had left care in the last six to seven years. Most (54.5%) identified as African American, followed by white (29.9%), multiracial (5.8%), and other races. Approximately 4% identified as Hispanic. More than two-thirds of youth (62.9%) reported feeling lucky to have been placed in foster care, compared with 15% who neither agreed nor disagreed with feeling lucky, and 22% who disagreed or strongly disagreed. Youth were also asked whether they felt prepared to be self-sufficient. Over one-quarter said that they felt somewhat prepared and 65.5% said they felt very prepared; the remaining 7% said they did not feel very prepared or did not feel prepared at all. When they exited foster care years earlier, only one-quarter had said they felt very prepared.

At ages 23 or 24, most youth reported strong family ties, with 94% having said that they felt somewhat or very close to at least one biological family member. The greatest shares of youth reported feeling very close to their siblings, followed by another relative (aunt, uncle, or cousin), grandparent, biological mother, and biological father. The surveyed youth were most likely to be in daily contact (in this order) with their siblings, biological mother, another relative, grandparent, or biological father. Overall, most youth reported that they had social support, based on a 5-point scale with 1 meaning that they had support none of the time and 5 meaning they had support most of the time. The youth had a mean score of a 3.8.

Emancipated Youth Compared to Youth in Care at Midwest Evaluation Wave 3

Findings from wave 3 of the Midwest Evaluation suggest that youth who remain in care as late as age 20 tend to experience an easier transition to adulthood than their counterparts who emancipate at age 18. The study found that the young adults from Illinois (who were more likely to remain in care than youth in Wisconsin and Iowa) were almost two times as likely to have ever attended college than their peers in the other two states; and were more likely to have higher earnings and delayed pregnancy. See the last section of this report for further information.

Youth at Midwest Evaluation Wave 4 Compared to Youth Ages 23 and 24 Generally

For each of the four data collection waves, wherever possible, researchers asked the same questions that were taken directly from the National Longitudinal Survey of Adolescent Health ("Add Health"), a nationally representative survey that tracks a cohort of youth over time. [23] The former foster youth surveyed at wave 4 in the Midwest Evaluation were less likely to have attained a four-year college degree compared to the Add Health youth (2.5% versus 19.4%). Youth in the Midwest evaluation who were not currently in school reported barriers to enrolling or staying in school, including that they could not pay (39.9%), needed to work full-time (19.7%), needed to care for a child (13.8%), or had no transportation (3.2%), among other reasons. While youth formerly in care were almost as likely to report ever holding a job as Add Health youth (94.7% versus 97.3%), a smaller share were currently employed (48.0% versus 75.5%) and they had lower median hourly wages ($9.45 versus $12.00) and mean annual incomes ($8,000 versus $18,300). About 47% of former foster youth reported having any savings or checking account, compared to 85% of youth generally. A greater share of former foster youth did not have enough money to pay rent (38.6%), compared to their counterparts in the Add Health survey (7.4%) and were more likely to report having received food stamps (67.7% versus 7.2% for females; 26.8% versus 1.5% for males).

Table A-1 in Appendix A presents the outcomes for youth surveyed in wave 4 and Add Health participants surveyed at ages 23 and 24 across ten domains—living arrangements, educational attainment, employment and income, economic hardships, health, sexual behavior and pregnancy, relationships and family formation, involvement with the criminal justice system, transition to adulthood, orientation to the future, and mentoring. Table A-1 indicates that at age 23, former foster youth and youth generally shared some common characteristics, but that the former foster youth experienced more negative educational and employment outcomes, among other outcomes.

In addition to assessing the outcomes of youth at ages 23 and 24, the Midwest researchers have classified these youth into four subgroups, based on their similar characteristics across multiple indicators.[24] The profiles of the youth vary based on their living arrangements, educational attainment, and current employment status; whether they have children and whether they live with their children; and whether they have been convicted of a crime since leaving care. The alumni were categorized as follows:

- Accelerated adults: The highest percentage of youth (36.3%) were classified under this category. These youth were most likely to live on their own in a fairly stable situation (83.5%). Almost all had a high school diploma and over half had attended some college (54.3%). Three quarters were employed (74.8%). About half had children (51.9%), and they reported one of the lowest rates of criminal conviction (13.7%) relative to the other groups. Although these youth were generally high functioning, about one-third had been homeless or couch surfed and over one-third receive food stamps at age 23 or 24.
- Struggling parents: Nearly one out of four youth were categorized as struggling parents. They tended to live on their own (45.6%) or with relatives or friends (44.2%), and to have obtained a high school diploma (52.4%). Few (3.4%) were attending college (3.4%). Nearly all had children (98.0%), most of whom lived with them. Most were unemployed (74.5%) and most had not been convicted of a crime since leaving care (85.3%).
- Emerging adults: Emerging adults comprised 21.1% of the sample. All lived with relatives, friends, or others. Almost half had attended some college (45.5%) and just over one-third were currently employed (36.6%). Most did not have children (73.2%) and almost none had been convicted of a crime since leaving care (94.3%).
- Troubled and troubling: Nearly one out of five (17.5%) of youth were categorized as troubled and troubling. The majority of the group had lived in multiple placements, were in jail or a treatment program, or had an unstable living situation (71.6%). Four out of 10 did not have a high school diploma, but most were employed (90.2%). About one out of five had been convicted of a crime since leaving care (17.6%).

Resiliency of Current and Former Foster Youth

Despite the generally negative findings from the two major evaluations on youth aging out of foster care, many youth have demonstrated resiliency by overcoming obstacles, such as limited family support and financial resources, and meeting their goals. As mentioned above, youth in the Northwest Evaluation have obtained a high school diploma or passed the general education development (GED) test at close to the same rates as 25-to-34-year-olds generally (84.5% versus 87.3%). Further, youth in the third wave of the Midwest Evaluation were just as likely as the general youth population to report being hopeful about their future. (See Table A-1.) Over one- third of the youth have been classified as fairly high functioning because they are attached to work or school and live on their own.

Current and former foster youth are also working to make improvements to the child welfare system. At hearings in the 110th Congress that focused on older youth in foster care, these young people highlighted their struggles, successes, and their advocacy work on behalf of foster children. At a February 27, 2008 hearing before the Ways and Means' Subcommittee on Income Security and Family Support, a foster care alumni chronicled her life in care with 11 placements through her recent graduation from college. In her testimony, she urged Congress to improve conditions for children in foster care:

> I have accomplished a lot, but it is in spite of all of the uncertainty I experienced in foster care—not because of it. I want something better for the youth who are currently in the foster care system. I want them to have families to love and protect them and homes they know they can always return to. I want them to leave foster care to live with a family, a relative—someone who will be permanent in their lives. I do not want the youth currently in foster care to age-out of foster care with no family and no one to turn to for help or support.... Congress has the power to do something, and I ask you on behalf of all of my brothers and sisters who cannot be sitting here with me to do something now.[25]

The next section of this report describes the federal services and supports available to youth in foster care, and demonstrates how some states have varied in their approaches to serving older foster youth and youth who have recently emancipated from care.

OVERVIEW OF FEDERAL CHILD WELFARE SUPPORT FOR FOSTER YOUTH

Historically, states have been primarily responsible for providing child welfare services to families and children that need them. While in out-of-home foster care, the state child welfare agency, under the supervision of the court (and in consultation with the parents or primary caretakers in some cases), serves as the child's parent and makes decisions on his or her behalf that are to promote his or her safety, permanence, and well-being.

Safety refers to the state child welfare system's goal of ensuring that children in foster care are protected from further abuse or neglect. *Permanence* refers to the state's goal of ensuring that children do not spend too many of their formative years in a foster care placement, and that the state either returns them to their families quickly and safely or quickly finds another safe and permanent home for them. *Well-being* is inextricably linked to safety and permanency. The term refers to efforts by the child welfare system to promote positive outcomes for children in care, including education and physical and mental health outcomes, as well as supportive families. In most cases, the state relies on public and private entities and organizations to provide these services. The federal government plays a role in shaping state child welfare systems by providing funds and linking those funds to certain requirements.

Title IV-E of the Social Security Act provides foster care, case planning, and services to older foster youth. Title IV-E foster care authorizes federal funding for eligible children, and requires states to follow certain case planning and management practices for all children in care (Section 472). The Chafee Foster Care Independence program authorizes funding for states to provide independent living services to older foster youth and those who have emancipated from care (Section 477). Both programs are discussed below.

FEDERAL FOSTER CARE

Federal support for foster care preceded, by several decades, the 1980 (P.L. 9 6-272) creation of Title IV-E foster care under the Social Security Act. However, the 1980 law established this support as an independent funding source for states to provide foster homes for children in foster care. The law also stressed the importance of case planning and review to achieve permanence for foster children.

Case Planning and Review

Federal child welfare provisions under Title IV-B and Title IV-E of the Social Security Act require state child welfare agencies, as a condition of receiving funding under these titles, to provide certain case management services to all children in foster care. These include monthly case worker visits to each child in foster care (Section 422(b)(17)); a written case plan for each child in care that documents the child's placement and steps taken to ensure their safety and wellbeing, including by addressing their health and educational needs (Section 475(1)); and procedures ensuring a case review is conducted not less often than every six months by a judge or an administrative review panel, and at least once every 12 months by a judge who must consider the child's permanency plan (Section 475(5)). Specific case plan and case review procedures pertain to older youth in care. For a child age 16 or older, the written case plan must also include a description of the programs and services that will help the child prepare for the transition to independent living (Section 475(1)(D)). Permanency plan hearings, which are to be conducted at least once a year after a child enters care, must consider for children age 16 and older, the services needed to assist them transition to independent living (Section 475(5)(C)). Further, the court or administrative body conducting the hearings is to consult, in an age-appropriate manner, with the child regarding the proposed permanency or transition plan for the child (Section 475(5)(C)).

The Fostering Connections to Success and Increasing Adoptions Act of 2008 added requirements about a transition plan for older youth. The law requires that a youth's caseworker, and as appropriate, other representative(s) of the youth, assist and support him or her in developing a transition plan. The plan is to be directed by the youth, and is to include specific options on housing, health insurance, education, local opportunities for mentors, workforce supports, and employment services. The plan must be implemented 90 days prior to a youth's 18th birthday (or the 19th, 20th , or 21st birthdays of youth in states that take up the option to extend foster care), "whether during that period foster care maintenance payments are being made on the child's behalf or the child is receiving benefits or services under [the Chafee Foster Care Independence Program]."

The new health care reform law, the Patient Protection and Affordable Care Act (P.L. 111-148), adds another element to the transition plan. The law requires that the plan addresses the importance of designating another individual to make health care treatment decisions on behalf of the youth if he or she becomes unable to participate in these decisions *and* does not have a relative who would be authorized to make these decisions under state law, or he or she does not want a relative to make those decisions. In addition, the transition plan must provide the youth with the option to execute a health care power of attorney, health care proxy, or other similar documents recognized under state law. As part of the program instructions issued by HHS on June 7, 2010, concerning implementation of PPACA, states and tribes that have submitted a Title IV-E plan or have been approved to operate a Title IV-E program must submit, by December 31, 2010, a Title IV-E amendment that reflects implementation of, and compliance with, the new requirement.[26]

Program instructions issued by HHS in July 2010 provide additional guidance on the transition plan.[27] The instructions encourage child welfare agencies to use the plan to build on earlier efforts to help young people make the transition from foster care, including through the case planning process and permanency hearings. Child welfare agencies are encouraged to begin engaging youth in the transition plan process "well in advance" of the 90-day period.

Title IV-E Reimbursement for Foster Care

Title IV-E currently reimburses states for a part of the cost of providing foster care to eligible children and youth, who, because of abuse or neglect (or some other reason), cannot remain in their own homes and for whom a court has consequently given care and placement responsibility to the state. Under this program, a state may seek partial federal reimbursement to "cover the cost of (and the cost of providing) food, clothing, shelter, daily supervision, school supplies, a child's personal incidentals, liability insurance with respect to a child, and reasonable travel to the child's home for visitation" (Section 475(4)). States may also seek reimbursement for related costs of administration, child placement (e.g., case planning), training, and data collection.

Under the Chafee Foster Care Independence Program (see below), states must certify that they will use Title IV-E foster care program funding (and Adoption Assistance program funding) to provide training relevant to foster parents and others (adoptive parents, workers in group homes, and case managers) to help them understand and address the issues confronting adolescents preparing for independent living and coordinating this training, where possible, with independent living programs.[28] Although case planning and review procedures (described above) apply to all foster children in state care, federal reimbursement to states under Title IV-E may be made only on behalf of a child who meets multiple federal eligibility criteria (Section 472), including those related to the child's removal and the income and assets of the child's family. For purposes of this report, the most significant eligibility criteria for the federal foster care program are the child's age and placement setting.

Eligibility

Under current law, once a child has reached his or her 18th birthday, he or she is no longer eligible for federal foster care assistance. The age limitation on Title IV-E eligibility is created by the program's eligibility link to the now-defunct Aid to Families with Dependent Children (AFDC) program.[29] Children qualified as dependents under the AFDC program until age 18. As was the case with AFDC, federal law does permit states to make continued claims for otherwise eligible foster youth until their 19th birthday provided that the youth is a full-time student and is expected to complete high school or an equivalent training program by age 19. States must have elected this option in its definition of "child" for purposes of the state's AFDC program.

Pursuant to P.L. 110-351, states have the option, as of FY2011, to seek reimbursement for the cost of providing foster care to eligible youth until age 19, 20, or 21. The law makes this change by inserting a definition of "child" as it pertains to older youth in care. This definition specifies that a state may seek reimbursement for a youth age 18 or older who is: completing high school or a program leading to an equivalent credential; enrolled in an institution that provides postsecondary or vocational education; participating in a program or activity designed to promote, or remove barriers to, employment; or employed at least 80 hours per month (i.e., part-time). States may exempt youth from these requirements due to a medical condition, as documented and updated in their case plan.

In its July 2010 program guidance, HHS advises that states and tribes can make remaining in care conditional upon whether youth pursue certain educational or employment pathways. For example, extended care could be provided only to those youth enrolled in post-secondary education. Still, the guidance advises that states and tribes should "consider how [they] can provide extended assistance to youth age 18 and older to the broadest population possible consistent with the law to ensure that there are ample supports for older youth."

P.L. 110-351 also authorizes states, for the first time, to provide Title IV-E subsidies on behalf of youth 18 or older (until age 19, 20, or 21, at the state's option) who left foster care after age 16 for adoption or kinship guardianship, and meet the criteria listed above. This change was made by adding a definition of "child" as it relates to these youth.

Eligible Placement Setting

Under current law, federal reimbursement of part of the costs of maintaining children in foster care may currently be sought only for children placed in foster family homes or child care institutions. States may not seek federal reimbursement of foster care costs for children who are in "detention facilities, forestry camps, training schools, or any other facility operated primarily for the detention of children who are determined to be delinquent."[30] As mentioned above, states will have the option of seeking federal maintenance payments for youth ages 18 to 21 beginning in FY2011. States that take up the option will be permitted to claim reimbursement for youth placed in a "supervised setting in which the individual is living independently." The act directs the Department of Health and Human Services (HHS) to establish in regulation what qualifies as such a setting. As part of the July 2010 program instructions issued by HHS, the department stated that it does not have plans "at this time" to issue "forthcoming regulations" that describe the kinds of living arrangements considered to be independent living settings, how these settings should be supervised, or any other conditions for a young person to live independently. The instructions advise that states and tribes have the discretion to develop a range of supervised independent living settings that "can be reasonably interpreted as consistent with the law, including whether or not such settings need to be licensed and any safety protocols that may be needed."

Chafee Foster Care Independence Program

A second Title IV-E program, the Chafee Foster Care Independence program (CFCIP), provides services to older youth in foster care and youth transitioning out of care.[31]

Overview

The Foster Care Independence Act of 1999 (P.L. 106-169) replaced the prior law Independent Living Program, established in 1985, with the John H. Chafee Foster Care Independence Program. The 1999 law doubled the annual funds available to states for independent living services from $70 million to $140 million. Youth served include those who are expected to leave foster care because they have not been placed in a permanent family before reaching the state's legal age of majority and those who have emancipated from care (until age 21). As enacted by P.L. 106-169, the purposes of the program are to—(1) identify youth who are likely to remain in foster care until age 18 and provide them with support services to help make the transition to self sufficiency; (2) assist these youth to obtain employment and prepare for and enter college or other postsecondary training or educational institutions; (3) provide personal and emotional support to youth aging out of foster care through mentors and other dedicated adults; (4) enhance the efforts of former foster youth ages 18 to 21 to achieve self sufficiency through supports that connect them to employment, education, housing, and other services; and (5) assure that youth receiving services recognize and accept personal responsibility for preparing for and then making the transition from adolescence to adulthood. As discussed below, the law has been amended twice to expand the purposes of the CFCIP and to create a new Education and Training Voucher program for eligible youth.

CFCIP-funded services may consist of educational assistance, vocational training, mentoring, preventive health activities, and counseling. States may dedicate as much as 30% of their program funding toward room and board for youth ages 18 to 21, including for those youth enrolled in an institution of higher education or who remain in foster care in states that provide care to youth until ages 19, 20, or 21.[32] Room and board are not defined in statute, but typically include food and shelter, and may include rental deposits, rent, utilities, and the cost of household startup purchases. CFCIP funds may not be used to acquire property to provide housing to current or former foster youth. [33] The act also required that youth in the program be actively involved in decisions about the services they receive.

In addition, the law changed the amount of earnings or other resources that foster youth may accumulate to assist in their transition to independent living. Eligibility for foster care maintenance payments under Title IV-E of the Social Security Act is based on whether the children's original families would qualify for AFDC, as it was in effect on July 16, 1996. Under those rules, children could not remain eligible for Title IV-E services if they accumulated assets of more than $1,000. P.L. 106-169, however, changed this asset limit to $10,000. The act also encouraged states to provide Medicaid coverage to youth ages 18, 19, and 20 who have emancipated from foster care by authorizing a new Medicaid eligibility pathway for "independent foster care adolescents," commonly called the "Chafee option" (see section on Medicaid in "Other Federal Support" below). In 2002 (P.L. 107-133), discretionary funds—up to $60 million annually—were authorized for eligible current and former foster care youth to receive education and training vouchers.

Legislative History

The CFCIP is the successor to earlier efforts by Congress to better support the transition of youth from foster care to independent living. In 1985, Congress established the Independent Living Program (ILP), under a new section 477 of the Social Security Act, in response to several surveys showing that significant number of individuals who used homeless shelters had been recently discharged from foster care. The ILP awarded grants to states to provide services that would prepare youth to live independently outside of the child welfare system. Youth ages 16 to 18 who met the eligibility criteria of Title IV-E qualified for ILP services. In 1988 (P.L. 100-647), ILP eligibility was expanded to include children ages 16 to 18 in foster care, regardless of their federal Title IV-E eligibility. The 1988 law also permitted states to use ILP funds to serve certain youth for six months after their emancipation from foster care. In 1990, P.L. 101-508 gave states the option of providing independent living services to any youth up to age 21 who had emancipated from care. In 1993 (P.L. 103-66), Congress permanently authorized funding for the program at $70 million annually.

Since the CFCIP was established in 1999 under P.L. 106-169, the program has been amended three times. In 2002, P.L. 107-133 authorized additional funding to provide education and training vouchers to youth who age out of foster care and youth who are adopted from care at age 16 or older. In 2008, P.L. 110-351 expanded eligibility for the program by adding as an additional program purpose that youth who are in foster care on their 16th birthday but who subsequently leave care for adoption or kinship are eligible for CFCIP services. The law also extended the ETV program to youth who leave care at age 16 or older for kinship guardianship; and made tribal entities eligible to apply directly for CFCIP and ETV funds directly from the federal government. In 2010, the program was amended for a third time by the Patient Protection and Affordable Care Act (P.L. 111-148) to require states to make assurances about educating young people aging out about a health care power of attorney and assisting the youth with executing the power of attorney.

Eligibility for CFCIP Benefits and Services

The Foster Care Independence Act of 1999 required states to ensure that independent living programs serve children of "various ages and various stages of achieving independence" and use objective criteria for determining eligibility for benefits and services under the program. The act further specified that states are to provide services under the CFCIP for children who are "likely to remain in foster care until 18 years of age" or are "aging out of foster care." It also addressed the responsibilities of the states to consult with American Indian tribes and provide services to tribal youth. Foster youth who are in runaway status or lose contact with their child welfare agency continue to be under the custody of the state, and therefore, are eligible for services upon returning. Those youth in care who have been adjudicated through the juvenile justice system are eligible for CFCIP services as long as they are not in a detention or related facility.[34] (The juvenile corrections facility is responsible for all services for foster youth who are confined in a locked setting.) Finally, foster children who are not citizens may be eligible for CFCIP services while under state custody.

The Foster Care Independence Act further requires states to provide certain services to youth who meet specific age and other criteria. States may provide room and board with CFCIP funds and Medicaid through the Chafee pathway (see below for further information) only to those youth who are eligible for CFCIP services. Youth are eligible for an education and training voucher (until age 23) if they emancipate from care or were adopted from care at age 16 or older. However, to be eligible for a voucher at age 22 or 23, they must have received one at age 21.

Youth Likely to Remain in Foster Care Until Age 18

Under the former ILP, states could provide services to current foster youth ages 16 and 17 who were eligible for Title IV-E foster care maintenance payments, or to "other children in care," regardless of Title IV-E status. P.L. 106-169 removed reference to a minimum eligibility age and required states to provide supports to children "likely to remain in foster care" until age 18. This phrase is not defined in the act, and states are to create eligibility standards using objective criteria. States can provide services to any child age 17 and younger regardless of their placement in a kinship care home, family foster home, pre-adoptive home, or any other state-sanctioned placement so long as the child is in state custody. HHS 's *Child Welfare Policy Manual* requires states that place children in foster care settings in other states to fund independent living services for foster youth ages 16 to 18 regardless of their placement in another state.[35]

According to the National Foster Care Coalition, a child welfare advocacy organization, many states have developed indicators to help determine the likelihood that a child will remain in care until his or her 18th birthday.[36] For example, Louisiana determines a child's eligibility for independent living services by reviewing his or her case history, presenting problems, and individual case goals. Kentucky and Alaska require that services be provided concurrently with permanency planning for young people over the age of 14. Alaska further defines the level of such services that should be provided at age 14 and older.

A 2008 survey of independent living coordinators in 45 states (including the District of Columbia) by the Chapin Hall Center for Children at the University of Chicago found that in about half of the states (24, 53.3%), youth as young as age 14 are eligible for CFCIP-funded services. Seven states provide these services at a younger age, while 13 provide services at an older age. One state said that the age depends on the county, and another state did not report on the minimum age for services.[37] Nearly all (40) of the surveyed states reported that foster youth are eligible for CFCIP-funded services regardless of their permanency plan. Further, nearly half of the states (22) said that young people who are placed with a permanent legal guardian are ineligible or are eligible under certain circumstances.

Permanency Planning

The Adoption and Safe Families Act of 1997 (ASFA, P.L. 105-89) amended the Social Security Act at Section 475(5), which required that all young people in foster care have a permanency plan. ASFA established that, in addition to reunification, adoption, placement with a relative, and legal guardianship, "another planned permanent living arrangement" (APPLA) is specified as a permanency option, and may include independent living. While the

CFCIP is intended to expand independent living services for older youth in foster care, Section 477 of the act encourages states to continue their efforts to achieve permanency for a young person, including by specifying that states should continue to locate and achieve placement in adoptive families for older youth in care. In his introductory remarks about the Senate version of P.L. 106-169 (S. 1327), Senator Jay Rockefeller described the intent of the legislation:

> "[A] youth's need for a family does not end at any particular age. Each of us can clearly recall times when we have had to turn to our own families for advice, comfort, or support long after our 1 8th or 21st birthdays. Many of us are still in the role of providing such support to our own children who are in their late teens or 20s. Therefore, an important provision in this Senate version of the Foster Care Independence Act states that Independent Living (IL) programs are not alternatives to permanency planning-young people of all ages need and deserve every possible effort made towards permanence, including adoption."[38]

Youth Aging Out of Foster Care

Prior to the enactment of the CFCIP, states had the *option* to serve young people who had emancipated from care until age 21. The Foster Care Independence Act *requires* states that receive CFCIP funds to provide independent living services to youth who have aged out of care between the ages of 18 through 21. According to HHS 's *Child Welfare Policy Manual*, this requirement does not preclude states from providing services to other former foster care youth ages 18 to 21 who exited care prior to their eighteenth birthday.[39] The 2008 Chapin Hall survey of 45 states found that than half of the states (19; 42.2%) reported that former foster youth are eligible for aftercare services if they were not in care on their eighteenth birthday. Slightly more states (about 21) reported that these youth could receive services if their discharge outcome was reunification, adoption, or legal guardianship.

Former foster youth continue to remain eligible for aftercare services until age 21 if they move to another state. The state in which the former foster youth resides—whether or not the youth was in foster care in that state—is responsible for providing independent living services to the eligible young person.[40] Separately, several states have developed recommitment policies for youth who have been discharged from care that specify a time limit in which they may be eligible for services. Under such a policy, youth who turn age 18 while in runaway status may reenter care to receive services.[41]

American Indian Youth

The prior federal Independent Living Program did not specify that states consult with American Indian tribes or serve Indian youth in particular. P.L. 106-169 required that under the CFCIP, states must certify that each federally recognized Indian tribal organization in the state has been consulted about the state's independent living programs and that there have been efforts to coordinate the programs with these tribes.[42] In addition, P.L. 106-169 provides that the "benefits and services under the programs are to be made available to Indian children in the state on the same basis as to other children in the state." "On the same basis" has been interpreted by HHS to mean that the state will provide program services equitably to children in both state custody and tribal custody.[43] The importance of tribal involvement was explained by Representative J.D. Hayworth during debate of the House version of P.L. 106-

169 (H.R. 1802) in June 1999, when he said that tribes are in the best position to identify the needs of tribal youth and local resources available for these young people.[44]

P.L. 110-351 added and modified provisions in the CFCIP pertaining to Indian youth. As of FY2010, the law permits an Indian tribe, tribal organization, or tribal consortium that receives direct funding from HHS to provide child welfare services or enters into a cooperative agreement or contract with the state to provide foster care, to apply for and receive an allotment of CFCIP and ETV funds directly from HHS. To be eligible, a tribal entity must be receiving Title IV-E funds to operate a foster care program (under a Title IV-E plan approved by HHS or via a cooperative agreement or contract with the state). Successful tribal applicants are to receive an allotment amount(s) out of the state's allotment for the program(s) based on the share of all children in foster care in the state under the custody of the tribal entity. Tribal entities must satisfy the CFCIP program requirements established for states, as HHS determines appropriate, and they must submit a plan to HHS that details their process for consulting with the state about their independent living or ETV programs, among other information. For example, in their state plans, tribal entities must discuss the process for consulting with the state to ensure that tribal youth who previously received independent living services through the state will continue to receive the same services through the tribal entity.

The law also requires that as of FY2010, a state must certify that it will negotiate in good faith with any tribal entity that does not receive a direct federal allotment of child welfare funds, but would like to enter into an agreement or contract with the state to receive funds for administering, supervising, or overseeing CFCIP and ETV programs for eligible Indian children under the tribal entity's authority.

National Child Welfare Resource Center for Youth Development Survey of Tribal Consultation and Independent Living Services

In 2007, the National Child Welfare Resource Center for Youth Development reviewed select parts of five-year state child welfare plans, known as the Child and Family Service Plan, to determine the extent to which (1) states have consulted tribes and involved tribal officials in the development of independent living programs and (2) tribal youth have accessed independent living services.[45] Based on a review of these five-year child welfare plans for 28 states, the NCWRCYD determined that the plans provided limited information about tribal consultation. In one-third of the plans, states did not provide a response about consulting tribes. (States may have provided this information in other parts of the plans that were not reviewed and/or may have in fact consulted widely with tribes.) However, some of the state plans detailed their consultation process with tribal entities. The NCWRCYD also reviewed annual child welfare progress reports (known as Annual Progress and Service Reports, which update the five-year plans) and found that 39 states reported consulting with tribes, but that only four states elaborated with additional information.

The Role of Youth Participants

Section 477 of the Social Security Act requires that states ensure youth in independent living programs participate directly in designing their own program activities that prepare them for independent living and further that they "accept personal responsibility for living up to their part of the program." This language builds on the positive youth development approach to serving youth. [46] Youth advocates that support this approach view youth as assets and promote the idea that youth should be engaged in decisions about their lives and communities.

States have also taken various approaches to involving young people in decisions about the services they receive. These include annual conferences, with young people involved in conference planning and participation; youth speakers' bureaus, with young people trained and skilled in public speaking; youth or alumni assisting in the recruitment of foster and adoptive parents; and young people serving as mentors for children and youth in foster care, among other activities.[47] Some states have also established formal youth advisory boards to provide a forum for youth to become involved in issues facing youth in care and aging out of care.[48] Youth-serving organizations for current and former foster youth, such as Foster Club, provide an outlet for young people to become involved in the larger foster care community and advocate for other children in care. States are not required to utilize life skills assessments or personal responsibility contracts with youth to comply with the youth participation requirement, although some states use these tools to assist youth make the transition to adulthood.[49]

Program Administration

States administer their independent living programs in a few ways. Some programs are overseen by the state independent living office, which employs an independent living coordinator and other staff. For example, in Maine, the state's independent living manager oversees six specialized life skills education coordinators assigned to cover all of the state's district offices for the Department of Health and Human Services. In some states, like California, each county (or other jurisdiction) administers its own program with some oversight and support from a statewide program. Other states, including Florida, use contracted service providers to administer their programs. Many jurisdictions have partnered with private organizations to help fund and sometimes administer some aspect of their independent living programs. For example, the Jim Casey Youth Opportunities Initiative has provided funding and technical assistance to multiple cities to provide financial support and training to youth exiting care.[50]

Education and Training Vouchers

As mentioned above, in 2002, Congress passed legislation (P.L. 107-133) to authorize discretionary funding to eligible current and former foster care youth for education and training vouchers worth up to $5,000 annually per youth (states may determine the annual period to which to apply the $5,000 ceiling[51]). Youth qualify for a voucher if they are eligible for CFCIP services or were adopted from foster care after 16 years of age. (Youth eligible for CFCIP services includes those who are ages 18 to 21 who have left foster care because they have aged out; youth likely to remain in foster care until age 18, as determined by the state;

and former foster care recipients age 21 and younger, as determined by the state.) In 2008, P.L. 110-351 extended the ETV program to youth who leave foster care at age 16 or older for kinship guardianship.

The vouchers are available for the cost of full-time or part-time attendance at an institution of higher education, as defined by the Higher Education Act of 1965.[52] (ETV funds may be used to pay for health insurance, which may cover mental health services; but they may not be used to pay directly for a doctor's visit or dental insurance.[53]) A current fiscal year's ETV funds may not be used to finance a youth's educational or vocational loans incurred prior to that current fiscal year.[54] Students may receive the vouchers if they are in good standing and making progress toward completing their program or graduating, though states may have additional requirements such as periodically meeting with a caseworker or limiting the funding to a certain number of semesters.[55] Only youth receiving a voucher at age 21 may continue to participate in the voucher program until age 23.

Funding received through the ETV program does not count toward the student's expected family contribution, which is used by the federal government to determine a student's need for federal financial aid (even for those students who are classified as *independent*, meaning that their parental financial information is not included in the financial aid analysis). However, the total amount of education assistance provided under the CFCIP and other federal programs may not exceed the total cost of attendance, and students cannot claim the same education expenses under multiple federal programs.

Program Administration

States and counties may use ETV dollars to fund the vouchers and the costs associated with administering the program, including for salaries, expenses, and training of staff who administer the state's voucher program. States are not permitted to use Title IV-E Foster Care or Adoption Assistance program funds for administering the ETV program. [56] They may, however, spend additional funds from state sources or other sources to supplement the ETV program or use ETV funds to expand existing post-secondary funding programs.[57] Several states have scholarship programs, tuition waivers, and grants for current and former foster youth that are funded through other sources.[58]

Generally, states administer their ETV program through their independent living program. Some states, however, administer the program through their financial aid office (e.g., California Student Aid Commission) or at the local level (e.g., Florida, where all child welfare programs are administered through community-based agencies). Some states contract with a non-profit service provider, such as the Orphan Foundation of America or the Student Assistance Foundation.

Youth Enrolled in the Program

Youth may enroll in the program if they are in care or have aged out of care. The state with the placement and responsibility for a youth in foster care is to provide the voucher to that youth. The state must also provide a voucher to any youth who is currently receiving a voucher and moves to another state for the *sole* purpose of attending an institution of higher education.[59] If a youth permanently moves to another state after leaving care and subsequently enrolls in a qualified institution of higher education, he or she can apply for a voucher in his or her current state of residence.[60]

HHS 's Administration for Children and Families reported that states provided vouchers to 11,365 youth in FY2006; 12,692 youth in FY2007; and 16,700 youth in FY2008 under the Education and Training Voucher program (these are the most recent data available and do not include all states).[61]

Funding for States

States must provide a 20% match (in-kind or cash) to receive their full federal CFCIP and ETV allotment. CFCIP funds are often mixed with state, local, and other funding sources to provide a system of support for youth likely to age out of care and those who have emancipated. To be eligible for CFCIP general and ETV funds, a state must submit a five-year plan (as part of what is known as the Child and Family Service Plan (CFSP) and Annual Progress and Service Report (APSR), discussed below) to HHS that describes how it intends to carry out its independent living program, including how it involves the public and private sectors to do so. Among other things, a state must ensure in the plan that CFCIP services are available statewide (although services do not have to be identical in all places), that the program serves children of various ages and stages of achieving independence, and that it uses objective criteria to determine eligibility for, and receipt of, CFCIP services. P.L. 110-351 added the requirement that states must ensure that eligible youth receive education about the importance of designating an individual to make health care treatment decisions for them and other information about a health care power of attorney.

The box below includes the full list of certifications that the state must make when submitting its plan. Under Section 477 of the Social Security Act, HHS must approve a state's plan for independent living services if it contains all of the required materials. The plan must be submitted on or before June 30 of the calendar year in which the plan is to begin. States may make amendments to the plan and notify HHS within 30 days of modifying the plan. HHS is to make the plans available to the public. Mandatory and discretionary funds provided under the CFCIP may only supplement, rather than supplant, any funds from other federal sources (e.g., Social Services Block Grant or Runaway and Homeless Youth program) or non-federal sources that may be available for independent living programs in the state.

The 2008 survey of 45 states by Chapin Hall (see above) found that 31 of the states (68.9%) spend additional funds—beyond the 20% match—to provide independent living services and supports to eligible youth. [62] Of the 31 states, 22 reported that they used funds to provide services for which CFCIP dollars cannot be used.[63]

Use of Funds

States may apply to receive mandatory funds for purposes specified in the CFCIP. Also as described in HHS's *Child Welfare Policy Manual*, states may also use CFCIP funding to establish trust funds for youth eligible under the program (Section 3.3E, Question 1). However, states may not use CFCIP funds to train foster parents, workers in group homes, and case managers in issues confronting adolescents; however, states may use funding under the Title IV-E Foster Care program or Adoption Assistance program for this purpose.

A comprehensive report on the development and implementation of the CFCIP was produced by the GAO in November 2004.[64] GAO found that a majority of states use CFCIP funds to provide training on employment-related skills; independent living skills; assistance with obtaining a high school diploma or its equivalent; assessments; and counseling for youth younger than 16. Nearly all states provide these same services, as well as independent living arrangements for youth ages 18 to 21, although provision of services varies within and across states. Separately, the 2008 survey by Chapin Hall asked states if they used CFCIP funding for matched savings accounts, which provide matching funds to youth who accumulate their own funds in a savings account (six states do use funds for this purpose); room and board for youth ages 18 to 21 (39 states); and room and board for current foster youth (11 states).[65]

CFCIP and ETV funds are distributed to each state based on its proportion of the nation's children in foster care. Table B-1 in Appendix B provides the CFCIP and voucher allotments for each state in FY2009 and FY2010 and for a small number of tribes in FY2010.

CFCIP State Plan Requirements

To receive funds under the CFCIP, a state must describe in its CFCIP plan how it will

- design and deliver programs to achieve the program purposes;
- ensure statewide, although not necessarily uniform, coverage by the program;
- ensure that the programs serve children of various ages and at various stages of achieving independence;
- involve the public and private sectors in helping adolescents in foster care achieve independence;
- use objective criteria for determining eligibility for and ensuring fair and equitable treatment of benefit recipients; and
- cooperate in national evaluations of the effects of the programs in achieving the purpose of the CFCIP.

The state must also certify that it will

- provide assistance and services to eligible former foster youth;
- use room and board payments only for youth ages 18 to 21;
- expend not more than 30% of CFCIP funds on room and board for youth ages 18 to 21;
- use funding under the Title IV-E Foster Care program and Adoption Assistance program (but not the CFCIP) to provide training to help foster parents and others understand and address the issues confronting adolescents preparing for independent living and coordinate this training, where possible, with independent living programs;
- consult widely with public and private organizations in developing the plans and give the public at least 30 days to comment on the plan;
- make every effort to coordinate independent living programs with other youth programs at the local, state, and federal levels, including independent living projects funded under the Juvenile Justice and Delinquency Prevention Act, abstinence education programs, local housing programs, programs for disabled youth, and school-to-work programs offered by high schools or local workforce agencies;

- consult each Indian tribe about the programs to be carried out under the plan, that there have been efforts to coordinate the programs with such tribes, and that benefits and services under the programs will be made available to Indian children in the state on the same basis as other children in the state (beginning in FY2010, states must also negotiate in good faith with any tribal entity that does not receive a direct federal allotment of child welfare funds, but would like to enter into an agreement or contract with the state to receive funds for administering, supervising, or overseeing CFCIP and ETV programs for eligible Indian children under the tribal entity's authority);
- ensure that eligible youth participate directly in designing their own program activities that prepare them for independent living and that they accept personal responsibility for living up to their part of the program;
- establish and enforce standards and procedures to prevent fraud and abuse in the programs carried out under its plan;
- ensure that the ETV program complies with the federal program requirements, including that (1) the total amount of education assistance to a youth provided through the ETV program and under other federal and federally supported programs does not exceed the total cost of attendance and (2) does not duplicate benefits under the CFCIP or other federal or federally assisted benefit program; and
- ensure that eligible youth receive education about (1) the importance of designating an individual to make health care treatment decisions for them (should they become unable to do so, have no relatives authorized under state law to do so, or not want relatives to make those decisions); (2) whether a health care power of attorney, health care proxy, or other similar document is recognized under state law; and (3) how to execute such a document.

Source: Section 477 of the Social Security Act.

Hold Harmless Provision

Section 477 of the Social Security Act's includes a "hold harmless" clause that precludes any state from receiving less than the amount of general independent living funds it received under the former independent living program in FY1998 or $500,000, whichever is greater. (There is no hold harmless provision for ETV funds.) The general funding for independent living services doubled nationally with the implementation of the CFCIP, however, the percentage change in funds received varies across states. This is because the distribution of funding was changed to reflect the most current state share of the national caseload (instead of their share of the 1984 caseload in all previous years). In FY2007 (the latest year for which final data are available), three states (the District of Columbia, Louisiana, and New York) received the same funding amount they received in FY1998. Eight states (Alaska, Delaware, Idaho, New Hampshire, North Dakota, South Dakota, Vermont, and Wyoming) each received $500,000 because their FY1998 allotments were this amount or less.

Unused Funds

States have two years to spend their CFCIP and voucher funds. For instance, funds allotted for FY2008 may be spent in FY2008 or FY2009. If a state does not apply for all of its allotment, the remaining funds may be redistributed among states that needs these funds as determined by HHS. If a state applies for all of its CFCIP allotted funds but does not spend them within the two-year time frame, the unused funds revert to the federal treasury.

Table B-2 in Appendix B shows the FY2007 (the latest year for which data for returned funds are available)[66] final allocations, dollars expended, and dollars returned to the federal treasury for general CFCIP allotments.[67] That fiscal year, the 50 states, Puerto Rico, and Washington, DC, were allocated a combined total of $137.9 million in general CFCIP funds, of which $230,000 (0.2%) was returned to the treasury. No states returned all of their funds. Five states (Kentucky, Massachusetts, Montana, North Carolina, and Wyoming) each returned between less than 1.0% and 26.6% of their allocations.

States initially received funds for education and training vouchers in FY2003. Table B-3, also in Appendix B, shows that in FY2007 (the latest year for which data are available), the 50 states, Puerto Rico, and Washington, DC, received $45.5 million in funds for the vouchers, of which 16 states collectively returned $1.5 million (3.4%).[68] States did not report to HHS the reasons for not spending ETV funds. Based on past Congressional Research Service (CRS) discussions with HHS staff, staff with the Orphan Foundation of America (which administers funds in a small number of states), and a small number of states, the reasons may include (1) the lack of infrastructure to absorb and distribute funds, including training child welfare workers and knowledge about educational financial aid; (2) mechanisms for distributing funds to youth and tracking youth outcomes; (3) federal fiscal year deadlines; and (4) youth's knowledge about the ETV program. [69]

Training and Technical Assistance

Training and technical assistance grants for the CFCIP and ETV program are awarded competitively every five years, with non-competitive grants renewed annually.[70] The most recent cooperative agreement was made for FY2010 through FY2014. The National Child Welfare Resource Center for Youth Development, housed at the University of Oklahoma, currently provides assistance under the grant.[71] The NCWRCYD helps states and tribes implement their independent living programs and involve foster youth in programming and services. The NCWRCYD emphasizes the principles of youth development, cultural competence, permanent connections, and collaboration in developing and carrying out state and tribal programs and services for youth in care. Training and technical assistance requests from states have involved providing assistance with more effective implementation of state CFCIP plans, including discussions around allowable expenditures of both CFCIP and ETV funds, permanency planning for adolescents, and educating the courts on laws affecting for older youth, among other types of issues.[72] Assistance is provided through national conferences and meetings, on-site technical assistance, and information made available on the NCWRCYD website and through publications.

National Youth in Transition Database

Section 477 requires that HHS consult with state and local public officials responsible for administering independent living and other child welfare programs, child welfare advocates,

Members of Congress, youth service providers and researchers to (1) "develop outcome measures (including measures of educational attainment, high school diploma, avoidance of dependency, homelessness, non-marital childbirth, incarceration, and high-risk behaviors) that can be used to assess the performance of states in operating independent living programs;" (2) identify the data needed to track the number and characteristics of children receiving services, the type and quantity of services provided, and state performance on the measures; and (3) develop and implement a plan to collect this information beginning with the second fiscal year after the passage of P.L. 106-169. The law further required that by December 2000, HHS was to submit to the House Ways and Means Committee and Senate Finance Committee a report detailing a plan and timetable for collecting the data from the states and a proposal to impose penalties of not less than 1% or more than 5% of the states' CFCIP funding for states that do not comply with the data collection requirements, based on the degree of noncompliance.

History

In its September 2001 *Report to the Congress*, "Developing a System of Program Accountability Under the John H. Chafee Foster Care Independence Program," HHS outlined a plan and timetable for developing a data collection system. The report stated that HHS administrators and an HHS working group consulted with stakeholders and reviewed child welfare literature to identify the data elements to be collected and reported in the database, as well as the outcomes relevant to assessing the CFCIP. The report discussed a penalty structure for states not in compliance with the reporting requirements. HHS also established a pilot test in 2001 involving seven states and an Indian tribe. In each of the jurisdictions, caseworkers collected data about older youth, identified unclear data elements, and described any difficulties encountered while collecting the information. According to HHS, the pilot test enabled the agency to assess the burden for workers collecting the data and to learn if the capacity to report data varied significantly across states and agencies.

Acting on the advice of the Department's General Counsel, HHS decided to produce formal regulations for this mandatory data collection process instead of following their initial plan of producing Program Instructions. The September 2001 report stated that HHS would publish the final outcomes and measures in the *Federal Register* and seek public comment by May 2002. The agency anticipated administering the database nationally in October 2003. However, a notice of proposed rulemaking (NPRM) for the data collection system was not published until July 14, 2006.

The NPRM provided for a 60-day comment period during which HHS heard from states and child welfare advocates. After this period, the final regulations underwent a full agency and department review as well as Office of Management and Budget (OMB) clearance before final publication on February 26, 2008.[73] The final rule establishing the NYTD became effective April 28, 2008, sixty days after publication and requires states to report data on youth beginning in FY2011.

Data Collection

HHS will use the NYTD to engage in two data collection and reporting activities.[74] First, states will collect information twice each fiscal year on eligible youth who currently receive independent living services whether they continue to remain in foster care, were in foster care in another state, or received child welfare services through an Indian tribe or privately operated foster care program. These youth are known as *served youth*. Second, states will also collect information on foster youth on or about their 17th birthday, two years later on or about their 19th birthday, and again on or about their 21st birthday. Foster youth age 17 are known as the *baseline youth* and at ages 19 and 21 are known as the *follow-up youth*. These current and former foster youth will be tracked regardless of whether they receive independent living services at ages 17, 19, and 21. States have the option of tracking a sample of youth who participated in the outcomes collection at age 17 to reduce the data collection burden. Information will be collected on a new group of foster youth age 17 every three years.

Consistent with the statutory requirement developed by Congress in P.L. 106-169, HHS will penalize any state not meeting the data collection procedures for the NYTD from 1% to 5% of its annual Chafee fund allotment, which includes any allotted or re-allotted funds for the general CFCIP program only. The penalty amount will be withheld from a current fiscal year award of the funds. ACF will evaluate a state's data file against data compliance standards, provided by statute. However, states will have the opportunity to submit corrected data.

Training and Technical Assistance[75]

Training and technical assistance for NYTD is provided to states through HHS; the National Child Welfare Resource Center for Youth Development (NCWRCYD) based at the University of Oklahoma; the National Resource Center for Child Welfare Data and Technology (NRCCWDT), housed at the Child Welfare League of America; and a contractor, ICF International, which was selected in September 2008. The contractor is developing and deploying the system used to receive and process states' NYTD data and provide technical assistance to states around data reporting. The Children's Bureau has annually convened national technical assistance meetings for states in each year since 2008. At the conferences, federal staff and staff from NCWRCYD and NCRCCWDT have assisted states in understanding the NYTD regulation and implementation requirements. In coordination with ICF, NCWRCYD, and NRCCWDT, HHS has developed a technical assistance strategy in preparing for NYTD implementation, including a technical assistance toolkit and a series of regional and national conference calls.

Evaluation of Innovative CFCIPs

Section 477 provides that HHS is to conduct evaluations of independent living programs funded by the CFCIP deemed to be innovative or of national significance. The law reserves 1.5% ($2.1 million) of total CFCIP funding annually for these evaluations, as well as CFCIP-related technical assistance, performance measurement, and data collection. For FY2007, HHS spent $1.4 million on research and evaluation and the remaining was set aside for technical assistance and other program support.

HHS has contracted with the Urban Institute and its partners to conduct the Multi-Site Evaluation of Foster Youth Programs. The goal of the evaluation is to determine the effects of independent living programs funded by P.L. 106-169 in achieving key outcomes, including increased educational attainment, higher employment rates and stability, greater interpersonal and relationship skills, reduced non-marital pregnancy and births, and reduced delinquency and crime rates. HHS and the evaluation team initially conducted an assessment to identify programs that could be evaluated rigorously, through random assignment to treatment and control groups, as required under Section 477 of the Social Security Act. The evaluation team, in coordination with HHS and a federally appointed technical work group, established criteria for selecting the sites. Such criteria included that the program should take in sufficient numbers of youth to allow for an adequate sample size; have excess demand so that random assignment is possible while serving the same number of youth as before the evaluation; and be reasonably stable, relatively intense, and consistently implemented; among other considerations.[76]

The evaluation team determined that it could use random assignment at four innovative programs in California and Massachusetts—an employment services program in Kern County, California; a one-on-one intensive, individualized life skills program in Massachusetts; and, a classroom-based life skills training program and tutoring/mentoring program, both in Los Angeles County, California.[77] The 1,400 youth participating in the evaluation at the four sites were assigned to intervention and control groups, and have been surveyed at three points: baseline, one year after baseline, and two years after baseline. The researchers have conducted in-person interviews with the youth to obtain information on youth characteristics, program interventions and services, and intermediate and longer-term outcomes. Researchers have also conducted interviews with program administrators, community advocates, and directors of community provider agencies. Further, the evaluation team has held focus groups with youth, independent living program staff, and other agency staff responsible for referring youth to the programs. The team is using extracts of state administrative data to determine child and family demographics, child welfare placement history, physical and mental health status, and delinquency history. Data specific to each site is also being collected by the team. The findings from the two Los Angeles sites were made available in July 2008. Findings from the other sites are forthcoming.

The life skills and tutoring programs in Los Angeles are administered by the Community College Foundation, a nonprofit organization that administers education and social service programs for foster youth and other vulnerable youth at community colleges throughout California, including Los Angeles County. The purpose of the life skills program is to prepare older foster youth to live independently and acquire the skills and resources needed for emancipation.[78] A second goal is to encourage these youth to complete high school and go on to post-secondary education and training. The life skills classes are held at the community colleges twice a week for five weeks and address education, employment, daily living skills, choices and consequences, and interpersonal social skills. Foster youth enrolled in the life skills program and participating in the study were 17 years old at the time of assignment, eligible for CFCIP services, and physically and mentally fit to participate.

The purpose of the tutoring program is to improve the educational outcomes of foster youth in reading and math and to empower them to use other educational services and resources that may be available to them. Another purpose of the program is to facilitate a mentoring relationship between the tutor and youth. Youth enrolled in the tutoring/mentoring program and participating in the study were ages 14 or 15 and were one to three years behind grade level in either reading or math.[79] The youth received up to 50 hours of remedial one-on-one tutoring in reading in math in their homes. The life skills program evaluated outcomes across several domains: education, employment, money management, housing, and health and hygiene. The tutoring evaluation measured impacts through the Woodcock Johnson educational assessment, grades, educational attainment, and school behavior.

The evaluation of the two programs found no statistically significant impact as a result of the life skills training and tutoring interventions. A limitation of the design for the evaluation is that some youth in the control group received life skills services or tutoring services through other programs, and some members in the treatment group did not receive the life skills or tutoring services through the Community College Foundation, as intended. Nonetheless, the evaluation team concluded that even if there were no challenges with the experimental design of the studies, the results would not likely change. According to the research team, the findings from the evaluations should not be generalized to other independent living programs, given that these other programs may be structured differently and provide distinct services.

PART Review

In calendar year 2004, the CFCIP was reviewed through the U.S. Office of Management and Budget's Program Assessment Rating Tool (PART) process.[80] The evaluation concluded that program results were "not demonstrated" because the CFCIP lacked long-term performance measures and time frames for these measures, as well as adequate progress in achieving its annual performance goals; and because some states did not use all of their CFCIP or ETV funding. OMB made the determination about the performance measurement because the National Youth in Transition Database, which will provide long-term performance and annual performance measurement beginning in FY2011, had not yet been implemented. The PART review also found that no independent evaluations of the program have been routinely conducted. While the Multi- Site Evaluation will provide information about outcomes for youth who receive independent living services, according to the PART review, it is not sufficiently national in scope.

The PART has established two goals for the program:

- Promote the efficient use of CFCIP funds by (1) increasing the percentage of states that completely expend their allocations within the two-year expenditure period, and (2) decreasing the percentage of funds that remain unexpended by states within that period.
- Increase the percentages of CFCIP youth who avoid high-risk behaviors which might otherwise lead to criminal investigations and incarceration. The baseline measurement will be taken in FY20 11, the first year the NYTD is implemented.

Assessments of the CFCIP

There does not appear to be a clear picture of the types of services provided through CFCIPfunded programs, although the National Youth in Transition Database and the evaluation of innovative independent living programs will provide a national overview about the number of youth served, the types of services provided, and best practices in assisting current and former foster youth make the transition to adulthood. Three sources—an evaluation of independent living services described in states' Child and Family Services Review documents, a GAO report on the CFCIP, and a report on ETV programs in six states—provide some insight into how states carry out their independent living programs.[81]

Child and Family Services Review

The U.S. Department of Health and Human Services determines state compliance with federal child welfare policies, and helps to ensure that positive outcomes are achieved for children and families involved in the child welfare system, by conducting reviews of state and child welfare programs.

The most comprehensive component of HHS 's review system is the Child and Family Services Reviews (CFSR).[82] Conducted by the Children's Bureau, the reviews assess state conformity with certain requirements of Title IV-B and Title IV-E.[83] During the review process, a joint federal and state team determines whether states are in substantial conformity with seven outcomes related to the safety, permanency, and well-being of children, and whether states have in place child welfare systems to achieve these goals. The team reviews statewide administrative data; conducts interviews with children and families served, as well as foster parents, service providers, case workers, court personnel, and other key stakeholders; and systematically reviews the cases of a random sample of children served.

The first round of reviews was conducted between 2001 and 2004 in all 50 states, the District of Columbia, and Puerto Rico, and a final report was prepared discussing the findings in each jurisdiction.[84] This initial round found that no state's child welfare programs met the criteria that HHS established as demonstrating "substantial conformity" with all of federal child welfare policy requirements. As a result, all states have or are implementing Program Improvement Plans (PIP). To avoid financial penalties associated with noncompliance, states must meet the improvement goals established in their PIP.

Analysis of First Round CFSR Findings[85]

An analysis of the CFSR findings for 45 jurisdictions found strengths in a few states related to increased involvement of youth in case planning and other relevant activities, as well as an increased focus on permanency issues for adolescents in care, including promoting family connections for older foster youth.[86] However, the analysis also found a number of barriers to effective youth services to be fairly common.

The most common identified barrier was inadequate or non-existent services, including service gaps related to life skills training, job skills training, substance abuse treatment, mental health treatment, general independent living services, inpatient mental health treatment services, services for pregnant or parenting teens, and independent living assessments. (Of the 45 final reports reviewed in this analysis 34 states reported the service gap barrier.) The second most common barrier (identified in 26 of the 45 reports analyzed) was a lack of placement resources for adolescents, including transitional living placements, homes for youth over 18, and homes for pregnant and parenting teens. Twenty-five of the 45 state final reports analyzed identified gaps in youth-specific training for staff and foster parents ranging from having no specialized adolescent training for any staff or foster parents to needing specialized training in assessing youths' needs. This training need was identified despite the fact that the majority of states received a positive rating relating to provision of training. Of the 45 states included in the analysis, 87% identified the need for additional training in adolescent issues despite the fact that they received an overall strength rating for their training program.

Inconsistency in services was found to be a barrier in a separate group of 25 states. This meant, for instance, that services related to life skills might be very strong in one part of the state but lacking in other areas of the state. In addition, in some places the service inconsistencies were found among contractors or providers within a specific region or area of the state. Finally, in 24 states the quality and consistency of independent living planning was identified as an issue. Specific problems included a lack of youth involvement in case planning, no independent living case plan completed, case plans not regularly updated, no transition planning, no youth assessment, poor placement matches, lack of individualized planning for youth in long-term care, and poor permanency goal selection.

A review of the initial 31 Program Improvement Plans approved for state implementation found that independent living and adolescent issues might not have been addressed. Researchers concluded that this might be the case because the language in the PIP was more general (services for all children not just adolescents) or because the specific concern was identified within an area for which the state might nonetheless have received a positive rating (e.g. quality of training program).[87]

Second Round CFSR

The second round of review for some jurisdictions are underway, and has a focus on older youth. For this second round, HHS has directed the federal and state evaluators to interview, at the state- level, youth being served by the state child welfare agency, especially those youth who are eligible to receive independent living services.[88] Also in the second round, 10 of 40 foster care cases reviewed must involve children who were ages 16 or 17 as of the last day of the 12-month review period or the date that they exited care, as applicable.[89] This is to ensure that the reviewers have enough applicable cases to determine whether states are adequately providing independent living services for youth with a goal of emancipation.[90]

GAO Report

The 2004 report by the GAO evaluated its implementation.[91] The report was based on survey data collected from independent living coordinators in all 50 states, the District of Columbia, and Puerto Rico as well as review of the jurisdictions' CFCIP plans for FY2001 through FY2004. After the 1999 passage of P.L. 106-169, forty states reported expanded independent living services to youth younger than they had previously served and 36 states reported serving older youth. In addition, 45 states reported offering assistance with room and board to emancipated foster youth. According to officials in the states GAO visited for the study, funds were also used to improve the quality of existing independent living services, refocus the attention of their programs, or develop new services to assist youth of all ages in the programs.

The GAO report also raised concerns about the implementation of the CFCIP. The report indicates that states varied in the percentage of eligible youth served. In 2003, forty states reported serving between 10% and 100% of eligible youth, with one-third of the states serving less than half of eligible youth. GAO also found gaps in the availability of mental health services, mentoring services, and securing safe and suitable housing, particularly in rural areas. Further, although 49 states reported increased coordination with a number of federal, state, and local programs that can provide or supplement independent living services, child welfare administrators and youth interviewed by GAO said that they were unaware of the services. Finally, the lack of uniformity among the states' CFCIP five-year plans precluded using them at the state and federal level to monitor how well the programs serve eligible youth.

Implementation of the ETV Program

In 2007, the National Foster Care Coalition, in partnership with Casey Family Programs, a foundation supporting child welfare research and advocacy, reported on six states' (California, Maine, Montana, New York, North Carolina, and Wyoming) experiences with implementing the ETV program.[92] These states serve as few as 31 youth to as many as nearly 2,000 youth in a given school year, with average awards ranging from $2,950 to $4,318 for each youth. Three of the states (Montana, New York, and North Carolina) contract with a non-profit service provider to administer the ETV program, while the other three states administer the program through the independent living coordinator or state financial aid office.

The report describes the best practices employed by the states in implementing their ETV programs, as well as the challenges they have encountered.[93] One promising approach was the application process for some states, which involves a web application process that allows students and schools to view application and approval status and deadlines. Other states reported providing extensive promotion and outreach about the program through information sessions, annual teen conferences for foster youth, and mailings; and providing additional educational supports to youth through financial aid counseling, mentoring, tuition waivers, and scholarships. Contracting through a third-party was also identified as an important practice that has lent to more efficient administration of the voucher program. The report also identified youth feedback about the program as another important feature of the programs.

In addition, the report also identified barriers to successfully administering the ETV program. Some of the challenges include (1) meeting the demand for the program; (2) recruiting youth to the program and ensuring that these youth have sufficient support to remain in school; (3) managing awards for youth whom schools are unable to locate once awards are issued or awarding funds to youth who have dropped out; (4) tracking how voucher funds are spent; (5) conveying to university financial aid staff the rules associated with the ETV program; (6) maintaining the confidentiality of youth's foster care experiences; (7) connecting non-collegebound youth to vocational programs; and (8) meeting the needs of parenting youth, among others. The states indicated that they are working to address these challenges.

OTHER FEDERAL SUPPORT FOR OLDER CURRENT AND FORMER FOSTER YOUTH

In addition to the federal programs under Title IV-E, other federal laws authorize some funding for service or assistance to older current and former foster youth. This section describes a Medicaid pathway for certain former foster youth; educational, workforce, and housing supports; and a grant to fund training for child welfare practitioners working with older foster youth and youth emancipating from care.

Medicaid

In the Foster Care Independence Act, Congress encouraged states to provide Medicaid coverage to children who were aging out of the foster care system. The law created a new optional Medicaid eligibility pathway for "independent foster care adolescents;" this pathway is often called the "Chafee option."[94] The law further defined these adolescents as individuals under the age of 21 and who were in foster care under the responsibility of the state on their 18th birthday. Within this broadest category of independent foster care adolescents, the law permits states to restrict eligibility based on the youth's income or resources, and whether or not the youth had received Title IV-E funding.[95]

In all states, youth age 19 or younger with family incomes at or below 100% of the federal poverty limit (or up to 250% in some states) are eligible for Medicaid or State Children's Health Insurance Program (SCHIP). Youth ages 18 to 21 in foster care who do not qualify for Medicaid or SCHIP may be eligible for Medicaid coverage through the "Ribicoff" pathway, named for the late former senator, Abraham Ribicoff. Ribicoff youth must meet the income and resource requirements for the former Aid to Families with Dependent Children program but do not meet other categorical requirements for AFDC. Older foster youth may also be eligible under a pathway for children under age 21 who are taken into state custody. This pathway allows the state to extend Medicaid eligibility to youth under age 21 in foster care regardless of the income or resources of their biological or foster parents.[96]

Former foster youth may also qualify for Medicaid through other eligibility pathways available to certain groups of adults, such as for pregnant women with family income equal to or less than 133% of the federal poverty limit (FPL), some low-income adults with children, and some adults with high medical expenses (i.e., "medically needy").[97] These youth may be also eligible for Medicaid or SCHIP coverage through waivers, known as Section 1115 waivers, that provide comprehensive coverage to categorically ineligible adults with incomes up to at least 100% of the FPL.

According to the 2008 survey by Chapin Hall of 45 states, 29 states (64.4%) have extended the Chafee option to eligible youth.[98] Of the 28 states that responded to a follow-up question about eligibility requirements, 25 states reported that to be eligible, youth must have been in foster care on their 18th birthday; 15 states reported that youth must complete an application to be eligible; one state said that youth are automatically eligible; and nine states reported other eligibility criteria. Another 14 states reported that former foster youth are eligible for SCHIP (six of the states) or Medicaid through other pathways (13 of the states). Youth are eligible for Medicaid by meeting the "medically needy" criteria (seven states), through a 100% state funded program (three states), and through other, unspecified pathways (three states). One state reported that former foster youth are not categorically eligible for Medicaid.

The Chafee option will likely become a moot pathway in the next few years. As part of the health care reform law, the Patient Protection and Affordable Care Act (P.L. 111-148), youth who were in foster care on their 18th birthday (or an older age allowed by the state) will be eligible under a new mandatory Medicaid pathway specifically for former foster youth until age 26 regardless of their annual income. [99] This provision is effective January 1, 2014. HHS has not issued guidance about this pathway.

Other Educational Support[100]

The Higher Education Opportunity Act (HEOA), was signed into law on August 14, 2008 as P.L. 110-315, and amended the Higher Education Act (HEA) to authorize services specifically for youth in foster care or recently emancipated youth, including housing services, among other related changes. The act authorizes that youth in foster care (including youth who have left foster care after reaching age 16) and homeless children and youth are eligible for what are collectively called the federal Trio programs. The Trio programs are designed to identify potential postsecondary students from disadvantaged backgrounds, prepare these students for higher education, provide certain support services to them while they are in college, and train individuals who provide these services. The programs are known individually as Talent Search, Upward Bound, Student Support Services, and Educational Opportunity Centers. P.L. 110-315 directs the Department of Education to require applicants seeking Trio funds to identify and make available services, including mentoring, tutoring, and other services, to these youth. In addition, the bill authorizes services for current and former foster youth (and homeless youth) through Student Support Services—a program intended to improve the retention and graduation rates of disadvantaged college students—that include temporary housing during breaks in the academic year.

Separately, HEOA allows additional uses of funds through the Fund for the Improvement of Postsecondary Education to establish demonstration projects that provide comprehensive support services for students who were in foster care (or homeless) anytime before age 13. As specified in the law, the projects can provide housing to the youth when housing at an educational institution is closed or unavailable to other students.

As of July 2009, the College Cost Reduction Act (P.L. 110-84) allows certain youth who have been in foster care to claim independent status when applying for federal financial aid. The act amended the definition of "independent student" in the Higher Education Act to include any child "who is an orphan, in foster care, or a ward of the court at any time when the individual is 13 years of age or older" and "is an emancipated minor or is in legal guardianship as determined by a court of competent jurisdiction in the individual's state of legal residence." [101] Students who claim independent status are typically able to access greater federal education assistance because they are exempt from including information about income and assets from their parents. An "independent" student's expected "family" contribution is the amount that the federal need analysis system determines should be contributed, based only on his or her available income (and assets, if applicable), as well as basic living expenses, federal income tax liability, and other expenses. The act does not specify the length of time that the child must have been in foster care or the reason for exiting care, to be eligible to claim independent status. The law first becomes effective for the 2009 to 2010 school year.

Workforce Support

Workforce Investment Act Programs

The Workforce Investment Act authorizes job training programs to unemployed and underemployed individuals through the Department of Labor (DOL). Two of these programs— Youth Activities and Job Corps—provide job training and related services to targeted low-income vulnerable populations, including foster youth. [102] The WIA Youth Activities program focuses on preventative strategies to help in-school youth stay in school and receive occupational skills, as well as on providing training and supportive services, such as assistance with child care, for outof-school youth. Job Corps is an educational and vocational training program that helps students learn a trade, complete their GED, and secure employment.

To be eligible, foster youth must meet age and income criteria as defined under the act. Young people current or formerly in foster care may participate in Youth Activities if they are ages 14 to 21, and in Job Corps if they are ages 16 to 24 (20% of participants must be ages 22 to 24).[103]

Foster Youth Demonstration Project

The Workforce Investment Act authorizes funding for pilot programs.[104] Under this authority, the Department of Labor's Employment and Training Administration awarded grants to five states in FY2005—California, Illinois, Michigan, New York, and Texas—to design and implement programs to improve the self sufficiency, education attainment, and employment skills of youth aging out of foster care. The purpose of the grant was to encourage states to develop best practices around serving foster youth in the workforce investment system, and integrate these practices across workforce investment boards across each state. The five states were required to target the programs to youth in areas with the largest foster care populations. These areas are Los Angeles, Chicago, Detroit, New York City, and Houston. DOL awarded each state $800,000 total for FY2005 and FY2006; states were required to provide 100% matching funds.

The sites have differed in their recruitment and delivery strategies, but all have provided youth with academic instruction and support, preparation for and exposure to the work place, support in developing skills for self-sufficiency, and the supportive services intended to help them succeed academically and in the work place.

With their own funding, Casey Family Programs and its partners conducted an evaluation of the program.[105] At all of the sites, youth formed strong relationships with staff, and staff remained relatively consistent over time. The sites also reported improvements in their programs. For example, multiple sites changed their program classes and activities to accommodate the individual needs of youth. Partnerships with workforce investment boards and other public agencies have also been formed to provide youth with job training experience, and at some sites, new relationships between the workforce agencies and the child welfare agencies have developed at the state level. These partnerships appear to have been difficult to build.

The evaluation concluded that no single agency can meet the needs of youth in foster care or aging out of care; case workers—who serve as social workers, counselors, mentors, and teachers—are highly valued by the youth; well-defined programs tended to be more successful in leveraging other services for youth; and the sites lacked consistency in they ways they defined and collected the data, among other findings. The programs are continuing to serve eligible youth, with funding from Casey Family Programs and a 100% match by the states and other lead partners.

Housing Support

Family Unification Vouchers Program

Current and former foster youth may be eligible for housing subsidies provided through programs administered by the Department of Housing and Urban Development's (HUD) Family Unification Vouchers program (FUP vouchers). The FUP vouchers were initially created in 1990 under P.L. 101-625 for families that qualify for Section 8 tenant-based assistance and for whom the lack of adequate housing is a primary factor in the separation, or threat of imminent separation, of children from their families or in preventing the reunification of the children with their families. [106] Amendments to the program in 2000 under P.L. 106-377 made youth ages 18 to 21 who left foster care at age 16 or older eligible for the vouchers. These youth are eligible for the vouchers for up to 18 months.

FUP vouchers were initially awarded from 1992 to 2001. Over that period, approximately 39,000 vouchers were distributed. [107] Each award included five years of funding per voucher and the voucher's use was restricted to voucher-eligible families for those five years. At the end of those five years, public housing authorities (PHAs), which administer the vouchers, were eligible to convert FUP vouchers to regular Section 8 housing vouchers for low-income families. While the five-year use restrictions have expired for all family unification vouchers, some PHAs may have continued to use their original family unification vouchers for FUP-eligible families and some may have chosen to use some regular-purpose vouchers for FUP families. Congress appropriated $20 million for new FUP vouchers in each of FY2008 and FY2009 and $15 million in FY2010.[108] Congress has specified that amounts made available under Section 8 tenant-based rental assistance and used for the FUP are to remain available for these purposes.

A survey of states in 2008 by Chapin Hall found that 12 states provided housing assistance through FUP vouchers, and another nine states gave youth priority access to Section 8 vouchers.[109] Finally, 18 states reported providing housing assistance through other housing programs, such as transitional living programs with a housing component.

Other Support

Older current and former foster youth may be eligible for housing services and related supports through the Runaway and Homeless Youth program, administered by the U.S. Department of Health and Human Services.[110] In FY2008, 974 of the 48,104 youth (2.0%) who used the program's Basic Center program or Transitional Living program were living in foster homes at the time they entered the program.[111] That same year, of the 45,907 youth who exited the program, 1,334 (2.9%) were placed in a foster home. (The number of youth who may have lived in other foster care settings before entering or at exit is not reported.) Youth transitioning out of foster care may also be eligible for select transitional living programs administered by HUD, though the programs do not specifically target these youth.[112]

The Foreclosure Prevention Act of 2008 (P.L. 110-289), was signed into law on July 30, 2008, and enables owners of properties financed in part with Low-Income Housing Tax Credits (LIHTCs) to claim as low-income units those units occupied by low-income students who were in foster care. Owners of LIHTC properties are required to maintain a certain percentage of their units for occupancy by low-income households; students (with some exceptions) are not generally considered low-income households for this purpose. The law does not specify the length of time these students must have spent in foster care nor require that youth are eligible only if they emancipated.

Grant to Support Curriculum for Supervising Older Youth in Care

In FY2006, the U.S. Department of Health and Human Services awarded grants under Title IV-B of the Social Security Act (Promoting Safe and Stable Families) to fund the development of curriculum for child welfare supervisors and their staff who work with older youth in foster care. The grants were awarded through FY2008 to six entities: the Hunter College School of Social Work; Massachusetts Department of Social Services; San Francisco State University; University of Iowa; University of Houston; and University of Louisville Research Foundation. Each of the entities provide at least a 25% match to the federal grant award of (up to) $250,000 annually for three years.

The six entities were directed to develop, implement, evaluate, and disseminate a training curriculum for public child welfare agency supervisors.[113] The purpose of the curriculum is to strengthen supervision of staff interactions with older youth in care and/or in independent living programs, and to ensure that staff adequately: (1) assess a youth's readiness for independent living services, support, and training; (2) identify culturally competent independent living program services and activities; (3) utilize positive youth development principles for involving youth in decisionmaking, implementation, and evaluation of training and program activities;[114] (4) identify areas of stress and its impact on youth in foster care; (5) work with youth to help them deal with crisis situations and to assess the results of the intervention; (6) work with youth to develop and maintain permanent connections; and (7) collaborate with both inter-and intraagency resource people to achieve positive outcomes for youth transitioning to adulthood. Each entity must conduct an evaluation of the project, either in-house or by contracting with a third-party evaluator.

APPENDIX A. OUTCOMES FOR YOUNG ADULTS FORMERLY IN FOSTER CARE

Table A-1. Comparison of Outcome Domains Between Young Adults in the Midwest Study and Young Adults in the Add Health Study

Outcome	Midwest Evaluation (Wave 4)—Former Foster Youth at Age 23 and 24	Add Health—Youth Surveyed at Age 23 and 24
Current Living Arrangement		
Lives in own place	49.0%	63.2%
Lives with biological parent(s)	7.0%	29.4%
Lives with other relative	14.1%	3.4%
Lives with non-relative foster parent(s)	3.8%	0%
Lives with spouse/partner	7.3%	0.7%
Lives with a friend	6.5%	1.2%
Lives in group quarters (e.g., dormitories, barracks)	1.7%	1.1%
In jail or prison	7.0%	0.1%
Homeless	0.7%	0.1%
Other living arrangement	3.0%	0.8%
Highest Educational Attainment		
No high school diploma or GED	24.4%	7.3%
High school diploma only	33.7%	26.2%
GED only	9.8%	5.4%
One or more years of college, but no degree	25.6%	27.6%
Two-year college degree	3.2%	9.4%
Four-year college degree	2.5%	19.4%
One or more years of graduate school	0.5%	4.8%
Employment, Income, and Assets		
Ever held a job	94.7%	97.3%
Currently employed[a] (nonincarcerated youth only)	48.0%	75.7%
Mean hourly wage[a]	$10.14	$13.94
Mean income[a]	$12,064	$20,349
Any savings/checking account[a]	47.3%	85.1%
Owns a vehicle[a]	44.9%	81.3%
Economic Hardships		
Not enough money to pay rent[a]	28.5%	7.4%
Not enough money to pay utility bill[a]	26.9%	11.8%
Gas or electricity shut off	8.7%	4.3%
Evicted[a]	8.6%	0.7%
Receipt of food stamps[a]	61.5%–females 19.9%–males	8.3%–females 1.2%–males

Table A-1. (Continued)

Outcome	Midwest Evaluation (Wave 4)—Former Foster Youth at Age 23 and 24	Add Health—Youth Surveyed at Age 23 and 24
Receipt of TANF	6.6%–females[a] 2.0%–males	6.5%–females[a] 1.5%–males
Health and Access to Health Care Services		
Description of general health as fair[a]	14.6%	3.6%
Description of general health as poor[a]	1.2%	0.3%
Health conditions or disability limits daily activities[a]	12.5%	5.0%
Has medical insurance[a]	57.0%	78.0%
Did not receive needed medical care[a]	13.0%	22.6%
Received psychological or emotional counseling[a]	11.3%	6.5%
Attended substance abuse treatment program	5.1%	2.4%
Sexual Behaviors and Pregnancy		
Age at first intercourse	16.0–female 15.0–male	17.0–female 16.0–male
Used birth control at time of most recent intercourse[a]	51.6%–females 51.9%–males	68.2%–females 68.4%–males
Ever paid by someone to have sex[a]	9.4%–females 12.4%–males	3.9%–females 3.1%–males
Ever pregnant (females only)[a]	77.0%	40.4%
Impregnated partner (males only)[a]	60.7%	28.4%
Received prenatal care (females only)[a]	94.2%	84.4%
Relationships and Parenting		
Ever married	16.1%–females[a] 13.2–males	30.2%–females[a] 18.2%–males
Currently married	13.4%–females[a] 11.8%–males	27.7%–females[a] 16.3%–males
Currently cohabiting	26.4%–females[a] 21.4%–males	15.7%–females[a] 16.3%–males
At least one living child[a]	66.8%–females 44.3%–males	30.1%–females 18.3%–males
Criminal Justice		
Ever arrested[a]	57.2%–females 81.2%–males	4.3%–females 17.4%–males
Arrested since age 18[a]	38.7%–females 64.0%–males	0.3%–females 2.9%–males
Ever convicted[a]	28.2%–females 58.8%–males	2.0%–females 10.3%–males
Convicted since age 18[a]	18.4%–females 42.8%–males	1.6%–females 9.1%–males

Table A-1. (Continued)

Outcome	Midwest Evaluation (Wave 4)—Former Foster Youth at Age 23 and 24	Add Health—Youth Surveyed at Age 23 and 24
Transition to Adulthood and Orientation Toward the Future		
Became socially mature[a]	69.4%–faster than others 23.4%–about the same rate as others 6.5%–slower than others	58.5%–faster than others 8.5%–about the same rate as others 32.8%–slower than others
Took on adult responsibilities[a]	67.8%–faster than others 25.4%–about the same rate as others 6.8%–slower than others	62.9%–faster than others 8.5%–about the same rate as others 28.5%–slower than others
Thinks of self as an adult[a]	Most or all of the time–88.2% Sometimes–7.3% Never or seldom – 4.3%	Most or all of the time–77.9% Sometimes–5.8% Never or seldom–2.0%
Will live to 35 (mean score based on 1 to 5 scale, with 1 being almost no chance to 5 being almost certain)[a]	4.49	4.66
Will be married within next 10 years (mean score based on 1 to 5 scale, with 1 being almost no chance to 5 being almost certain)[a]	3.40	3.96
Will have a middle-class income by age 30 (mean score based on 1 to 5 scale, with 1 being almost no chance to 5 being almost certain)[a]	3.66	4.17
Mentoring		
Maintained a positive relationship with a caring adult since age 14[a]	66.4%	76.2%
Closeness to mentor[a]	9.3%–not at all to a little close 26.5%–somewhat close 64.1%–very or quite close	10.7%–not at all to a little close 31.5%– somewhat close 57.8%–very or quite close

Source: Congressional Research Service presentation of data in Mark E. Courtney et al., *Midwest Evaluation of the Adult Functioning of Former Foster Youth: Outcomes at Ages 23 and 24*, Chapin Hall Center for Children, University of Chicago, 2010.

Note: The Midwest Evaluation has tracked the outcomes of foster youth at ages 17 and 18, age 19, age 21, and ages 23 and 24. For each of the four data collection waves, wherever possible, researchers asked the same questions that were taken directly from the National Longitudinal Survey of Adolescent Health ("Add Health"), a nationally representative survey that tracks a cohort of youth over time.

a. Indicates that the difference between the youth in the Midwest Evaluation and youth in the Adolescent Heath Survey is statistically significant.

APPENDIX B. FUNDING FOR THE CHAFEE FOSTER CARE INDEPENDENCE PROGRAM (CFCIP) AND EDUCATION AND TRAINING VOUCHER (ETV) PROGRAM

Table B-1. Final FY2009 and Estimated FY2010 CFCIP General and ETV Allotments by State (Excludes Funding for CFCIF Technical Assistance and ETV Set Asides)

State	Final FY2009			Estimated FY2010		
	CFCIP	ETV	Total	CFCIP	ETV	Total
Alabama	$1,947,161	$654,771	$2,601,932	$2,020,511	$677,380	$2,697,891
Alaska	587,392	197,522	784,914	627,046	210,218	837,264
Arizona	2,623,829	882,314	3,506,143	2,995,850	1,004,364	4,000,214
Arkansas	969,425	325,988	1,295,413	1,012,123	339,316	1,351,439
California	20,375,619	6,851,700	27,227,319	19,346,731	6,486,023	25,832,754
Colorado	2,084,961	701,109	2,786,070	2,276,271	763,124	3,039,395
Connecticut	1,550,651	521,437	2,072,088	1,545,485	518,127	2,063,612
Delaware	500,000	104,305	604,305	500,000	90,369	590,369
District of Columbia	1,091,992	198,063	1,290,055	1,091,992	213,590	1,305,582
Florida	7,067,742	2,376,666	9,444,408	6,375,916	2,137,537	8,513,453
Georgia	3,280,389	1,103,095	4,383,484	2,869,119	961,877	3,830,996
Hawaii	520,101	174,894	694,995	500,000	153,280	653,280
Idaho	501,335	168,583	669,918	500,000	165,997	665,997
Illinois	4,772,059	1,604,698	6,376,757	5,132,172	1,720,569	6,852,741
Indiana	3,048,757	1,025,204	4,073,961	3,559,387	1,193,290	4,752,677
Iowa	2,209,089	742,849	2,951,938	1,980,853	664,084	2,644,937
Kansas	1,777,727	597,795	2,375,522	1,812,230	607,553	2,419,783
Kentucky	2,025,445	681,095	2,706,540	2,094,365	702,139	2,796,504
Louisiana	1,429,741	480,778	1,910,519	1,455,538	487,972	1,943,510
Maine	565,888	177,599	743,487	565,888	180,641	746,529
Maryland	2,863,236	962,819	3,826,055	2,226,843	746,553	2,973,396
Massachusetts	2,813,371	946,051	3,759,422	2,996,999	1,004,749	4,001,748
Michigan	5,584,382	1,877,857	7,462,239	5,812,955	1,948,803	7,761,758
Minnesota	1,811,238	609,064	2,420,302	1,729,978	579,978	2,309,956
Mississippi	892,214	300,024	1,192,238	942,292	315,905	1,258,197
Missouri	2,641,523	888,263	3,529,786	2,760,494	925,460	3,685,954
Montana	500,000	156,593	656,593	500,000	155,014	655,014
Nebraska	1,575,048	529,640	2,104,688	1,607,101	546,933	2,154,034
Nevada	1,354,675	455,536	1,810,211	1,442,032	483,443	1,925,475
New Hampshire	500,000	97,724	597,724	500,000	98,847	598,847
New Jersey	2,502,114	841,385	3,343,499	2,537,781	850,795	3,388,576
New Mexico	649,590	218,437	868,027	638,253	213,975	852,228
New York	11,585,958	2,711,038	14,296,996	11,585,958	2,841,411	14,427,369
North Carolina	2,902,646	976,071	3,878,717	2,828,025	948,100	3,776,125
North Dakota	500,000	113,861	613,861	500,000	119,464	619,464
Ohio	4,561,875	1,534,019	6,095,894	4,844,801	1,624,227	6,469,028

Table B-1. (Continued)

State	Final FY2009			Estimated FY2010		
	CFCIP	ETV	Total	CFCIP	ETV	Total
Oklahoma	3,174,760	1,067,575	4,242,335	3,044,704	1,020,742	4,065,446
Oregon	2,563,507	862,029	3,425,536	2,583,757	866,209	3,449,966
Pennsylvania	5,591,889	1,880,381	7,472,270	5,577,023	1,869,706	7,446,729
Puerto Rico	1,745,019	586,797	2,331,816	1,815,903	608,784	2,424,687
Rhode Island	729,750	245,393	975,143	691,704	231,895	923,599
South Carolina	1,374,514	462,207	1,836,721	1,436,571	481,613	1,918,184
South Dakota	500,000	141,448	641,448	500,000	142,779	642,779
Tennessee	2,077,991	698,765	2,776,756	2,074,536	695,492	2,770,028
Texas	8,079,527	2,716,898	10,796,425	8,088,940	2,711,831	10,800,771
Utah	734,307	246,925	981,232	747,741	250,682	998,423
Vermont	500,000	118,008	618,008	500,000	115,610	615,610
Virginia	2,005,337	674,334	2,679,671	1,937,748	649,633	2,587,381
Washington	2,977,712	1,001,314	3,979,026	3,199,303	1,072,572	4,271,875
West Virginia	1,182,292	397,568	1,579,860	1,267,884	425,060	1,692,944
Wisconsin	1,996,222	671,269	2,667,491	2,127,412	713,219	2,840,631
Wyoming	500,000	110,977	610,977	500,000	111,179	611,179
Total for states	$137,900,000	$44,670,735	$182,570,735	$137,808,215	$44,648,113	$182,456,328
Tribes	N/A	N/A	N/A	$91,785	$22,622	$114,407
Total for states and tribes	**N/A**	**N/A**	**N/A**	**$137,900,000**	**$44,670,735**	**$182,570,735**

Sources: Congressional Research Service presentation of data from the U.S. Department of Health and Human Services (HHS), Administration on Children, Youth and Families, Administration for Children and Families, *FY2010 Justification of Estimates for Appropriations Committees*, pp. 151-152, 364-365; and U.S. Department of Health and Human Services, Administration on Children, Youth and Families, Administration for Children and Families, Children's Bureau, *Program Instruction: Title IV-B Annual Progress and Services Report; Child Abuse Prevention and Treatment State Plan; Chafee Foster Care Independence Program; Educational Training Vouchers Program*, ACYFCB-PI-10-09, April 20, 2010, http://www.acf.hhs.gov/programs/cb/laws

Note: The Fostering Connections to Success and Increasing Adoptions Act (P.L. 110-351) permits, as of FY2010, an Indian tribe, tribal organization, or tribal consortium that receives direct funding from HHS to provide child welfare services or enters into a cooperative agreement or contract with the state to provide foster care to apply for and receive an allotment of CFCIP and ETV funds directly from HHS. To be eligible, a tribal entity must be receiving Title IV-E funds to operate a foster care program (under a Title IV-E plan approved by HHS or via a cooperative agreement or contract with the state). For FY2010, the following tribes received CFCIP funding: Prairie Band of Potawatomi (Kansas), Santee Sioux Nation (Nebraska), Confederated Tribe of Warm Springs (Oregon), and Port Gamble S'Klallam Tribe (Washington). For FY2010, the following tribes received ETV funding: Prairie Band of Potawatomi (Kansas), Confederated Tribe of Warm Springs (Oregon), and Port Gamble S'Klallam Tribe (Washington).

Table B-2. FY2007 Chafee Foster Care Independence Program: Final Funds Allotted, Expended, and Returned to Federal Treasury, by State

State	Dollar Amount Allocated	Dollar Amount Expended	Dollar Amount Returned to Treasury	Percent of Allotment Returned to Treasury
Alabama	$1,784,444	$1,784,444	$0	0%
Alaska	500,000	500,000	0	0
Arizona	2,600,648	2,600,648	0	0
Arkansas	833,756	833,756	0	0
California	20,953,350	20,953,350	0	0
Colorado	2,120,011	2,120,011	0	0
Connecticut	1,815,162	1,815,162	0	0
Delaware	500,000	500,000	0	0
District of Columbia	1,091,992	1,091,992	0	0
Florida	7,566,271	7,566,271	0	0
Georgia	3,604,768	3,604,768	0	0
Hawaii	713,984	713,984	0	0
Idaho	500,000	500,000	0	0
Illinois	5,015,701	5,015,701	0	0
Indiana	2,905,756	2,905,756	0	0
Iowa	1,753,727	1,753,727	0	0
Kansas	1,506,181	1,506,181	0	0
Kentucky	1,880,984	1,873,714	7,270	0.4
Louisiana	1,358,131	1,358,131	0	0
Maine	596,019	596,019	0	0
Maryland	2,805,086	2,805,086	0	0
Massachusetts	3,160,529	3,159,197	1,332	<0.1
Michigan	5,291,124	5,291,124	0	0
Minnesota	1,801,223	1,801,223	0	0
Mississippi	843,823	843,823	0	0
Missouri	2,928,213	2,928,213	0	0
Montana	573,562	452,945	120,617	26.6
Nebraska	1,608,401	1,608,401	0	0
Nevada	1,205,461	1,205,461	0	0
New Hampshire	500,000	500,000	0	0
New Jersey	3,108,387	3,108,387	0	0
New Mexico	591,373	591,373	0	0
New York	11,585,958	11,585,958	0	0
North Carolina	2,761,462	2,679,637	81,825	3.1
North Dakota	500,000	500,000	0	0
Ohio	4,502,283	4,502,283	0	0
Oklahoma	2,965,641	2,965,641	0	0
Oregon	2,844,837	2,844,837	0	0
Pennsylvania	5,599,072	5,599,072	0	0
Puerto Rico	1,751,663	1,751,663	0	0
Rhode Island	647,646	647,646	0	0

Table B-2. (Continued)

State	Dollar Amount Allocated	Dollar Amount Expended	Dollar Amount Returned to Treasury	Percent of Allotment Returned to Treasury
South Carolina	1,227,919	1,227,919	0	0
South Dakota	500,000	500,000	0	0
Tennessee	2,327,548	2,327,548	0	0
Texas	7,455,535	7,455,535	0	0
Utah	589,825	589,825	0	0
Vermont	500,000	500,000	0	0
Virginia	1,812,581	1,812,581	0	0
Washington	2,598,840	2,598,840	0	0
West Virginia	1,117,956	1,117,956	0	0
Wisconsin	2,093,167	2,093,167	0	0
Wyoming	500,000	480,908	19,092	4.0
Total	137,900,000a	137,669,864	230,136	0.2

Source: Congressional Research Service presentation of data from the U.S. Department of Health and Human Services, Administration for Children and Families, September 2009.

a. Training and technical assistance, research and evaluation, and set asides are not included in the total funding.

Table B-3. FY2007 Chafee Education and Training Vouchers: Estimated Funds Allotted, Expended, and Returned to Federal Treasury, by State

State	Dollar Amount Allocated	Dollar Amount Expended	Dollar Amount Returned to Treasury	Percent of Allotment Returned to Treasury
Alabama	611,903	577,399	34,504	6.0
Alaska	158,530	158,530	0	0
Arizona	891,786	891,786	0	0
Arkansas	285,903	285,903	0	0
California	7,185,099	7,185,083	16	0
Colorado	726,972	726,972	0	0
Connecticut	622,436	622,436	0	0
Delaware	85,151	85,151	0	0
District of Columbia	221,730	221,730	0	0
Florida	2,594,545	2,594,545	0	0
Georgia	1,236,109	1,236,109	0	0
Hawaii	244,832	244,832	0	0
Indiana	996,411	996,411	0	0
Iowa	601,369	601,369	0	0
Kansas	516,484	516,484	0	0
Kentucky	645,007	427,362	217,645	50.9

Table B-3. (Continued)

State	Dollar Amount Allocated	Dollar Amount Expended	Dollar Amount Returned to Treasury	Percent of Allotment Returned to Treasury
Idaho	160,920	146,264	14,656	10
Illinois	1,719,931	1,719,931	0	0
Louisiana	427,792	346,896	80,896	23.3
Maine	204,381	204,381	0	0
Maryland	961,890	961,890	0	0
Massachusetts	1,083,775	1,083,775	0	0
Michigan	1,814,376	1,758,787	55,589	3.2
Minnesota	617,656	617,656	0	0
Mississippi	289,355	287,884	1,471	0.5
Missouri	1,004,112	1,004,112	0	0
Montana	196,680	196,680	0	0
Nebraska	551,536	551,536	0	0
Nevada	413,364	413,364	0	0
New Hampshire	104,270	104,270	0	0
New Jersey	1,065,895	1,065,895	0	0
New Mexico	202,787	170,750	32,037	18.8
New York	2,692,620	2,692,620	0	0
North Carolina	946,931	930,943	15,988	1.7
North Dakota	120,734	118,039	2,695	2.3
Ohio	1,543,875	1,543,875	0	0
Oklahoma	1,016,946	932,317	84,629	9.1
Oregon	975,521	975,521	0	0
Pennsylvania	1,919,974	1,459,142	460,832	31.6
Puerto Rico	600,661	600,661	0	0
Rhode Island	222,084	222,084	0	0
South Carolina	421,065	383,278	37,787	9.9
South Dakota	151,537	124,499	27,038	21.7
Tennessee	798,138	798,138	0	0
Texas	2,556,573	2,154,597	401,976	18.7
Utah	202,256	202,256	0	0
Vermont	127,107	127,107	0	0
Virginia	621,551	621,551	0	0
Washington	891,167	891,167	0	0
West Virginia	383,358	371,037	12,321	3.3
Wisconsin	717,766	717,766	0	0
Wyoming	111,794	109,170	2,624	2.4
Total	**45,464,645**[a]	**43,981,941**	**1,482,704**	**3.4**

Source: Congressional Research Service, Administration for Children and Families, presentation of data from the U.S. Department of Health and Human Services, September 2009.

a. Training and technical assistance, research and evaluation, and set asides are not included in the total funding.

Author Contact Information

Adrienne L. Fernandes-Alcantara
Specialist in Social Policy
afernandes@crs.loc.gov, 7-9005

End Notes

[1] U.S. Department of Health and Human, Administration for Children and Families, Children's Bureau. *The AFCARS Report #16: Preliminary FY2008 Estimates*, October 2008, at http://www.acf.hhs.gov/ programs/cb/stats_research/ index.htm#afcars. (Hereafter referenced as U.S. Department of Health and Human Services, *AFCARS Report #16.*)

[2] Ibid.

[3] Using data from 2002 through 2008 on children in foster care in 15 states, researchers have projected that the number of youth who are expected to leave foster care upon turning age 18 will likely decline between 2009 and 2013, due primarily to the decrease in the number of entries in foster care among children ages 10 through 17; Fred Wulczyn and Linda Collins, *A 5-Year Projection of the Number of Children Reaching Age 18 While in Foster Care*, University of Chicago, Chapin Hall Center for Children, 2010, http://chapinhall.org/ research/report/5-year-projection-numberchildren-turning-age-18-while-foster-care.

[4] For further information about implementation of the youth provisions of the act, see CRS Report R40218, *Youth Transitioning from Foster Care: Issues for Congress*, by Adrienne L. Fernandes-Alcantara.

[5] U.S. Department of Health and Human Services. *National Survey of Child and Adolescent Well-Being, Overview*, available, along with the NSCAW reports, at http://www.acf.hhs.gov/programs/opre/abuse

[6] U.S. Department of Health and Human Services. *National Survey of Child and Adolescent Well-Being, Adolescents Involved with Child Welfare: A Transition to Adulthood*, April 2008, at http://www.acf.hhs.gov/ programs/opre/ abuse_neglect/nscaw/reports/transition_adult/transition_adult.pdf.

[7] Fred Wulczyn, Lijun Chen, Kristen Brunner Hislop, *Foster Care Dynamics 2000-2005: A Report from the Multistate Foster Care Data Archive*, Chapin Hall Center for Children, University of Chicago, 2007.

[8] Bob Schoeni and Karen Ross, "Material Assistance Received from Families During the Transition to Adulthood." In Richard A. Settersten, Jr., Frank F. Furstenburg, Jr., and Rubén Rumbaut, eds., *On the Frontier of Adulthood: Theory, Research, and Public Policy*, pp. 404-405. Chicago: University of Chicago Press, 2005.

[9] According to the National Longitudinal Survey of Adolescent Health ("Add Health"), a nationally representative survey that tracks a cohort of youth over time, approximately 41% of surveyed youth age 21 in the study's third wave (200 1-2002) lived with their parents. See Mark E. Courtney et al., *Midwest Evaluation of the Adult Functioning of Former Foster Youth: Outcomes at Age 21*, Chapin Hall Center for Children, University of Chicago, December 2007, p. 1, at http://www.chapinhall.org/article_abstract.aspx?ar=1355. (Hereafter referenced as Courtney et al., *Midwest Evaluation at Age 21.*)

[10] For a compendium of outcome studies and their methodologies, see Mark E. Courtney and Darcy Hughes Heuring. "The Transition to Adulthood for Youth "Aging Out" of the Foster Care System" in Osgood et al., eds., *On Your Own Without a Net*, appendix. (Hereafter referenced as Mark E. Courtney and Darcy Hughes Heuring, The Transition to Adulthood for Youth "Aging Out" of the Foster Care System.")

[11] Fred Wulczyn et al. *Beyond Common Sense: Child Welfare, Child Well-Being, and the Evidence for Policy Reform* (New Brunswick: AldineTransaction, 2005), p. 116. (Hereafter referenced as Wulczyn et al., *Beyond Common Sense.*)

[12] Mark E. Courtney et al., *Midwest Evaluation of the Adult Functioning of Former Foster Youth: Outcomes at Age 19*, Chapin Hall Center for Children, University of Chicago, May 2005, pp. 68-70, at http://www.chapinhall.org/ article _abstract. aspx?ar=13 55.

[13] Peter J. Pecora et al., *Improving Foster Family Care: Findings from the Northwest Foster Care Alumni Study*, Casey Family Programs, 2005, at http://www.casey.org/Resources/Publications/pdf/ ImprovingFamilyFosterCare_FR.pdf. (Hereafter referenced as Peter J. Pecora et al., Improving Foster Family Care.) See also Peter J. Pecora et al., *What Works in Foster Care?: Key Components of Success From the Northwest Foster Care Alumni Study* (Oxford, U.K.: Oxford University Press, 2010).

[14] U.S. Department of Health and Human, *AFCARS Report #16.*

[15] These youth were placed in care prior to the enactment of the Foster Care Independence Act (P.L. 106-169) and most entered care because of sexual abuse and other type of maltreatment, which is not a primary reason for most children entering care (though the definition of sexual abuse in the U.S. Department of Health and

Human Services' data collection system for children in foster care is not identical to the definition in this study). For additional information about the sample of youth, see pages 18 to 21 and 25 to 31 of the study.

[16] In a nationally representative study of children ages 11 to 14 entering foster care, 56.1% had a clinical/borderline score on the total problem behaviors checklist. Researchers often use this list as a proxy for mental health issues. Wulczyn et al., *Beyond Common Sense*, p. 108.

[17] Courtney et al., *Midwest Evaluation at Age 21*.

[18] Iowa amended its child welfare statute in 2006 to create a program that provides continuing support to foster youth ages 18 to 21. The Iowa youth in the Midwest study were already too old to benefit from the program when it was implemented.

[19] Mark E. Courtney, Sherry Terao, and Noel Bost, *Midwest Evaluation of the Adult Functioning of Former Foster Youth: Conditions of Youth Preparing to Leave State Care*, Chapin Hall Center for Children, University of Chicago, May 2005, pp. 28-30, at http://www.chapinhall.org/article_abstract.aspx?ar=1355.

[20] Mark E. Courtney et al., *Midwest Evaluation of the Adult Functioning of Former Foster Youth: Outcomes at Age19*, Chapin Hall Center for Children, University of Chicago, and Partners for Our Children, University of Washington, May 2005, pp. 17-19, at http://www.chapinhall.org/article_abstract.aspx?ar=1355.

[21] Courtney et al., *Midwest Evaluation at Age 21*, pp. 22-25.

[22] Mark E. Courtney et al., *Midwest Evaluation of the Adult Functioning of Former Foster Youth: Outcomes at Ages 23 and 24*, Chapin Hall Center for Children, University of Chicago, 2010, http://www.chapinhall.org/research/report/ midwest-evaluation-adult-functioning-former-foster-youth.

[23] The Add Health sampled young adults from across the country, the majority (about 75%) of whom were white. Data from the Add Health survey were collected six to seven years before wave 4 of the Midwest Evaluation. As a result, data on earnings and income have been adjusted by the Consumer Price Index (CPI) for comparison purposes.

[24] Mark E. Courtney, Jennifer L. Hook, and JoAnn S. Lee, *Distinct Subgroups of Former Foster Youth During Young Adulthood: Implications for Policy and Practice,* University of Chicago, Chapin Hall Center for Children, and University of Washington, Partners for Our Children, March 2010, http://www.chapinhall.org/research/brief/distinctsubgroups-former-foster-youth-during-young-adulthood

[25] U.S. Congress, House Ways and Means Committee, Income Security and Family Support Subcommittee, "Hearing on Improving the Child Welfare System," February 27, 2008, available at http://waysandmeans.house.gov/hearings. asp?formmode=detail&hearing=6 12.

[26] U.S. Department of Health and Human Services, Administration on Children, Youth and Families, Administration for Children and Families, Children's Bureau, *Program Instruction: Public Law (P.L.) 111-148, the Patient Protection and Affordable Care Act*, ACYF-CB-PI-10-10, June 7, 2010, http://www.acf.hhs. gov/programs/cb/laws policy/pi/2010/pi1010.htm.

[27] U.S. Department of Health and Human Services, Administration on Children, Youth and Families, Administration for Children and Families, Children's Bureau, *Program Instruction: Guidance on Fostering Connections to Success and Increasing Adoptions Act of 2008*, ACYF-CB-PI-10-1 1, July 9, 2010, http://www.acf.hhs.gov/programs/cb/ laws_policies/policy/pi/2010/pi101 1.htm.

[28] Section 477(b)(3)(D).

[29] For additional information, see Section 8.3A, Question 2 of the *Child Welfare Policy Manual*.

[30] Section 472(c) of the Social Security Act.

[31] See Appendix E for proposed legislative changes to the CFCIP.

[32] U.S. Department of Health and Human Services, *Child Welfare Policy Manual*, Section 3. 1G, Questions 1 and 4.

[33] Ibid, Section 3. 1G, Questions 1 and 3.

[34] U.S. Department of Health and Human Services, *Child Welfare Policy Manual*, Section 3.4, Question 5.

[35] U.S. Department of Health and Human Services, *Child Welfare Policy Manual*, Section 3.1F, Question 2.

[36] National Foster Care Awareness Project, *Frequently Asked Questions II: About the Foster Care Independence Act of 1999 and the John H. Chafee Foster Care Independence Program*, December 2000, p.16, at http://www.nrcys.ou.edu/ yd/programs/pdfs/faq2_final.pdf. (Hereafter referenced as National Foster Care Awareness Project, Frequently Asked Questions II.) Some of the members of the National Foster Care Awareness Project, which no longer exists, are now members of the National Foster Care Coalition. The National Foster Care Coalition produced the Frequently Asked Questions III publication about the program.

[37] Amy Dworsky and Judy Havlicek, *Review of State Policies and Programs to Support Young People Transitioning Out of Foster Care*, University of Chicago, Chapin Hall Center for Children, 2009, pp. 7-8, at http://www.wsipp.wa.gov/pub.asp?docid=08-12-3903. (Hereafter referenced as Amy Dworsky and Judy Havlicek, *Review of State Policies and Programs to Support Young People Transitioning Out of Foster Care*.)

[38] U.S. Congress, *Congressional Record*, July 1, 1999, p. S8124.

[39] U.S. Department of Health and Human Services, *Child Welfare Policy Manual*, Section 3. 1B, Question 2.

[40] U.S. Department of Health and Human Services, *Child Welfare Policy Manual*, Section 3. 1F, Question 3.

[41] National Foster Care Coalition, *Frequently Asked Questions III*, p. 9.

[42] U.S. Department of Health and Human Services, *Child Welfare Policy Manual*, Section 3.1I, Question 4.

[43] U.S. Department of Health and Human Services, *Child Welfare Policy Manual*, Section 3.1I, Question 5.

[44] U.S. Congress, *Congressional Record*, June 25, 1999, p. H4969.

[45] University of Oklahoma, National Child Welfare Resource Center for Youth Development, *Tribal Youth Transitioning to Adulthood: Current Status of Independent Living Services Provided to Indian Youth*, November 2007. The NCWRCYD reviewed at least one of the following documents for each state: Child and Family Service Plans (CFSP) for FY2005-FY2009 and Annual Progress and Service Reports (ASPR) for FY2005 and FY2006.

[46] For additional information about the positive youth development movement in youth policy, see CRS Report CRS Report RL33975, *Vulnerable Youth: Background and Policies*, by Adrienne L. Fernandes-Alcantara.

[47] National Foster Care Coalition, *Frequently Asked Questions II*, pp. 30-31.

[48] For a list of jurisdictions with youth advisory boards, see http://groups.fosterclub.com/.

[49] U.S. Department of Health and Human Services, *Child Welfare Policy Manual*, Section 3. 1A, Question 1.

[50] For further information about the Jim Casey Youth Opportunities Initiative, see http://www.jimcaseyyouth.org/ communities.htm.

[51] U.S. Department of Health and Human Services, *Child Welfare Policy Manual*, Section 3.5C, Question 7.

[52] Section 472 of the Higher Education Act, as amended defines "cost of attendance" as tuition, fees, and other equipment or materials required of all students in the same course of study; books, supplies, and allowance for transportation and miscellaneous personal expenses, including computers; room and board; child care expenses for a student who is a parent; accommodations related to the student's disability that is not paid for by another source; expenses related to the youth's work experience in a cooperative education program; and student loan fees or insurance premiums on the loans. Section 102 of the Higher Education Act of 1965, as amended identifies "institutions of higher education" for purposes of student assistance (under Title IV of the Higher Education Act) to include traditional higher education institutions (i.e., public or private, nonprofit two- and four-year colleges and universities) as well as other postsecondary institutions (i.e., proprietary or for-profit schools offering technical training programs usually of less than two-years' duration, and vocational schools).

[53] National Foster Care Coalition, *Frequently Asked Questions III*, p. 12.

[54] U.S. Department of Health and Human Services, *Child Welfare Policy Manual*, Section 3.5C, Question 5.

[55] National Foster Care Coalition, *Frequently Asked Questions III*, p. 7.

[56] Ibid, Section 3.5C, Question 5.

[57] Ibid, Section 3.5C, Question 6.

[58] For example, see National Governors Association, Center for Best Practices, *State Policies to Help Youth Transition Out of Foster Care*, Issue Brief, December 2007. (Hereafter referenced as National Governors Association, *State Policies to Help Youth Transition Out of Foster Care*.)

[59] U.S. Department of Health and Human Services, *Child Welfare Policy Manua*l, Section 3.5, Question 1.

[60] National Foster Care Coalition, *Frequently Asked Questions III*, p. 7.

[61] U.S. Department of Health and Human Services, Administration for Children and Families, *FY2009 Justification of Estimates for Appropriations Committees,* p. D-87; and information provided to the Congressional Research Service by the U.S. Department of Health and Human Services, Administration for Children and Families, September 2009 and March 2010.

[62] Amy Dworsky and Judy Havlicek, *Review of State Policies and Programs to Support Young People Transitioning Out of Foster Care,* p. 14.

[63] The authors of the survey note that some of the services for which states reported spending non-CFCIP dollars can, in fact, be funded through the CFCIP.

[64] U.S. Government Accountability Office. *HHS Actions Could Improve Coordination of Services and Monitoring of States' Independent Living* Programs, GAO-05-25, November 2004, p. 17, at http://www.gao.gov/new.items/ d0525.pdf. (Hereafter referenced as U.S. Government Accountability Office. *HHS Actions Could Improve Coordination of Services and Monitoring of States' Independent Living* Programs.)

[65] Amy Dworsky and Judy Havlicek, *Review of State Policies and Programs to Support Young People Transitioning Out of Foster Care*, pp. 12-13.

[66] This information was provided to the Congressional Research Service by the U.S. Department of Health and Human Services, Administration for Children and Families in January 2010.

[67] Ibid, September 2009.

[68] Ibid.

[69] This information was provided to the Congressional Research Service in June 2007.

[70] This information was provided to the Congressional Research Service by the U.S. Department of Health and Human Services, Office of the Secretary in July 2008.

[71] For more information about the type of assistance that is provided, see http://www.nrcys.ou.edu/yd/about.html.

[72] This information was provided to the Congressional Research Service by the U.S. Department of Health and Human Services, Administration for Children and Families, Children's Bureau in December 2008.

[73] U.S. Department of Health and Human Services, "Chafee National Youth in Transition Database," 73 *Federal Register* 10338, February 26, 2008.

[74] For additional information, you may request a copy of a Congressional Distribution Memorandum, *Chafee Foster Care Independence Act National Youth in Transition Database*, by Adrienne L. Fernandes.

[75] This information was provided to the Congressional Research Service by the U.S. Department of Health and Human Services, Office of the Secretary in July 2008, December 2008, and January 2010.

[76] U.S. Department of Health and Human Services, *Evaluation of the Life Skills Training Program: Los Angeles County*, July 2008, at http://www.acf.hhs.gov/programs/opre/abuse. (Hereafter referenced as U.S. Department of Health and Human Services, *Evaluation of the Life Skills Training Program: Los Angeles County*.)

[77] Additional information regarding the Multi-Site Evaluation of Foster Youth Programs is available at http://www.acf.hhs.gov/programs/opre/abuse

[78] U.S. Department of Health and Human Services, *Evaluation of the Life Skills Training Program: Los Angeles County*.

[79] U.S. Department of Health and Human Services, *Evaluation of the Early Start to Emancipation Preparation—Tutoring Program Los Angeles County*, July 2008, at http://www.acf.hhs.gov/programs/opre/abuse reports/eval_estep/eval_estep.pdf.

[80] U.S. Office of Management and Budget, *Detailed Information on the Independent Living Program Assessment*, 2004, at http://www.whitehouse.gov/omb/expectmore/summary/10002146.2004.html.

[81] Other resources illustrate how select jurisdictions and programs provide independent living services for older current and former foster youth. See, for example, U.S. Government Accountability Office, *Disconnected Youth: Federal Action Could Address Some of the Challenges Faced by Local Programs That Reconnect Youth to Education and Employment,* GAO-08-3 13, February 2008; National Governors Association, Center for Best Practices, *State Policies to Help Youth Transition Out of Foster Care,* Issue Brief, January 2007; Wilhelmina A. Leigh et al., *Aging Out of the Foster Care System to Adulthood: Findings, Challenges, and Recommendations*, Joint Center for Political and Economic Studies and Black Administrators in Child Welfare Inc., December 2007; and Rachel H. Sherman, "Serving Youth Aging Out of Foster Care," Welfare Information Network Issue Note, vol. 8, no. 5 (October 2004), pp. 5-7. See also the University of Chicago Law School, "Transition From Foster Care to Adulthood Wiki" at http://fostercaretoadulthood.wikispaces.com/ and the University of Oklahoma, National Child Welfare Resource Center for Youth Development, "State by State Facts Page," at http://www.nrcys.ou.edu/yd/state

[82] For additional information, see CRS Report RL32968, *Child Welfare: State Performance on Child and Family Services Reviews*, by Emilie Stoltzfus.

[83] In 2000, HHS published a final rule to establish a formal review process consistent with legislative mandates to improve federal oversight of state child welfare programs. The final rule established the CFSR and Title IV-E Foster Care Eligibility Reviews. The Foster Care Eligibility Reviews are conducted to validate a state's claim for federal reimbursement of payments made on behalf of eligible children, and are not discussed in this report.

[84] The reports are available at http://basis.caliber

[85] This section was written by Emilie Stoltzfus, Specialist in Social Policy.

[86] Edi Winkle, Dorothy Ansell, and Ann Newman, An Analysis of State's Child and Family Services Reviews and *Program Improvement Plans From a Youth Development Perspective*, National Resource Center for Youth Development, University of Oklahoma, March 25, 2004, at http://www.nrcys.ou.edu/yd/ resourcessummaryv2.2.pdf. This analysis was based on 45 Dorothy Ansell, and Ann Newman, *An Analysis of State's Child and Family Services Reviews and* of the final reports that were available as of March 15, 2004.

[87] Ibid.

[88] U.S. Department of Health and Human Services, *Child and Family Services Review Stakeholder Interview Guide*, June 2008, available at http://www.acf.hhs.gov/programs/cb/cwmonitoring/tools_guide/stakeholder.htm.

[89] U.S. Department of Health and Human Services, *Child and Family Services Review Procedures Manual, Chapter 4,* available at http://www.acf.hhs.gov/programs/cb/cwmonitoring/tools_guide/proce_manual.htm.

[90] U.S. Department of Health and Human Services, *Child and Family Services Review Onsite Review Instrument and Instructions*, July 2008, available at http://www.acf.hhs.gov/programs/cb/cwmonitoring/tools_guide/ proce_manual.htm.

[91] U.S. Government Accountability Office. *HHS Actions Could Improve Coordination of Services and Monitoring of States' Independent Living* Programs, pp. 18-19.

[92] National Foster Care Coalition, *The Chafee Education and Training Voucher Program: Six States' Experiences*, National Foster Care Coalition and Casey Family Programs, 2007, at http://www.casey.org/ Resources/Publications/pdf/ ChafeeETV.pdf.

[93] In a separate publication, from 2005, the National Foster Care Coalition identified promising practices for ETV programs. These include (1) a clearly defined application process and a funding process transparent to stakeholders, including informing students of the amount of funding they receive; (2) open lines of communication between applicants/participants and ETV administrators, including multiple methods for contacting the ETV office; and (3) individual assessments for all applicants to ensure that ETV funds are based on their unmet financial need as calculated by their educational institution; among other approaches. See

National Foster Care Coalition, *Frequently Asked Questions III: About the Chafee Foster Care Independence Program and the Chafee Educational and Training Program*.

[94] Section 1902(a)(10)(A)(ii)(XVII) of the Social Security Act.

[95] Section 1905(w)(1)) of the Social Security Act.

[96] Sonja Schwartz and Melanie Glascock, *Improving Access to Health Coverage for Transitional Youth*, National Academy for State Healthy Policy, p. 5, July 2008, at http://www.nashp.org/sites/default/files/transitional_youth.pdf.

[97] For information about Medicaid eligibility pathways, see CRS Report RL33019, *Medicaid Eligibility for Adults and Children*, by Jean Hearne.

[98] Amy Dworsky and Judy Havlicek, *Review of State Policies and Programs to Support Young People Transitioning Out of Foster Care*, p. 11. A 2006 survey of state human service officials by the American Public Human Services Association (APHSA) found that 17 states reported extending Medicaid coverage to eligible youth through the Chafee option. See Sonali Patel and Martha A. Roherty, *Medicaid Access for Youth Aging Out of Foster Care*, American Public Human Services Association, 2007, at http://www.aphsa.org/Home/Doc/Medicaid-Access-for-Youth-AgingOut-of-Foster-Care-Rpt.pdf. Puerto Rico was not included in this analysis.

[99] Youth will be eligible if they are not eligible or enrolled under existing (at the time P.L. 110-351 was passed) Medicaid mandatory eligibility groups (or described in any of the existing Medicaid mandatory eligibility groups), regardless of whether they have income that exceeds the upper income eligibility limit established under any such group; and they were enrolled in the Medicaid state plan or under a waiver while in such foster care. Children in foster care who are not Title IV-E eligible generally still qualify for Medicaid coverage because all states have implemented one or more mandatory or optional Medicaid eligibility categories that allow them to cover children in care regardless of their IV-E eligibility status. Rob Geen, Anna Sommers, and Mindy Cohen, *Medicaid Spending on Foster Children*, The Urban Institute, August 2005, http://www.urban

[100] Though not discussed here, a small part of the allocation formula population factor for the Title I-A program of Education for the Disadvantaged (authorized under the Elementary and Secondary Education Act, as amended) accounts for the number of children ages five to 17 who are in institutions for delinquent children or foster homes when making grants to local education agencies (LEAs). For additional information, see CRS Report RL3373 1, *Education for the Disadvantaged: Reauthorization Issues for ESEA Title I-A Under the No Child Left Behind Act*, by Rebecca R. Skinner.

[101] The previous definition included an individual who is an orphan or ward of the state (or was until age 18). 29 U.S.C. 1087vv(d). The College Cost Reduction and Access Act Technical Amendments of 2007 (H.R. 4153), would make a correction to the definition of independent student to include any child who "is an orphan, in foster care, or a ward of the court, or was an orphan, in foster care, or a ward of the court any time when the individual was 13 years of age or older." The Higher Education Opportunity Act (P.L. 110-315) makes additional changes to the definition of independent student to include "an orphan, in foster care, or a ward of the court, or was an orphan, in foster care, or a ward of the court at any time when the individual was 13 years of age or older;" and "is, or was immediately prior to attaining the age of majority, an emancipated minor or in legal guardianship as determined by a court of competent jurisdiction in the individual's state of legal residence."

[102] Authorization of appropriations under WIA expired in FY2003 but is annually extended through appropriations acts. Youth in foster care are also eligible for WIA's Youth Opportunity program, however, Congress has not appropriated funding for the program since FY2003.

[103] 29 U.S.C. 2801(13) and 29 U.S.C. 2884(1).

[104] 29 U.S.C. 2916.

[105] Institute for Educational Leadership, *Foster Care Youth Demonstration Project: Final Evaluation Report, Executive Summary*, July 2008, at http://www.casey.org/Resources/Publications/EmPLOY/pdf/DOL and http://iel.org/programs/casey.html.

[106] 42 U.S.C. 1437(f)(x).

[107] This information is based on correspondence with the National Center for Housing and Child Welfare, a child welfare organization, in August 2008.

[108] U. S. Congress, House Committee on Appropriations, *Joint Explanatory Statement, Division K.* report to accompany FY2008 Consolidated Appropriations Amendment to H.R. 2764/P.L. 110-161, 1 10th Cong., 1st sess., p. 2396; U.S. Congress, House Committee on Appropriations, *Omnibus Appropriations Act, 2009, Division I, committee print of the House Committee on Appropriations on H.R. 1105/P.L. 111-8*, 111th Cong., 1st sess., p. 1987; and U.S. Congress, House Committee on Appropriations, *Departments of Transportation and Housing and Development, and Related Agencies Appropriations Act, 2010*, report to accompany H.R. 3288/P.L. 111-117, 111th Cong., 1st sess., December 8, 2009, H.Rept. 111-366, p. 46.

[109] Amy Dworsky and Judy Havlicek, *Review of State Policies and Programs to Support Young People Transitioning Out of Foster Care*, p. 13.

[110] For additional information, see CRS Report RL33785, *Runaway and Homeless Youth: Demographics and Programs*, by Adrienne L. Fernandes-Alcantara.

[111] Data on youth served by the program are provided in HHS's National Extranet Optimized Runaway and Homeless Youth Management Information System (NEO-RHYMIS), at http://extranet.acf.hhs.gov/rhymis/.

[112] National Alliance to End Homelessness, "Federal Funding for Youth Housing Programs," information presented at National Alliance to End Audio Conference, March 9, 2006, available at http://naeh.org/content/article/browse/?type= 24&topic=Youth.

[113] U.S. Department of Health and Human Services, "Training of Child Welfare Agency Supervisors in the Effective Delivery and Management of Federal Independent Living Service for Youth in Foster Care," 70 *Federal Register* 35087, June 16, 2005.

[114] In the fall of 2000, HHS awarded twelve grants for Independent Living Training for Child Welfare practitioners. One of the findings from the completed projects was that child welfare supervisors needed training on youth development to understand the unique developmental and service needs of youth in care.

In: Children and Youth Transitions from Foster Care
Editor: Joseph A. Ferrari
ISBN: 978-1-61209-705-3

Chapter 2

YOUTH TRANSITIONING FROM FOSTER CARE: ISSUES FOR CONGRESS

Adrienne L. Fernandes-Alcantara

SUMMARY

Recent research has demonstrated that compared to their peers, current and former foster youth are more likely to experience negative outcomes in adulthood. This research, along with the efforts of policymakers and child welfare advocates, has brought greater attention to the challenges facing youth transitioning from foster care. In response, Congress has sought to improve existing services and provide additional supports for this population. Most recently, the 110th Congress passed, and President George W. Bush enacted, the Fostering Connections to Success and Increasing Adoptions Act of 2008 (P.L. 110-351), which is arguably one of the most significant laws passed in recent history that expands services and supports for older youth in care. This reports presents issues around implementation of P.L. 110-351. It also describes other issues affecting older youth as they transition from foster care into adulthood.

As enacted, the new law extends eligibility, beginning in FY20 11, for federal foster care assistance to youth who remain in care after age 18 (at state option until 19, 20, or 21). P.L. 110-351 additionally authorizes this assistance on behalf of older youth eligible for federal foster care if they reside in an independent living setting (as well as foster family homes or other eligible settings). The law requires the Department of Health and Human Services (HHS) to define independent living settings in regulation.

P.L. 110-351 also expands the purposes of the Chafee Foster Care Independence Program (CFCIP). The CFCIP was established in 1999 (P.L. 106-169) to provide supports and services to current and former foster youth who are likely to be emancipated from care. Changes made by P.L. 110-351 explicitly permit states to provide CFCIP services to youth who leave care at age 16 or older through kinship guardianship or adoption. Funding for the CFCIP was not increased, and whether states will expand their independent living programs to include this population remains to be seen. In addition, the new law requires child welfare agencies to assist youth who are leaving foster care in developing a transition plan so that they have specific options on housing, employment, education, and mentoring. In July 2010, HHS issued program instructions that provide guidance to states on the implementation of P.L. 110-351.

One possible challenge in implementing the law is that even with assistance from the federal government, states (and tribes, pursuant to P.L. 110-351) may be hesitant to extend care to older youth because of the cost. Child welfare agencies may also face difficulties in retaining youth in care, even if remaining in care would be beneficial. Further, despite the passage of the new law and issuance of accompanying guidance, policymakers and advocates remain concerned that older foster youth and those who have aged out will continue to experience challenges during the transition to adulthood. Emancipated youth face particular obstacles in fostering permanent connections with caring adults, securing health insurance and housing, and staying connected to work and school. Further, little is known about youth as they transition from foster care, although a new national database will likely provide some insight into their outcomes across a number of areas, such as education, employment, and contact with social service and criminal justice systems.

This report will be updated as programmatic and regulatory activity occurs. For background information about older foster youth and the current federal policies and programs for this population, see CRS Report RL34499, *Youth Transitioning from Foster Care: Background and Federal Programs*, by Adrienne L. Fernandes-Alcantara.

INTRODUCTION

Since the mid-1980s, Congress has passed legislation that is intended to support older youth in foster care who are expected to leave care without a permanent family placement. At the center of these policies is the Chafee Foster Care Independence Program (CFCIP), authorized in 1999 (P.L. 106-169) to provide services, including housing, for older foster youth.[1] With funding from the CFCIP and other sources, states have developed independent living programs that supplement youth's own efforts to attain self sufficiency. Additionally, federal law directs child welfare agencies to develop policies, where appropriate, targeted to older youth that assist in their transition from care, such as written case plans outlining the services they will receive to prepare for independent living. Despite these services and supports, research has demonstrated that compared to their counterparts in the general population, current and former foster youth are more likely to have difficulty making the transition to adulthood. During their early adult years, foster care alumni youth are much more likely than their peers to forego higher education, describe their general health as fair or poor, become homeless, and rely on public supports. This research, along with the efforts of policymakers and child welfare advocates, has brought greater attention to the challenges facing youth transitioning from care.

Congress has recently focused on efforts to ensure that youth have connections to caring adults and can continue to receive support from the state after they reach the legal age of majority— usually age 1 8—to help ease the challenges associated with the transition to adulthood. Arguing that most youth are not ready to live independently at age 18, federal policymakers have expressed special interest in providing a safety net for youth who are wards of the state. The 110th Congress conducted a series of hearings on child welfare reforms, some of which focused on older youth in care. These hearings culminated in the passage of the Fostering Connections to Success and Increasing Adoptions Act of 2008 (P.L. 110-351), an omnibus child welfare bill that addresses several aspects of the child welfare system. [2] P.L. 110-351 is arguably one of the most significant laws passed in the last several Congresses that pertain to older youth in foster care.

This reports presents issues around implementation of P.L. 110-351, as well as other ongoing issues affecting older youth as they transition from foster care into adulthood. Perhaps the most pressing implementation issue is whether states should extend foster care to older youth. The new law encourages states, as of FY2011, to extend care after age 18 by authorizing partial reimbursement for the cost of that continued support.[3] One possible challenge in implementing this provision is that even with assistance from the federal government, states may be hesitant to extend foster care to young adults because of the cost. The law also raises questions about whether youth who initially choose to emancipate from care may return before their 21st birthday, and how the transition plan requirement should be carried out by states. P.L. 110-351 also makes other significant reforms to the CFCIP and child welfare requirements pertaining to older youth.

In July 2010, the Department of Health and Human Services (HHS) issued program instructions to address the youth (and other) provisions of P.L. 110-351. Even with the passage of the new law and issuance of accompanying guidance, policymakers and advocates remained concerned that older foster youth and those who have aged out will continue to experience challenges during the transition to adulthood. Emancipated youth face particular obstacles in fostering permanent connections with caring adults, securing health insurance and housing, and staying connected to work and school. Further, little is known about youth as they transition from foster care, although a new national database will likely provide some insight into their outcomes across a number of areas, such as education, employment, and contact with social service and criminal justice systems.

After a brief background on existing and new federal child welfare policies concerning transitioning youth, this report will include discussions about implementation of the new law and other ongoing issues. The report is a companion to another report that provides context about older foster youth and related federal policy. See CRS Report RL34499, *Youth Transitioning from Foster Care: Background and Federal Programs*.

BACKGROUND

The Share of Youth in Care Is Increasing

The overall number of children in foster care has been declining in recent years. On any given day in FY2002, approximately 523,000 children were in foster care, while the corresponding figure for FY2009 was 423,773.[4] Over this same period, the share of older children in care increased. Children ages 13 through 17 comprised 28.7% of the caseload in FY2002 and 37.4% in FY2009.[5] Further, a greater share of youth who exited care were not reunited with their families or placed in another permanent arrangement, and instead were emancipated because they reached the state's legal age of majority. In FY2002, just over

20,000 children "aged out" of foster care, making up 7.2% of all children who exited care that year. These figures increased in each subsequent year through FY2009, when over 29,000 were youth who aged out, making up 10.4% of all children who exited that year.

Despite this increase, child welfare researchers have projected that the number of children who are expected to emancipate from foster care by 2013 will likely decline, due to the decrease in the number of entries in foster care among children ages 10 through 17.[6] This analysis is based on data from 2002 through 2008 on children in foster care in 15 states, and may not be representative of all states.

Youth in Care Face Challenges during the Transition to Adulthood

A growing body of research on youth who spend some of their teenage years in foster care demonstrates that they tend to experience more negative outcomes in adulthood than their peers generally. A leading study of former foster youth—known as the Midwest Evaluation on the Adult Functioning of Former Foster Youth ("Midwest Evaluation")—is tracking outcomes of former foster youth in three states: Illinois, Iowa, and Wisconsin. All of the surveyed youth entered care prior to their 16th birthday. Surveyed youth responded to researcher questions about outcomes in three data collection waves: at wave 1, when they were ages 17 and 18, at which time most were in foster care; at wave 2 when they were ages 19 and 20, at which time some remained in care; at wave 3, when they were age 21 and no longer in care; and wave 4, when they were ages 23 and 24 and at least a couple of years out of care. Of those who remained in care beyond age 18, all were in Illinois, the only state of the three that retains court jurisdiction of foster youth (with the youth's permission) until age 21.[7]

The most recent results of the study, based on survey data of youth at age 23 or 24, found that the foster care alumni were less likely to have attained a four-year college degree compared to youth overall (2.5% versus 19.4%).[8] Youth in the Midwest evaluation who were not currently in school reported barriers to enrolling or staying in school, including that they could not pay for school (39.9%), needed to work full-time (19.7%), needed to care for a child (13.8%), or had no transportation (3.2%), among other reasons. While youth formerly in care were almost as likely to report ever holding a job as youth in the general population (94.7% versus 97.3%), a smaller share were currently employed (48.0% versus 75.5%) and they had lower median hourly wages ($9.45 versus $12.00) and mean annual incomes ($8,000 versus $18,300). About 47% of former foster youth reported having any savings or checking accounts, compared to 85% of youth generally. A greater share of former foster youth did not have enough money to pay rent (38.6%), compared to their counterparts overall (7.4%) and were more likely to report having received food stamps (67.7% versus 7.2% for females; 26.8% versus 1.5% for males).

Federal Child Welfare Support for Youth

The state child welfare agency, with oversight by the court, is responsible for the care and placement of children who have been removed from their homes due to abuse, neglect, or for some other reason that does not allow them to remain in their homes. The child welfare agency uses both federal and state funds to facilitate children reuniting successfully and safely with their parents, and when this is not possible, to find them a permanent and safe home. A primary federal source is Title IV-E foster care, authorized under the Social Security Act (see below for further discussion). To be eligible to receive federal funds (under both the Title IV-E foster care program and Title IV-B child welfare services program), states must agree to carry out activities that are intended to promote the safety, permanency, and well-being of all children in foster care. These include that a state has a written case plan detailing, among other things, where the child is placed and what services are to be provided to ensure that a permanent home is re-established for the child.[9] Further, for each child in foster care, this plan must be reviewed on a regular basis. The case review is to be conducted not less often than every six months by a judge or an administrative review panel, and at least once every 12 months by a judge who must consider the child's permanency plan.[10] Specific case plan and case review procedures pertain to older youth in care. "Where appropriate," for a child age 16 or older, the written case plan must include a description of the programs and services that will help the child prepare for the transition to independent living,[11] and the permanency plan hearing must consider "the services needed to assist the child to make the transition from foster care to independent living."[12] As required by P.L. 110-351, states must also assist youth in developing what is known as a transition plan that addresses housing and other needs when they have emancipated from foster care.

For many children who enter foster care, returning to their parents is the way permanence is reestablished. For some children, however, it is not safe or possible to reunite with their parents. In those cases, states must work to find adoptive parents or legal guardians who can provide a permanent home and family. Yet despite efforts to find a permanent home for older youth while they are in care, some age out upon reaching the state's legal age of majority. The Chafee Foster Care Independence Program is designed to provide services that will prepare these youth for when they are no longer under the custody and care of the state. The discussion below of Title IV- E foster care and the CFCIP briefly mentions the changes made by P.L. 110-351, which are described in greater detail in a later section.

Title IV-E Foster Care

Title IV-E of the Social Security Act authorizes the federal foster care program.[13] Under this program, a state (and now Indian tribes, pursuant to P.L. 110-351)[14] may seek federal funds for partial reimbursement of the room and board costs needed to support eligible children who are in out-of-home foster care. Funding for the Title IV-E foster care program is appropriated out of the general treasury and is available on an open-ended entitlement basis. This means the federal government is obligated to reimburse states for every eligible cost made on behalf of an eligible child.[15] A child or youth is eligible for Title IV-E foster care if he or she is in the care and responsibility of the state and, among other things:

- the child or youth is a citizen or qualified alien[16] and meets certain income/assets tests, age, and family structure/living arrangement rules in the home he/she was removed from;[17]
- a judge has determined that (1) the home the child was removed from was "contrary to the welfare" of the child; (2) the state made reasonable efforts to prevent the

child's placement; and (3) on a continuing basis, the state makes reasonable efforts to secure a permanent home for the child;[18] and
- the child is placed in an eligible licensed setting with an eligible provider.

The state or tribal child welfare agency must provide a "foster care maintenance payment" on behalf of every Title IV-E eligible child in foster care. This payment is made to the licensed foster family home or institution where the eligible child is placed to provide for his or her care and safety. A child remains eligible for Title IV-E foster care maintenance payments until his or her 18th birthday (or 19th birthday if the child is still completing secondary school or equivalent training). Beginning with FY2011, P.L. 110-351 permits states and tribes to provide these payments up to age 21.

A Title IV-E maintenance payment is defined as "payments to cover the cost of (and the cost of providing) food, clothing, shelter, daily supervision, school supplies, a child's personal incidentals, liability insurance with respect to a child, reasonable travel to the child's home for visitation," and as added by P.L. 110-351, "reasonable travel for the child to remain in the school in which the child is enrolled at the time of placement."[19] Federal reimbursement of these costs may only be sought for children placed in a licensed child care institution or foster care home (although P.L. 110-351 adds that eligible young people who remain in extended care may be placed in an independent living setting, as described further below.) States and tribes that receive federal child welfare funds must also carry out activities that are designed to promote the safety, permanency, and well-being of all youth in care, regardless of whether they are eligible for a federal maintenance payment.[20]

Chafee Foster Care Independence Program

The federal Chafee Foster Care Independence Program funds services to assist youth who are expected to emancipate from foster care. As enacted by the Foster Care Independence Act of 1999 (P.L. 106-169), the purposes of the CFCIP are to—identify youth who are likely to remain in foster care until age 18[21] and provide them with support services to help make the transition to self sufficiency; assist these youth in obtaining employment and prepare for and enter postsecondary training and educational institutions; provide personal and emotional support to youth aging out of foster care through mentors and other dedicated adults; enhance the efforts of former foster youth ages 18 to 21 to achieve self sufficiency through supports that connect them to employment, education, housing, and other services; and assure that these former foster youth recognize and accept personal responsibility for preparing for and then making the transition from adolescence to adulthood. (P.L. 110-351 explicitly enables states and tribes to provide independent living services to youth who leave foster care after attaining age 16 for placement in an adoptive home or with a legal kinship guardian.)

The CFCIP is a capped entitlement with an annual ceiling set at $140 million. States (and now tribes, pursuant to P.L. 110-351) are entitled to an amount based on their share of the nation's foster care population, in the most recent year for which information is available. However, no state may receive less than the greater of $500,000 or the amount received by the state in FY1998. States must provide a 20% match. With funding from the CFCIP and other sources, states have developed independent living programs consistent with the purposes of the law. These programs provide direct services to youth such as housing, career exploration, education services, preventative health activities, counseling, mentoring, training in financial management, and other services. To be eligible for CFCIP funds, states and tribes must describe in their five-year Child and Family Services Plan[22] how they will carry out their independent living program. Among other things, they must ensure statewide coverage (although not necessarily uniform) of the program and ensure that the program serves children of various ages and at various stages of achieving independence. States and tribes must also certify in their plans that they meet certain requirements pertaining to the youth served and how funding will be spent. For example, no more than 30% of program funds may be used for the room and board of youth ages 18 to 21.

Separately, the Chafee Education and Training Voucher Program (ETV) was authorized by the Promoting Safe and Stable Families Amendments of 2001 (P.L. 107-133) for children who have emancipated from care or were adopted from care at age 16 or older. (P.L. 110-351 also permits youth who leave foster care for guardianship at age 16 or older to be eligible.)[23] Congress authorized $60 million in discretionary funds for the program, which is allocated to states based on their relative share of the foster care population. Congress has appropriated approximately $45 million each year for the program. The program authorizes vouchers worth up to $5,000 annually per eligible youth for the cost of full-time or part-time attendance at an institution of higher education, as defined by the Higher Education Act of 1965. "Cost of attendance" refers to tuition, fees, books, supplies, equipment and materials, room and board, and related expenses. Students are eligible for the vouchers if they are in good academic standing and making progress toward completing their program or graduating, though states may have additional requirements. Only youth receiving a voucher at age 21 may continue to participate in the voucher program until age 23.

FOSTERING CONNECTIONS TO SUCCESS AND INCREASING ADOPTIONS ACT OF 2008

Background

The 110th Congress held a series of hearings on reforms to the child welfare system, which culminated in the passage of the Fostering Connections to Success and Increasing Adoptions Act on October 7, 2008. Three of the hearings, all conducted by the House Ways and Means Subcommittee on Income Security and Family Support, focused on proposals to further support older youth in care. The topic of a June 19, 2007 hearing was disconnected (i.e., not working or in school) youth, including those in foster care.[24] Witnesses raised the concern that youth in foster care and other vulnerable populations are at risk of becoming disconnected. Chairman Jim McDermott and then Ranking Member Jerry Weller described the challenges of disconnected youth in securing employment and earning a living wage in an increasingly global economy. Also at the hearing, Representative Michele Bachmann and another witness emphasized that additional educational support is needed for the foster care population.[25] They cited information that foster children and youth are more likely to experience multiple school placements, which may lead to gaps in learning and lowered educational attainment, and that a disproportionate share of the population has Individualized Education Plans (IEPs), which are required under the Individuals with Disabilities Act (IDEA), to accommodate their learning disabilities.

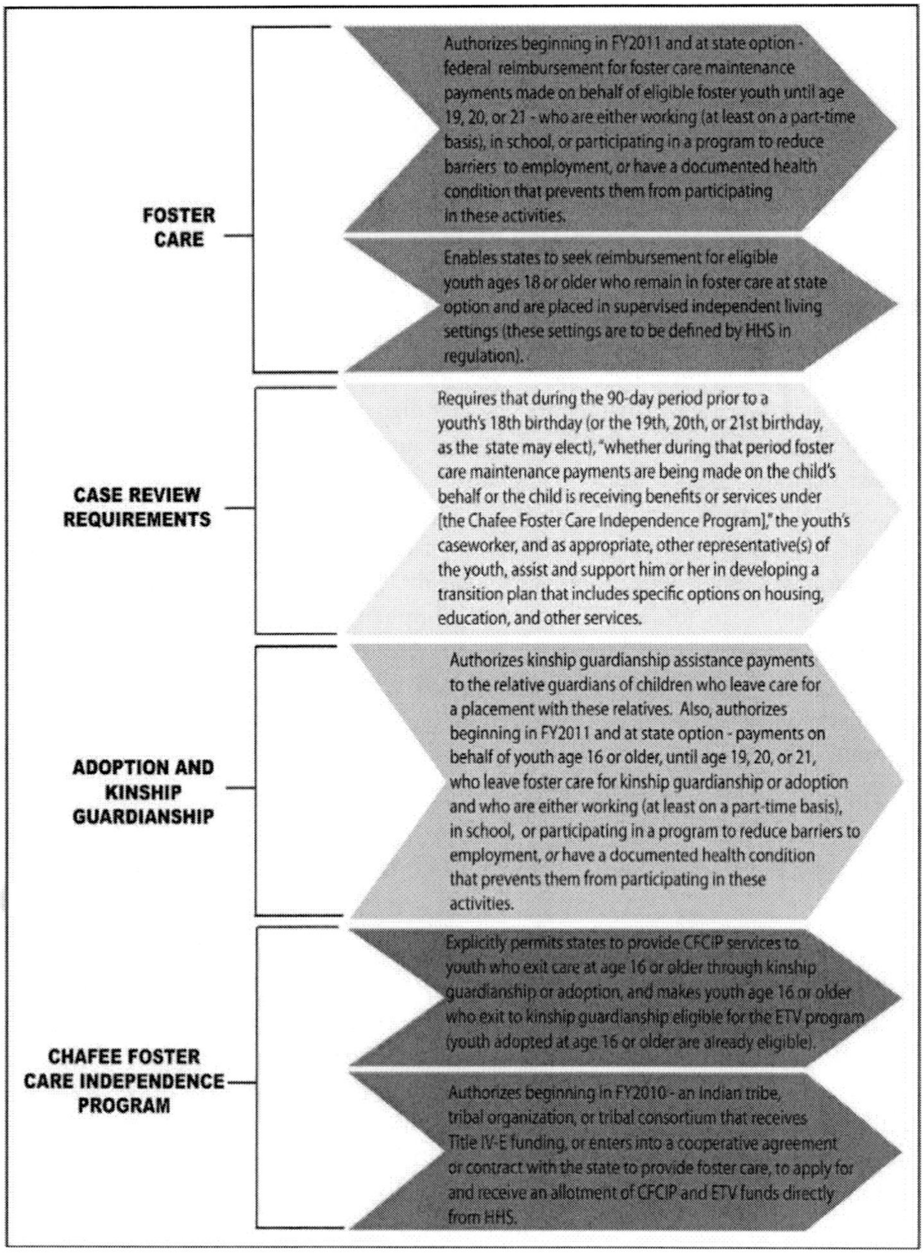

Source: Prepared by the Congressional Research Service.

Figure 1. Provisions in the Fostering Connections to Success and Increasing Adoptions Act (P.L. 1 10-351) That Pertain to Older Youth in Foster Care.

At a July 12, 2007 hearing on youth who age out of foster care and a February 27, 2008 hearing on improving the child welfare system, witnesses—youth, child welfare practitioners, and researchers—argued that youth should have the option to remain in foster care after their 18th birthday.[26] They explained that foster care services end abruptly for many older youth in care when they reach age 18. One practitioner at the July 12 hearing testified that a county child welfare agency buys luggage for youth aging out to replace the garbage bags they were using to haul their few belongings.[27] He went on to say that this practice is merely a band-aid and does not address the bigger issue that youth often lack housing and other support upon aging out of care. One of the youth witnesses at the same hearing described the difficulty she faced in college with finding housing when her dorm was closed: "I waited in limbo for a friend to extend an invitation as I wondered where I would go for holidays and school breaks."[28]

Finally, at both the July 12, 2007, and February 27, 2008, hearings, former foster youth and others testified about the need for youth to establish permanent, genuine connections with caring adults before leaving foster care. A recently emancipated youth said that permanency can help young people avoid poor outcomes. He said, "[p]ermanency is having someone there to help you when you need it, someone you don't need an appointment to talk to. Permanency is having someone to lean on for support when obstacles come your way."[29]

The Fostering Connections to Success and Increasing Adoptions Act of 2008 addresses some of the concerns that were raised in the hearings during the 110th Congress, and makes significant changes to federal child welfare statutes. Several changes pertain to older youth in foster care and those transitioning out of care. Figure 1 summarizes these changes. These provisions focus not on youth living independently, but rather on their connections to adults and the state as they transition to adulthood. Some of the issues raised in the hearings, however, were not fully addressed in the law. Emancipated youth face particular challenges in fostering permanent connections with caring adults, securing health insurance and housing, and staying connected to work and school. These issues are discussed following the next section on implementation of P.L. 110-351.

OPTION TO EXTEND FEDERAL FOSTER CARE PAYMENTS FOR YOUTH AGES 18 TO 21

The existing Title IV-E foster care program partially reimburses states for foster care maintenance payments to cover the cost of providing room, board, and incidentals for youth until age 18, or age 19 in most states if the youth is expected to complete high school or a training program. P.L. 110-351 authorizes, beginning in FY2011 reimbursement for the cost of providing foster care to eligible youth until age 19, 20, or 21, at the state or tribe's option. P.L. 110-351 authorizes the extension of care until 21 by inserting a definition of "child" as it pertains to older youth in care. This definition effectively permits a state to seek reimbursement for a youth age 18 or older who is Title IV-E eligible and (1) completing high school or a program leading to an equivalent credential; (2) enrolled in an institution that provides post-secondary or vocational education; (3) participating in a program or activity designed to promote, or remove barriers to, employment; or (4) employed at least 80 hours per month (i.e., at least part-time). States and tribes may also seek reimbursement for an older youth's foster care if the youth has a medical condition that makes him or her incapable of participating in the activity and this incapacity is supported by regularly updated information in the youth's case plan. The law does not describe programs that may help to remove barriers to employment, or what constitutes a medical condition that could preclude a youth from working or attending school.

States are permitted to seek federal foster care reimbursement for all eligible youth (including those who remain in care) who live in licensed foster homes or a licensed "child care institution." A child care institution is defined as a private child care institution or a public child care institution for no more than 25 children that is licensed by the state.[30] The definition excludes a detention facility, forestry camp, training school, or any other facility operated primarily to detain delinquent children and youth. As authorized by P.L. 110-351, beginning with FY2011 states may also seek reimbursement for youth ages 18 or older who remain in foster care at state option and are placed in a "supervised setting in which the individual is living independently." The act directs HHS to establish in regulation what qualifies as such a setting.

Federal Program Instructions on Extended Care

On July 9, 2010, HHS issued program instructions on certain provisions of P.L. 110-351, including extended care.[31] HHS encourages states and tribes to extend federal foster care assistance to eligible youth until age 21, and if they extend to a lower age (19 or 20), they must describe the rationale for doing so.[32]

Youth Eligibility for Extended Care

According to the guidance, states and tribes must establish the criteria they will use to determine whether young people meet the employment or education conditions and/or whether youth have a medical condition that renders them incapable of pursuing these options. States and tribes must also determine how they will verify or obtain assurances that the youth continues to meet the conditions of remaining in care. The program instructions give examples of education or employment activities that youth in extended care can pursue, such as finishing high school; taking classes to prepare for the general equivalency diploma (GED) exam; enrolling in a college, university, or vocational or trade school; enrolling in a Job Corps program; attending interview and resume-writing classes; and working part-time or full-time. Students are considered enrolled in school even when they are on a summer or other break.

Notably, HHS advises that states and tribes can establish certain requirements for extended foster care that are more restrictive than the federal requirements. For example, extended care could be provided only to those youth enrolled in post-secondary education. Still, the guidance advises that states and tribes should "consider how [they] can provide extended assistance to youth age 18 and older to the broadest population possible consistent with the law to ensure that there are ample supports for older youth."

Separately, the program instructions address issues related to four separate criteria pertaining to Title IV-E foster care eligibility. It appears that these instructions apply to young people who reach the state age of majority *and* either continue in care, seek to reenter care, or seek to enter care[33] even if they do not have a prior history of placement in foster care.

- ***AFDC Program Criteria:*** To continue to be eligible for federal foster care, a youth who remains in care must have met the Title IV-E requirements pertaining to income, assets, and living arrangements at the time of removal.[34] For a youth age 18 or older "entering or reentering care," eligibility is based on the youth without regard to the parents, legal guardians, or others in the home "from which the youth was removed as a younger child."[35]
- ***Removal from Home:*** Youth in extended care must also have entered care via a court order or voluntary placement agreement.[36] The program instructions state that for youth who came into care before age 18 and remain in care after age 18, the court ordered removal or the voluntary agreement that was in place before age 18 still stands. The instructions also address removal criteria for youth who are age 18 or older. The instructions specify that (1) a court can make a determination about whether the home from which the youth was removed is "contrary to the welfare" of the youth, to the extent that the court has the jurisdiction to do so; or (2) the youth can sign a voluntary placement agreement, so long as it meets Title IV-E requirements for voluntary placement agreements. (This includes the requirement that there be a judicial determination that remaining in care is in the child's best interest if Title IV-E payments extend beyond the first 180 days of the agreement). (It is unclear what applies to youth who are returning to care and/or youth who are seeking to enter care, possibly for the first time.)
- ***Placement and Care:*** The instructions also address the ways that state and tribal child welfare agencies can meet the placement and care rules[37] for older youth— that is, with written authorization by the youth prior to reaching age 18; or through a voluntary placement agreement or court order for youth who have already reached age 18 (it is unclear if this applies to youth who are returning to care and/or youth who are seeking to enter care, possibly for the first time).
- ***Placement Setting:*** P.L. 110-351 permits youth in extended care to be placed in a supervised independent living setting or, like all younger children in care, in a licensed foster family home or child care institution. The program instructions state that HHS does not "at this time" have "forthcoming regulations" that describe the kinds of living arrangements considered to be independent living settings, how these settings should be supervised, or any other conditions for a young person to live independently. The instructions advise that states and tribes have the discretion to develop a range of supervised independent living settings that "can be reasonably interpreted as consistent with the law, including whether or not such settings need to be licensed and any safety protocols that may be needed." The instructions give examples of the types of settings that could be eligible for reimbursement, such as host homes, college dormitories, shared housing, and supervised apartments, among other settings. Child welfare agencies are to ensure that youth in supervised independent living settings have opportunities to form connections to caring adults, such as through guardianship arrangements, adoption, or living with caring adults.

According to the program instructions, Title IV-E foster care maintenance payments, which must otherwise be paid to the foster care provider (i.e., the foster parent or child care institution), can be paid directly to a young person who is living in an independent living setting.

State Requirements Related to Providing Extended Care

States and tribes are further advised that they must apply "in a developmentally appropriate manner" the same case planning and case review requirements to youth in extended care as they already do for children under age 18. The program instructions explain that case plan and case review requirements for youth age 18 and older should address a youth's needs. For example, the case plan is to be developed jointly with the youth and include benchmarks that indicate how the youth and child welfare agency "both know when independence can be achieved." Further, periodic reviews (every six months) are to involve youth and focus on whether the youth is safe in his or her placement. States and tribes are also to make reasonable efforts to finalize a permanency plan every 12 months for older youth who were removed through a court-ordered placement agreement. According to the guidance, the permanency plan may reflect the goal of emancipation or independence[38] and address the child welfare agency's efforts to prepare the young person for this goal. As allowed under law for children of any age in foster care, the court overseeing the child's case can make a determination regarding reasonable efforts to finalize a permanency plan without calling a court hearing, so long as an authorized member of the judiciary makes that determination.

The program guidance goes on to advise that states and tribes that choose to extend care to youth who are *ineligible* for federal foster care *are not required* to fulfill the IV-E requirements, including those related to case planning and case review and certain data collection and reporting requirements, for these youth (although they must continue to do so for all children under the age of 18, or age 19 for children completing school). Given that children in foster care who are IV-E eligible are also categorically eligible for Medicaid, the guidance states that this eligibility is to be extended to youth who remain in care after age 18 (up to the age the state or tribe elects) and receive federal foster care maintenance payments.

Implementation of Extended Care

In taking up the option to extend care, states and tribes could look to how a small number of states that have extended care before P.L. 110-351 was enacted when deciding whether to extend care. States and tribes would likely consider a number of factors: (1) the outcomes of youth who remain in care; (2) potential costs; (3) which youth are permitted to stay in care; (4) whether they can actually facilitate youth remaining in care; (5) the extent to which older youth can return to care after they initially leave; (6) the extent to which older youth in general can be placed in foster care settings after age 18; and (7) the type of placements that qualify as independent living settings. Another issue, for both states and the federal government, concerns the changes that may need to be made to existing federal child welfare policy.

States That Currently Provide Extended Foster Care

The age of majority in nearly all states is 18, and most youth emancipate from foster care at that age. In 2008, the Chapin Hall Center for Children at the University of Chicago surveyed independent living coordinators in 45 states (including Washington, DC) about whether youth may remain in foster care beyond age 18, among other related questions.[39] Most states (43) reported that youth could remain in care beyond their 18th birthday. Five states allowed youth to remain until age 19; three until age 20; 27 states until age 21; two until age 22; and one until age 24. Another two states reported that youth become ineligible to remain in care upon reaching their 18th birthday; four reported that it depends on the situation; and one did not know, though it had indicated in another question on the survey that youth can remain in care after their 19th birthday. In total, the researchers counted these 43 states as allowing youth to remain in care beyond their 18th birthday.

The 43 states were asked about the circumstances under which youth are permitted to remain in care. States most frequently cited that youth must be on track to graduate from high school or obtain a GED (35 states), have physical or mental disabilities or other special needs (25 states), or be enrolled in school or vocational training (24 states); *or* the court determined that remaining in care is in the youth's best interest (21 states), among other, less frequently cited circumstances. To remain in care beyond their 18th birthday, youth must meet certain requirements, including live in an approved or licensed placement (27 states), comply with the case plan (26 states), be enrolled in school (19 states), or sign a voluntary placement agreement (17 states), among other requirements. In nearly half (20) of the 43 states that extend care beyond a youth's eighteenth birthday, the court retains legal jurisdiction of his or her case.[40]

Despite states reporting that they allow youth to remain in foster care for a limited period following their 18th birthday, child welfare researchers and advocates believe that a small number of states actively facilitate youth remaining in care.[41] Based on the information provided in the survey, it's not clear to what extent states encourage and facilitate youth remaining in care.

Also in 2008, the Congressional Research Service contacted four jurisdictions—Illinois, New York, Vermont, and Washington, DC—that are known to facilitate youth remaining in foster care until at least age 21.[42] The four jurisdictions provide state foster care maintenance payments, funded by state, local, and/or private dollars, on behalf of older youth. The four programs are similar but have distinguishing features. While Illinois, New York, and Washington, DC, provide more traditional foster care maintenance payments to foster families on behalf of youth ages 18 to 21, Vermont provides stipends (much like foster care maintenance payments) to caring adults (including, but not limited to, foster care families) who pledge to assist youth who have aged out of care. Another major difference is that in Washington, DC, youth must remain in care until their 21st birthday unless they meet narrow criteria. In contrast, eligible youth in Illinois and New York may decide to seek emancipation before reaching age 21. (Former foster youth ages 18 to 21 in Vermont are not required to participate in the stipend program.) Further, New York and Vermont require youth to be enrolled in an educational or workforce program as a condition for remaining in care; Illinois and Washington, DC, do not. In all cases, with the exception of Vermont, youth ages 18 and older in care continue to be wards of the state. The juvenile courts retain jurisdiction and social workers make routine visits to assist youth in achieving their case goal, which is often independent living. Still, case workers in Vermont continue to visit with youth and help them plan for the future. For additional information about the foster care programs for older youth in these states, see the Appendix. Note that this is not an exhaustive review of states that facilitate youth remaining in care beyond their 18th birthdays.

Outcomes of Youth in Extended Care

The Midwest Evaluation demonstrates that youth who remained in care as late as age 20 tended to have somewhat more positive outcomes, at least while they were still in care, than their counterparts who emancipated at age 18.[43] The study examined outcomes for former foster youth in three states: Illinois, Iowa, and Wisconsin. These three states offered a natural experiment for comparing youth outcomes: Iowa and Wisconsin emancipated nearly all of their foster youth in the study by age 18, while approximately three-fourths of foster youth in Illinois who reached age 18 in care remained under the custody of the state until age 21.[44] Remaining in care appeared to be associated with higher earnings and delayed pregnancy. The Midwest Evaluation found that while the young people in Illinois were less likely to be employed at age 21, likely due to being in school, each additional year in care after age 18 was associated with a $470 increase in average annual earnings. Average annual earnings for youth who remained in care longer increased by $924 after controlling for certain characteristics of the young adults (measured when they were age 17) that are likely to affect later earnings (e.g., work history, education attainment, mental health problems, and criminal behavior), as well as unobserved characteristics. Further, young people in Illinois were 38% less likely to become pregnant between ages 17 and 19. Although there was a reduction in the risk of pregnancy after age 19 for youth in care compared to their counterparts, this difference was not statistically significant. Youth in Illinois were also much more likely than their peers to have received a variety of transitional living services between ages 19 and 21, such as those services funded through the CFCIP.

Some of the benefits of remaining in care appear to have faded two years after the youth in Illinois aged out. While the study found that by age 23 these young people were more likely to have completed one year of college, they were no more likely than their peers to have earned a two- or four-year degree.[45] Researchers suggest that this could be because they lost access to the services and supports that made it possible for them to pursue their educational goals. In addition, these young people may have had to refocus their efforts on meeting their basic needs, like securing and maintaining housing. Further, even with assistance from the Chafee Education and Training Voucher (ETV) program and programs in some states that waive college tuition, these youth may not have necessarily received other support to help them in school, such as academic and social/emotional support.

Potential Benefits and Costs

The advantages of youth remaining in foster care after age 18 appear significant, as demonstrated by the Midwest Evaluation and a small number of studies that hypothesize about the benefits and costs of extending care. Still, little is known about these benefits and costs. A small number of studies posit that extending foster care or providing intensive transitional living services can offset the costs that individuals or society would incur, such as in the form of admissions to state prison and welfare payments, in the absence of these interventions.[46] One of these studies evaluated the cost to government and benefits to individual youth of extending foster care.[47]

Researchers calculated the costs of extending care based on the experience of Illinois in providing care beyond age 18 (as reported in the Midwest Evaluation) and data on public assistance receipt in Illinois. Based on the average length of stay in care beyond age 18 in Illinois—until approximately age 20, or two years total—researchers estimated the cost to be about $20,800 annually, or about $19,000 if the costs of providing certain public assistance to youth (if they did not remain in care) were subtracted. According to the study, the cost of extending care for up to two years would be shared among the federal government, state, and counties. The distribution of the cost would depend on the state's IV-E reimbursement rate, the share of these youth who were IV-E eligible, and any cost sharing between the state and counties.

The benefits (to youth) of remaining in care were evaluated only in the context of additional wages that the youth could earn because remaining in care would enable them to attend at least some college. Based on several factors,[48] the analysis found an average return of about $2 for every $1 spent on a youth remaining in care, which translates into an average of approximately $72,000 additionally earned over the course of his or her lifetime.

The analysis did not examine any cost to the state of extending the courts' oversight of the youths' cases. In addition, the analysis did not examine the potential benefits to society of extending care, such as higher tax revenues and reductions in homelessness, as well as nonmarket benefits to former foster youth, such as improved personal and familial health choices.

The cost of providing foster care to eligible youth after age 18 will likely be a consideration for most states. Given the expense, states that choose to extend care may decide to cover only youth who are IV-E eligible. (The federal government does not explicitly require that a state make foster care maintenance payments on behalf of children who are ineligible for federal foster care.)[49]

Based on administrative data, just under half of children meet the criteria to be eligible for federal foster care maintenance payments (this share varies greatly by state).[50] With the exception of eligibility determination and certain data collection costs (both counted as administrative costs), state foster care expenditures may only be partially reimbursed by the federal government if incurred on behalf of Title IV-E eligible children and youth. A child or youth is eligible for Title IV-E if he or she (1) meets income/assets tests and family structure/living arrangement rules in the home he/she was removed from, (2) has specific judicial determinations made related to reasons for the removal and other aspects of his/her removal and placement; and (3) is placed in an eligible licensed setting with an eligible provider(s). Currently, the reimbursement rate for federal foster care maintenance payments is pegged to a state's Federal Medical Assistance Percentage (FMAP), which ranges from a low of 50% (for highest per capita income states) to as high as 76% (for lowest per capita income states).[51] The reimbursement rate for program administration costs, including child placement activities is 50%; and the reimbursement rate for training costs is 75%.

States are expected to pay the full costs for children and youth who do not meet the Title IV-E eligibility criteria, either out of state or local treasuries or, if allowable, some other federal funding source. Whether states would also pay the full costs for youth ages 18 to 21 who are not Title IV-E eligible remains to be seen. Although permissible under law, extending care only to certain youth who meet the eligibility criteria established in the new law would likely raise equity concerns. States that extend care to all youth beyond their 18th birthday could in practice establish different levels of reimbursement for those youth who are Title IV-E eligible than for those who are not, and possibly different levels of services and supports.

The cost of Medicaid coverage is a related issue. Youth eligible for Title IV-E foster care maintenance payments are automatically eligible for Medicaid coverage. [52] Thus, because

P.L. 110-351 expands eligibility for Title IV-E foster care maintenance payments it automatically extends mandatory Medicaid coverage to any youth who elects to remain in foster care after his 18th birthday and who meets the Title IV-E eligibility criteria. As long as the youth remains in foster care and is otherwise Title IV-E eligible, this Medicaid coverage would continue until the youth's 21st birthday, or whichever earlier age the state elects. The costs of Medicaid are shared by the federal government and states. States incur Medicaid costs by making payments to service providers (e.g., for beneficiaries' doctor visits) and performing administrative activities (e.g., making eligibility determinations).[53] They then submit expense reports in order to receive federal reimbursement for a share of these costs. As with foster care maintenance payments, the FMAP is the rate at which states are reimbursed for most Medicaid costs. (Most states are reimbursed for administrative costs at 50%.) Youth who are ineligible for federal foster care would not automatically be eligible for Medicaid, however, most children in foster care who do not qualify for federal maintenance payments receive Medicaid through another pathway.

Nonetheless, the cost of Medicaid will likely become less of a consideration to states, since they will soon be required to extend Medicaid to all youth who age out, regardless of whether they stay in care after age 18. As part of the health care reform law, the Patient Protection and Affordable Care Act (PPACA, P.L. 111-148), these youth will be eligible under a new mandatory Medicaid pathway, beginning on January 1, 2014.[54] HHS has not issued guidance on how this pathway is to be implemented.

Establishing Criteria for Youth to Remain in Care

P.L. 110-351 specifies the circumstances under which youth may remain in care after age 18, such as by attending school; working part-time or full-time; participating in a program or activity designed to promote, or remove barriers to, employment; or having a condition that would preclude them from these activities. As noted earlier in its July 2010 program instructions, HHS advises that states and tribes can make remaining in care conditional upon whether youth pursue certain pathways. For example, extended care could be provided only to those youth enrolled in post-secondary education. However, it appears that P.L. 110-351 allows youth to remain eligible for extended care so long as they are pursuing any one of the conditions. This could raise equity concerns if states and tribes preclude youth who have pursued other opportunities allowed under the law. These youth may decide that college is not the right choice for them, or they may decide to work now and pursue college later. If states were, for example, to make extended care available only to those youth in post-secondary education, they may be reinforcing that only some youth should have the opportunity to stay in care. Youth who attend college may already be at an advantage relative to other youth in care who could not get into college or chose to work instead.

A somewhat related issue is that states choosing to extend foster care to all youth are not required to meet the case plan and case review requirements (or other Title IV-E requirements, such as data reporting and monitoring) for non IV-E eligible youth that must be fulfilled for all children in care under the age of 18, regardless of their IV-E eligibility. In states that choose to extend care to all youth beyond their 18th birthday, this could, in practice, establish different levels of services and supports, depending on whether the child is IV-E eligible. For example, the requirements for background checks of foster parents and monthly caseworker visits may not be enforced for non-IV-E eligible youth. In addition, these young people may not have the same level of oversight and supervision as IV-E eligible youth. Little may be known about the young people who remain in care and are IV-E ineligible, which may in turn preclude policymakers and others from determining whether the needs of *all* young adults in extended care are being met. Another consideration is that states would not need to report to the federal foster care data reporting system (known as AFCARS) on these youth. Therefore, the true number of youth in care ages 18 to 21 would be unknown.

Facilitating Youth Remaining in Care

States that decide to extend foster care to youth up to age 21 may face challenges actually keeping youth in care after their 18th birthday. In a recent study by the Chapin Hall Center for Children at the University of Chicago, researchers identified the reasons a significant share of youth in some parts of Illinois do not remain in care despite the state's policies to retain youth beyond age 18.[55] Child welfare services in the state are administered by the Department of Child and Family Services' (DCFS) four regional offices. In the Cook County region, which includes Chicago, over 81% of youth remain in care beyond age 18 (and nearly 60% until age 21), compared to the 54% of youth who are collectively retained in the three other regions (and about 15% to just over 40% until age 21, for each of the three regions).[56]

To determine the factors that influence whether some youth leave care before age 21, Chapin Hall evaluated administrative data, conducted a statewide survey of caseworkers, held focus groups with caregivers and youth, and interviewed court personnel across the state. The study identified five such factors:

- Court advocacy: Some juvenile courts in the state play an active role in retaining youth by keeping their cases open, even with resistance from stakeholders—caseworkers, caregivers, youth, and court personnel—involved in the case. According to the study, court advocacy is a key factor that influences the other four variables.
- Awareness of laws and policies: The study found that stakeholders in the child welfare system did not have a uniform understanding of laws and DCFS policy that allow youth to remain in care until age 21. A number of professionals, especially in two regions, believed that the nature of the laws and the state's implementation of the laws, presented obstacles to youth remaining in care beyond age 18 or 19. Further, stakeholders were not consistently aware of the independent living options that are available, or potentially available, to encourage extending foster care.
- Availability of resources: In regions where caseworkers believed that there were few appropriate foster care placements for the oldest youth in care, youth tended not to stay in care after age 18.[57] This was especially true in the state's Southern region. In contrast, caseworkers in the Cook County region were more confident about the availability of placements, and sought such placements. In addition, despite the availability of independent living services, some caregivers and youth did not believe them to be worthwhile. These stakeholders and others felt that services were most often geared toward either very low-functioning youth or college-bound youth.
- Adult Involvement: Youth who had stable and supportive relationships with adults—foster parents, relatives, caseworkers, or other professionals—tended to remain in care longer. However, youth and others reported that maintaining these relationships

is difficult due to high caseworker turnover, behavioral problems, and conflicts between youth and their biological parents.

- Attitudes toward remaining in care: Youth attitudes about staying in care beyond the age of majority was identified as a challenge in keeping them in care. Youth often request to leave or become uncooperative because of the restrictions imposed by their case worker. The study found that some agencies and court personnel sometimes support the youth's request to leave because their negative behavior would not otherwise change. Some adult stakeholders expressed the concern that remaining in care might encourage dependency on state services. Finally, some youth expressed that attending court hearings is bothersome and irrelevant, especially for those who live far from the courthouse or do not feel they are in control about decisions concerning their futures.

Though Illinois is not necessarily representative of all states, these factors may be relevant to other states, particularly those that currently do not extend care beyond age 18, and have not yet had to address these issues.

Older Youth Who Want to Return to Care

In states that extend foster care, youth age 18 or older who emancipate from foster care may later determine, prior to their state's optional older age, that they would like to return to care because of the challenges they face living on their own, or for other reasons. The July 2010 program instructions issued by HHS permit states and tribes to extend foster care assistance in a way that permits a youth to stay in care continuously or "leave care and return at some point after attaining age 18" (up to age 19, 20, or 21, depending on the state) so long as the original court order remains in effect and other IV-E eligibility criteria are satisfied. It appears that in at least a small number of states, youth are already permitted to reenter care.

The Chapin Hall Center for Children's 2008 survey of 45 state independent living coordinators found that 15 states permit youth to reenter care and another seven permit reentry under certain circumstances. In some of these states, youth can return by signing a voluntary placement agreement.[58] In other states, the court must decide that it is in the best interest for the youth to remain. Further, some states limit the amount of time that can elapse between exit and re-entry.

Texas permits youth to return if they are attending high-school, a GED course, or a vocational or technical program; or are on a one- to four-month break from college or a technical or vocational program.[59] Youth may participate in extended care subject to the availability of an appropriate licensed placement, certain age and time criteria, their criminal history, and signing a voluntary placement agreement. Other states, like New York, discharge youth on a trial basis, which enables them to return to care at any point before age 21. In New York, trial discharge means the youth remains in the custody of the child welfare system while living in the community in a non-foster care placement.[60] The same case planning and casework contact requirements apply as if the youth were still in a foster care placement, and permanency hearings are held. If a youth loses housing during the period of trial discharge, the local child welfare district must assist the youth to find other appropriate housing or place the youth in a foster care setting. While such a process could be adapted for use by states that extend foster care under the provisions of P.L. 110-351, youth would need to be placed in an eligible foster care setting—such as an independent living setting—for the state to receive Title IV-E funding on his or her behalf.

Older Youth Who Want to Be Placed in Care

The July 2010 program instructions appear to permit IV-E eligibility for young people who have reached the state age of majority and would like to enter care (up to the oldest age permitted by the state) even if they do not have a prior child welfare history. The instructions appear to allow these young people to enter care so long as they meet IV-E eligibility requirements. Arguably, youth ages 18 through 20 may want to be placed in foster care if they lack adequate housing and/or are otherwise not able to live independently. If any older youth sought foster care placement with a child welfare agency, states (and tribes) could be required, for the first time, to establish a system of care for young adults who do not necessarily have a history of foster care placement.[61] If this is not the case, HHS may wish to provide further clarification.

Supervised Independent Living Setting

P.L. 110-351 amends the definition of "child care institution" to include "a supervised setting in which the individual is living independently" for youth who remain in care after age 18 in states that take up the extended care option. The law directs HHS to clarify this phrase through the rulemaking process; however, HHS has signaled that it does not plan to issue a regulation "at this time" on independent living settings and the July 2010 instructions do not provide guidance on what independent living settings entail or how they should be overseen. In the absence of instructions on oversight of youth in these settings, states could establish very distinct protocols for supervising older youth in care.

Although not defined in law or regulation, "independent living" could refer to a variety of settings, including apartments or homes where youth live with or without a roommate(s); an apartment building where other older foster youth live; college dorms; group homes; and host or boarding homes where youth live with an older adult(s). The term "supervised" is also open to interpretation. This could mean that the youth's case worker visits him or her regularly onsite, and/or the landlord/dorm supervisor/host family checks in with the youth and provides updates to the case worker, among other arrangements.

States with foster youth in independent living settings would need to consider several issues: Should the child welfare agency purchase independent living units and/or contract with organizations that own such units? To what extent would the child welfare agency (or its contractor(s)) screen other youth and adults who live with youth in care? What share of the rent and utilities, if any, should youth cover? How often should case workers visit youth at the independent living setting, and where would the case worker visit the youth?[62] To what extent would the youth be responsible if he or she violated the terms of a lease or damaged his or her placement? Can youth move to less or more restrictive independent living settings depending on their progress?

States have already had to address at least some of these questions during their process in establishing independent living programs that provide housing to emancipated youth ages 18 to 21 under CFCIP-funded independent living programs. In a 2004 survey, the Government Accountability Office (GAO) found that 46 states offered assistance with room and board to emancipated youth, and provided a range of housing options to meet the needs of youth, including group homes, supervised apartment sites, and unsupervised apartment sites with periodic visits from cases managers.[63] (See the Appendix for a discussion of the types of settings that are funded in three states and Washington, DC, for youth who remain in care beyond age 18.)

Changes to Other Child Welfare Policies

The option to extend foster care to older youth will likely affect other federal child welfare policies regarding data collection and oversight of states' compliance with federal child welfare law.

AFCARS

To incorporate the potentially expanded foster care population allowed under P.L. 110-351, changes made to the Adoption and Foster Care Reporting and Analysis System (AFCARS), the federal system that collects national foster care data, are under consideration. States are required to report data twice each year to HHS on the number and characteristics of children in care and those who have been adopted. These figures are compiled to create a national profile of these children. Currently, states are required to report data on all children until age 18. States must also report data on youth ages 18 or older if they have not reached the state's legal age of majority; or for youth who are age 18, but not yet 19 and on whose behalf Title IV-E foster care maintenance payments are being made.[64] The July 2010 instructions on P.L. 110-351 require that states and tribes that exercise the option to extend federal foster care to youth age 18 or older must collect and report data to AFCARS on those youth. States would not be required to report on older youth who are receiving only state-funded foster care maintenance payments, which could result in an incomplete picture of all older youth in care. HHS is currently considering modifications to AFCARS. On January 11, 2008, HHS published a notice of proposed rulemaking (NPRM) that would restructure the AFCARS data and add new data reporting requirements.[65] That rule was never finalized and on July 23, 2010, HHS announced its intent to publish a new NPRM in light of the changes made by P.L. 110-351.[66] This rulemaking process could offer an opportunity for HHS to modify the AFCARS reporting requirements if it wants to ensure that youth in care who are older than the age of majority, including youth whose foster care is not funded through IV-E, are included in the data system.

Child and Family Services Review

The Child and Family Services Review (CFSR) is conducted by HHS to determine whether states are in compliance with programs and policies authorized under Title IV-B and Title IV-E of the Social Security Act.[67] States completed their first review round in 2004, and the second round began in 2007. During the review process, a joint federal and state team determines whether states are in substantial conformity with seven outcomes related to the safety, permanency, and well-being of children, and whether states have in place child welfare systems to achieve these goals. The team reviews statewide administrative data; conducts interviews with children and families served, as well as foster parents, service providers, case workers, court personnel, and other key stakeholders; and systematically reviews the cases of a random sample of children served.

For the second round of reviews, HHS has placed an emphasis on older youth. HHS directed the federal and state evaluators to interview, at the state-level, youth being served by the state child welfare agency, especially those youth who are eligible to receive independent living services.[68] Also in the second round, 10 of 40 foster care cases reviewed must involve children who were ages 16 or 17 as of the last day of the 12-month review period or the date that they exited care, as applicable. [69] This is to ensure that the reviewers have enough applicable cases to determine whether states are adequately providing independent living services for youth with a goal of emancipation.[70]

The CFSR is an ongoing process. For the third round, the agency could consider requiring that at least some of the sample cases reviewed by the team involve older youth who have remained in care after age 18, and that these youth also be included in the review process interviews.

Option to Extend Support for Youth Leaving Care for Permanent Homes after Reaching Age 16

Other provisions of the law address the connection of youth to caring adults, through adoption or placement with relatives. With limited exceptions, monthly federal (Title IV-E) assistance has not generally been available for a child who has reached his or her 18th birthday and who left foster care for a permanent family via adoption or kinship guardianship.[71] However, P.L. 110-351 permits states and tribes, as of FY2011, to choose to provide adoption or kinship guardianship subsidies on behalf of eligible children who leave foster care after their 16th birthday, so long as those youth have not yet reached their 21st birthday and are enrolled in school, employed at least 80 hours a month, or participating in an activity designed to promote or remove barriers to employment.[72] States and tribes may also cover an older youth with a medical condition that makes him or her incapable of participating in the activity and this incapacity is supported by regularly updated information in the child's case plan. In addition, a state or tribe is allowed to continue this assistance up to the 21st birthday on behalf of any child, regardless of the age at which the child left foster care, if the state determines that "the child has a mental or physical handicap that warrants the continuation of assistance." (This was and remains true with regard to adoption assistance; P.L. 110-351 will also extend it, as of FY2011, to kinship guardianship assistance.)

The July 2010 program instructions on P.L. 110-351 require that states opting to extend foster care beyond age 18 must also provide adoption and guardianship subsidies to youth age 18 and older, up to the age the state has elected. The instructions advise that the term "relative" for purposes of guardianship assistance can include biological and legal familial ties or refer more broadly to tribal kin, extended family and friends, or other "fictive" kin.[73] States and tribes are further advised that they may establish conditions under which a person may qualify to be a child's guardian or enter into a legal guardianship arrangement. For example, such conditions can include requiring a child to be in care for a certain period, and targeting certain age groups for guardianship, such as children over age 12.

CHANGES TO THE CHAFEE FOSTER CARE INDEPENDENCE PROGRAM

The Fostering Connections to Success and Increasing Adoptions Act of 2008 (P.L. 110-351) extended the purposes of the CFCIP to include serving youth exiting foster care to adoption or kinship guardianship at age 16 or older, in addition to youth who age out of care without a permanent home. This means that the law now explicitly authorizes states to provide CFCIP services to youth who leave care for a permanent placement. Similarly, youth age 16 or older who exit to kinship guardianship are now eligible for the Chafee Education and Training Voucher (ETV) program (youth adopted from foster care at age 16 or older continue to remain eligible, as authorized under P.L. 106-169).

The act also added and modified provisions in the CFCIP pertaining to Indian youth. As of FY2010, the law permits an Indian tribe, tribal organization, or tribal consortium that receives Title IV-E funding,[74] or enters into a cooperative agreement or contract with the state to provide foster care, to apply for and receive an allotment of CFCIP and ETV funds directly from HHS. Successful tribal applicants are to receive an allotment out of the state's allotment that is based on the share of all children in foster care in the state under the custody of the tribal entity. Tribal entities must satisfy the CFCIP program requirements established for states, as HHS determines appropriate, and they must submit a plan to HHS that details their process for consulting with the state about their independent living or ETV programs, among other information.[75] For example, in their state plans, tribal entities must discuss the process for consulting with the state to ensure that tribal youth who previously received independent living services through the state will continue to receive the same services through the tribal entity. The law also requires that as of FY20 10, a state must certify that it will negotiate in good faith with any tribal entity that does not receive a direct federal allotment of Title IV-E funds but would like to enter into an agreement or contract with the state to receive funds for administering, supervising, or overseeing CFCIP and ETV programs for eligible Indian children under the tribal entity's authority.

P.L. 110-351 explicitly authorizes states to provide independent living services to youth who have left foster care under a permanent arrangement before reaching age 18, either by adoption or kinship guardianship, in addition to the traditional CFCIP population of foster youth who age out without a permanent home. This means that independent living services—with their focus on connecting youth to school, work, and other resources—may be available to these youth until they reach age 21. A significant number of youth may be eligible. In FY2007, just over 2,000 youth ages 16 and 17 left foster for a guardianship arrangement (with relatives or non-relatives), and another 1,500 were adopted.[76] Further, states may extend CFCIP education and training vouchers to youth who leave care for guardianship at age 16 or older (youth adopted from care at age 16 or older were permitted under the authorizing law to receive the vouchers).

States currently provide CFCIP services to youth "likely to remain in foster care until age 18," and they have broad discretion in defining this term. Going forward, as states prioritize which youth to serve in the program, they may need to determine whether independent living programs have the capacity to serve any additional youth, given that authorized funding for the CFCIP has not increased.

TRANSITION PLAN REQUIREMENT

The Fostering Connections to Success and Increasing Adoptions Act of 2008 (P.L. 110-351) adds a case review requirement pertaining to older youth in care. The law requires that a youth's caseworker, and as appropriate, other representative(s) of the youth, assist and support him or her in developing a transition plan. The plan is to be directed by the youth, and is to include specific options on housing, health insurance, education, local opportunities for mentors, workforce supports, and employment services. The plan must be implemented 90 days prior to a youth's 18th birthday (or the 19th, 20th , or 21st birthdays of youth in states that take up the option to extend foster care), "whether during that period foster care maintenance payments are being made on the child's behalf or the child is receiving benefits or services under [the Chafee Foster Care Independence Program]."

As described earlier in the report, the new health care reform law, the Patient Protection and Affordable Care Act (PPACA, P.L. 111-148), adds another element to the transition plan. The law requires that the plan must address the importance of designating another individual to make health care treatment decisions on behalf of the youth if he or she becomes unable to participate in these decisions *and* does not have a relative who would be authorized to make these decisions under state law, or he or she does not want a relative to make these decisions. In addition, the transition plan must provide the youth with the option to execute a health care power of attorney, health care proxy, or other similar document recognized under state law. As part of program instructions issued by HHS on June 7, 2010, concerning implementation of PPACA, states and tribes that have submitted a Title IV-E plan or have been approved to operate a Title IV-E program must submit, by December 31, 2010, a Title IV-E amendment that reflects implementation of, and compliance with, the new requirement.[77]

The *transition plan* is distinct from a *case plan*,[78] which is required for every child and youth in foster care, but the two would appear to be somewhat complementary. In the *case plan*, the child welfare agency must describe in a written document the youth's placement and a plan for ensuring the youth receives safe and proper care, among other items. For youth ages 16 or older, the *case plan* must also address the programs and services that will help the youth develop independent living skills before emancipating from care. The *case plan* is implemented and modified as needed while the youth is in care. In contrast, the new *transition plan* is to include options about the services and supports that the youth may receive (presumably) when he or she is no longer in the custody of the state or receiving CFCIP-funded independent living services. While the *case plan* requirements do not outline the supports that are to be in place for older youth, the *transition plan* requires that youth and other stakeholders identify specific options that will help youth live independently. For example, the plan must specify which type of housing options the youth will have (and presumably alternative options if housing is not available). Further, the *case plan* requirements are silent on the youth's role in participating in decisions about their plan; on the other hand, the *transition plan* is to be directed by the youth in consultation with others, and can be as detailed as the youth would like.[79] Finally, the *case plan* is reviewed by a court as part of annual hearings to review the youth's (or child's) permanency goal(s). The *transition plan* is not reviewed by a court or other body.

The July 2010 program instructions issued by HHS on P.L. 110-351 provide additional guidance on the transition plan. The instructions encourage child welfare agencies to use transition planning to build on earlier efforts to assist young people in making the transition from foster care, including through the case planning process and permanency hearings. Child welfare agencies are encouraged to begin engaging youth in the transition plan process "well in advance" of the 90-day period.

The July 2010 program instructions state that the transition plan is *not required* for a youth who leaves foster care more than 90 days before his or her 18th birthday, or an older age in states that elect to extend care. This raises questions about those youth who emancipate at any earlier age. Thousands of youth emancipate from care at age 17,[80] raising the possibility that without a transition plan, they could leave care less prepared than their peers in care who are emancipated at ages 18 or older. (These youth might also be less likely to benefit from the Medicaid pathway for emancipated youth, who must have been in care on their 18th birthday to be eligible for this pathway, effective in 2014.) Similarly, states and tribes would not necessarily help develop transition plans for youth who remain in care beyond age 18 but leave at least 90 days before reaching age 19, 20, or 21 (depending on the state).

OTHER ONGOING ISSUES

Even with the passage of the new law, policymakers and child welfare advocates remained concerned that older foster youth and those who have aged out face challenges as they transition to adulthood. The Midwest Evaluation and other research demonstrate that youth have difficulty in fostering permanent connections with caring adults, securing health insurance and housing, and staying connected to work and school. Further, little is known about youth as they transition from foster care and the effectiveness of the services they receive, although a new national database will likely provide some insight into their outcomes across a number of areas, such as education, employment, and contact with social service and criminal justice systems.

Permanent Relationships

The Midwest Evaluation shows that youth who aged out of foster care are less likely to have permanent, positive relationships with caring adults, and that youth continue to remain in close contact with their biological families after emancipating. Still, they also appear to be estranged from these family members. The Midwest Evaluation on the Adult Functioning of Former Foster Youth, a study that is tracking young people who emancipated from care in three states, shows that at age 23 or 24, these youth were slightly less likely than their peers to be married (13.0% vs. 15.0%) and much less likely to live with relatives (21.1% vs. 32.8%).[81] Further, about half or less than half of alumni reported being "very close" or "somewhat close" to their biological mother (53.8%), biological father (30.2%), grandparents (49.5%), or "other relatives" (44.4%). (Comparable data were not reported for youth generally.) This suggests that a significant share of former foster youth in the study did not have strong relationships with at least some of their relatives after having been out of care for a few years. The study also suggests that some young people go back to living with their biological families. It is unclear the extent to which states facilitate youth in achieving and maintaining healthy relationships with their parents and other family members.

Despite federal protections to ensure that child welfare agencies help youth plan for their futures, child welfare practitioners and young people in care continue to advocate for additional policies that improve the transition to adulthood by encouraging strong, long-term connections to caring adults.[82] They argue that these connections can help youth achieve more successful outcomes by providing emotional, financial, and other support. In some jurisdictions, the child welfare agency plays an active role to ensure permanent adult connections for youth aging out. According to practitioners, permanency can mean different types of relationships for a youth in foster care, but generally refers to a connection with at least one committed adult who provides a safe, stable, and secure relationship, unconditional commitment, and a legal relationship where possible.[83] Practitioners point out that relationships can be developed by (1) connecting youth to family members such as grandparents and aunts, as well as others who have been involved in the youth's life, even many years ago; (2) establishing legal guardianships or some other permanent arrangement with a caring adult in the youth's life; (3) helping youth develop relationships with caring adults such as teachers or mentors; (4) when appropriate, exploring the viability of reunification with biological parents; and (5) assisting youth, up to their early twenties, pursue adoptive relationships with adults.[84]

Advocates have urged policymakers and practitioners to require that permanency planning be initiated before a youth leaves care. They argue for case planning and decision-making that concurrently address a youth's permanency needs and his or her needs for life skills, services, and supports, and they warn against only providing youth with links to resources and social service professionals.[85] According to Casey Family Services, a national child welfare provider: "All too often youth with a goal of independent living do not have a concurrent plan for permanent family relationships, and youth with a goal of [another] planned permanent living arrangement (APPLA) may have the commitment of a permanent place, but not a permanent person. Consequently, these youth lose out on two fronts: they will more than likely "age out" of the system without a permanent family, and be launched into adulthood unprepared and unsupported to successfully meet its challenges."[86]

The new transition plan requirement may be one way to help ensure that youth are fostering permanent connections in adulthood. The requirement directs youth and other stakeholders to consider local opportunities for mentoring. This could mean that, at minimum, youth and others have a conversation about the relationships the youth can forge as they leave care. Further, as proposed in previous Congresses, changes could be made to federal child welfare law to assist youth achieve permanency. For example, written case plan requirements could be amended to include the steps taken to ensure that a child has a permanent living arrangement if they emancipate, and for older youth, documentation of the permanent living arrangement the youth will enter after foster care. Further, the case plan requirements could include documentation of the steps the agency takes to find a permanent placement with a family or other adult connection for the youth, as well as a permanent living arrangement. Some existing transition processes in particular focus heavily on permanent connections. During the transition process in Texas, youth receive assistance in determining which caring adults can provide them support when they leave care.[87] As part of the youth's case plan, a youth is asked to identify someone who is over age 18 and not necessarily a placement option, but will provide consistent and significant support and help the youth make important decisions and work through emergency situations.

Foster Club, a child welfare organization, has developed what is known as a Permanency Pact, which is intended to help youth aging out connect with caring adults.[88] The pact is a tool that can be used to "define, substantiate, and verbalize" a lifelong commitment of an adult to a youth leaving care. The pact seeks to ensure that the young person leaving care has emotional and tangible supports. These supports can take several forms, including a home for the holidays, a place to do laundry, job search assistance and career counseling, educational assistance, clothing, spiritual support, use of a phone, help with moving into an apartment, someone to co-sign, mental health support, babysitting, and emergency cash, among other examples. At least one state, Oklahoma, has incorporated the Permanency Pact as part of the transition planning process for older youth expected to emancipate from care.[89]

Other efforts to support permanency have focused on adoption for older youth. Beginning in 2005, HHS funded a five-year pilot demonstration project to support adoption for older youth, known as Adoption Opportunity Grants.[90] Two of the multiple purposes of the grants are to demonstrate effective strategies of open adoption for youth who prefer to maintain contact with their biological families, and to demonstrate effective implementation strategies for securing permanent connections for youth, particularly through adoption, open adoption, guardianship, and kinship care. The grants funded 10 projects throughout the country.

Other changes could be made at the federal level to achieve permanency for current and former foster youth. For example, federal grants could be funded to provide mentoring. Currently, the Department of Justice is administering a pilot program that provides funding to a small number of grantees for mentoring teens in care.[91] In prior Congresses, bills were introduced that sought to permanently authorize funding for grants that provide mentoring to foster children. The bills proposed to authorize grants to states (or to a political subdivision of the state if it serves a "substantial number" of youth in foster care) to support, establish, and expand networks of public and private community entities to provide this mentoring.

Child welfare researchers advise that practitioners should be cautious in designing and implementing policies that help foster youth develop lasting connections with adults.[92] For example, young people in care have experienced failed relationships with adults who were supposed to care for them, and youth could be harmed if they form unsustainable relationships with other adults. Further, as the Midwest Evaluation and other studies have shown, youth who age out tend to have regular contact with their biological family. Little research has been conducted on how best foster youth facilitate healthy relationships with existing family members.

Housing

Among the most often cited concerns for youth aging out of foster care is the lack of adequate and affordable housing.[93] According to one study of former foster youth ages 20 to 33 in Oregon and Washington, about one out of five (22.5%) reported being homeless for one day or more within a year of leaving foster care.[94] (This figure is slightly higher than the 18% of 21-year-olds in the Midwest Evaluation who reported being homeless at least once since existing care.)[95] The housing status of former foster youth is often affected by their connection to caring adults, as well as their education and employment.[96] Reciprocally, youth who lack housing may have difficulty staying in school and/or maintaining employment.

Although the CFCIP authorizes states to spend up to 30% of their allotment on room and board for youth ages 18 to 21 who emancipate from care, child welfare researchers point out that these funds alone cannot adequately cover the cost of housing for many former foster youth.[97] Nonetheless, several jurisdictions appear to be using innovative strategies to connect youth to both temporary and permanent housing through a combination of federal, state, local, and private funding sources. These strategies have involved providing a continuum of housing that allows the youth to choose from various housing options; permitting youth to have multiple opportunities to remain in a housing program even if they fail to meet the terms of a housing agreement or lease; and providing housing to former foster youth with mental health issues and other barriers to living independently.[98] In addition, youth who live in states that take up the extended foster care option under P.L. 110-351 would be housed in a foster home or independent living setting, as defined in forthcoming regulations.

Another housing issue concerns current and former foster youth in college who are unable to stay with family or friends over school breaks, when college facilities are often closed. Some states require public universities to provide housing for these youth. For example, California law requires that the California State University system and the community college system, "review housing issues for those emancipated foster youth living in college dormitories to ensure basic housing during the regular academic school year, including vacations and holidays other than summer break."[99] In at least one state, Vermont, the child welfare agency attempts to secure housing for emancipated youth when they return from college on breaks (see Appendix).

A recently enacted law seeks to address some of these housing concerns, even in small part, by authorizing (but not necessarily providing) housing for current and former foster youth. The Higher Education Opportunity Act (HEOA, P.L. 110-315), enacted on August 14, 2008, authorizes services specifically for youth in foster care or recently emancipated youth, including housing services, among other related changes. The bill authorizes services for these youth (and homeless youth) through Student Support Services—a program intended to improve the retention and graduation rates of disadvantaged college students—that include temporary housing during breaks in the academic year. The HEOA further allows additional uses of funds through the Fund for the Improvement of Postsecondary Education to establish demonstration projects that provide comprehensive support services for students who were in foster care (or homeless) anytime before age 13. As specified in the law, the projects can provide housing to the youth when housing at an educational institution is closed or unavailable to other students. Nevertheless, authority to fund housing during breaks does not mean that universities and colleges will necessarily use funds from the two programs for this purpose.

Another law, the Foreclosure Prevention Act of 2008 (P.L. 110-289), enacted on July 30, 2008, enables owners of properties financed in part with Low-Income Housing Tax Credits to claim as low-income units those units occupied by low-income students who were in foster care. Owners of LIHTC properties are required to maintain a certain percentage of their units for occupancy by low-income households; students (with some exceptions) are not generally considered low- income households for this purpose. The law does not specify the length of time these students must have spent in foster care nor require that youth are eligible only if they emancipated.

Health Insurance

The Midwest Evaluation indicated that about half of all youth who were in foster care up to age 17 or 18 (primarily in Iowa and Wisconsin) did not have health insurance when they were surveyed one year after leaving care, at age 18 or 19, even though current and former foster youth in the study tended to need health and mental health services.[100] These youth (as well as their counterparts who stayed in care) described their overall health less favorably than youth in the general population and were more likely to report that health conditions limited their ability to engage in moderate activity. They also reported more visits to the emergency room and more hospitalizations during the prior five years, and were more likely to report being hospitalized for drug use or emotional problems.

Some child welfare advocates support expansion of the option to provide Medicaid for youth who age out of foster care, known as the Chafee option. [101] (Youth ages 18 to 21 who remain in care, pursuant to P.L. 110-351, and who are Title IV-E eligible will be categorically eligible to also receive Medicaid.) According to the 2008 survey by Chapin Hall of 45 states, 29 states (64.4%) have extended the Chafee option to eligible youth. [102] Of the 28 states that responded to a follow- up question about eligibility requirements, 25 states reported that to be eligible, youth must have been in foster care on their 18th birthday; 15 states reported that youth must complete an application to be eligible; one state said that youth are automatically eligible; and nine states reported other eligibility criteria. Another 14 states reported that former foster youth are eligible for SCHIP (six of the states) or Medicaid through other pathways (13 of the states). Youth are eligible for Medicaid by meeting the "medically needy" criteria (seven states), through a 100% state funded program (three states), and through other, unspecified pathways (three states). One state reported that former foster youth are not categorically eligible for Medicaid.[103]

The Chafee option will likely become a moot pathway in the next few years. As part of the health care reform law, the Patient Protection and Affordable Care Act (PPACA, P.L. 111-148), youth who were in foster care on their 18th birthday (or an older age allowed by the state) will be eligible under a new mandatory Medicaid pathway specifically for former foster youth until age 26 regardless of their annual income.[104] This provision is effective January 1, 2014. HHS has not issued guidance about this pathway.

Employment and Education

In its February 2008 report on disconnected youth, the U.S. Government Accountability Office defined this population as individuals ages 14 to 24 who are not in school and not working, or lack family or other support networks.[105] According to the report, youth in care and certain other groups of youth are more at risk of becoming disconnected from employment and education.

Young people who have aged out of care tend to have low rates of employment and low earnings. One study of youth who emancipated in three states—California, Minnesota, and North Carolina—linked child welfare, Unemployment Insurance (UI), and public assistance administrative data to determine the employment outcomes of these young people. [106] At age 24, about three out of five youth who aged out in the three states were working, a rate lower than that of youth nationally and youth from low-income families. These young people were also less likely to earn as much as their counterparts. The average monthly earnings for emancipated youth in all three states ($690 in California, $575 in Minnesota, and $450 in North Carolina) were substantially lower than earnings for youth nationally, who earned $1,535 a month on average. Similarly, the Midwest Evaluation also found that by age 23 or 24, about half of the young people who had aged out of care in Iowa, Illinois, and Wisconsin were employed, compared to about 75% of their counterparts in the general population.[107] Those foster care alumni who were employed tended to have poverty-level earnings.

On the education front, young people in care or who have aged out face numerous challenges. While in care, youth tend to experience multiple school placements, delays in enrollment, loss of academic credit, and lack of a consistent education advocate who is knowledgeable about their needs in the special education process, among other challenges.[108] Foster care alumni, even those who remain in care beyond age 18, are far less likely to attend college. The Midwest Evaluation demonstrates that by age 23 or 24, only about 7% of the young people who aged out of care at 18 and about 5% of the young people who aged out of care at a later age (up to 21) attained an associate's degree or bachelor's degree.[109] This suggests that young foster care alumni may need additional supports to facilitate completing their education. For example, they may benefit from academic, social/emotional, and logistical support, including year-round housing.

The federal government has taken steps to address the educational and workforce needs of youth who are in or were in foster care.[110] The Higher Education Opportunity Act (P.L. 110-315), enacted in 2008, includes provisions that authorize supportive educational services for foster youth. The law stipulates that youth in foster care (including youth who have left foster care after reaching age 16) and homeless children and youth are eligible for what are collectively called the federal Trio programs.[111] P.L. 110-315 directs the Department of Education to require applicants seeking Trio funds to identify and make available services, including mentoring, tutoring, and other services, to these youth. The Trio programs are designed to identify potential postsecondary students from disadvantaged backgrounds, prepare these students for higher education, provide certain support services to them while they are in college, and train individuals who provide these services. The programs are known individually as Talent Search, Upward Bound, Student Support Services, and Educational Opportunity Centers.

In addition, the act amends the Student Support Services program by changing one of its purposes—pertaining to fostering an institutional climate to support certain students—to include youth in foster care or recently emancipated youth. HEOA also make changes to the Education Opportunity Centers program to require that strategies for recruiting and serving hard-to-reach populations be targeted to students who are in foster care or aging out. Separately, HEOA directs the Secretary of Education to conduct a public awareness campaign about the availability of federal financial aid. The Secretary is to coordinate with, among other entities, organizations that provide services to individuals in foster care, that are or were homeless, or other disconnected individuals.

Separately, federal agencies are working together to address the multiple needs of vulnerable youth populations, including the education and employment needs of current and former foster youth. The U.S. Departments of Education Health and Human Services, Justice, and Labor, and the Social Security Administration have partnered to improve communication and collaboration across programs that target at-risk youth groups under an initiative called the "Shared Youth Vision." Together, the agencies have convened an Interagency Work Group and conducted regional forums in 16 states to develop and coordinate policies and research on foster youth and other vulnerable youth groups. Representatives from federal and state agencies in workforce development, education, social services, and juvenile justice have participated in the forums. The purpose of these forums was to create and implement plans to improve communication and collaboration between local organizations that serve at-risk youth.

Following the forums, the Department of Labor competitively awarded grants totaling $1.6 million to these states to assist them in developing strategic plans to link their systems that serve youth. For example, Arizona is using this initiative to bring together state and county agencies that can assist youth exiting foster care or the juvenile justice system in two counties connect to education and employment services and supports.[112] The Department of Health and Human Services has funded a solutions desk, administered by the National Child Welfare Resource Center for Youth Development, to provide the 16 states a single point of access to information on federal resources available to assist them in implementing Shared Youth Vision activities.

Additional Information on Youth in Foster Care

The Chafee Foster Care Independence Program is a major source of funding for independent living services for youth who are in care or have aged out. Yet little is known about the effectiveness of these services or the outcomes of foster youth after they leave care.[113] The few studies of independent living programs and other interventions have not been rigorous, or have shown that the interventions have not been effective at improving outcomes for youth.[114] Further, no studies have provided a national picture of how well former foster youth make the transition to adulthood. The Midwest Evaluation and other studies have focused on the transition for youth in select regions of the country. Though a new national database—known as the National Youth in Transition Database (NYTD)—will provide insight into the lives of youth when they leave care, full implementation of the database will likely take several years.

Background on the National Youth in Transition Database

The National Youth in Transition Database, authorized by the Chafee Foster Care Independence Act (P.L. 106-169), is intended to track demographic and outcome information of current and former foster youth. P.L. 106-169 required that HHS consult with state and local public officials responsible for administering independent living and other child welfare programs, child welfare advocates, Members of Congress, youth service providers and researchers to (1) "develop outcome measures (including measures of educational attainment, high school diploma, avoidance of dependency, homelessness, non-marital childbirth, incarceration, and high-risk behaviors) that can be used to assess the performance of States in operating independent living programs;" (2) identify the data needed to track the number and characteristics of children receiving independent living services, the type and quantity of services provided, and state performance on the measures; and (3) develop and implement a plan to collect this information beginning with the second fiscal year after the passage of P.L. 106-169.

In its September 2001 Report to the Congress, "Developing a System of Program Accountability Under the John H. Chafee Foster Care Independence Program," HHS outlined a plan and timetable for developing a data collection system.[115] HHS explained that it would publish the final outcomes and measures in the Federal Register and seek public comment by May 2002, and implement the database nationally in October 2003. However, a notice of proposed rulemaking (NPRM) for the data collection system was not published until July 14, 2006. The NPRM provided for a 60-day comment period, during which time HHS heard from states and child welfare advocates. After this period, the final regulations underwent a full agency and department review as well as Office of Management and Budget (OMB) clearance before final publication on February 26, 2008.[116] The final rule establishing the NYTD became effective April 28, 2008, sixty days after publication. The rule requires states to begin collecting data on youth in FY2011.

HHS will use NYTD to engage in two data collection and reporting activities.[117] First, states will collect and report information twice each fiscal year on eligible youth who currently receive independent living services (provided or funded by the state). Information will include whether they continue to remain in foster care, were in foster care in another state, or received child welfare services through an Indian tribe or privately operated foster care program. Second, states will also collect data on the outcomes of current and former foster youth on or about their 17th birthday, two years later on or about their 19th birthday, and again on or about their 21st birthday. These youth will be tracked regardless of whether they receive independent living services at ages 17, 19, and 21. States have the option of tracking a sample of youth who participated in the outcomes collection at age 17 to reduce the data collection burden. The rule imposes financial penalties on states that do not meet data and data submission requirements.

Independent Living Services for Youth in Care

The Chafee Foster Care Independence Program is the only dedicated source of funding for independent living services for transition-age young people in and recently emancipated from foster care. An annual appropriation of $140 million for the program is distributed to states based on their relative share of children in care. States must provide a 20% match in order to receive the funds. Nearly all states routinely draw down their maximum amount of CFCIP dollars.[118] Based on a 2008 survey of 45 states by the University of Chicago's Chapin Hall Center for Children, 31 of the states (68.9%) spend additional funds—beyond the 20% match—to provide independent living services and supports to eligible youth.[119] This suggests that federal funding alone is not likely enough for states to carry out their independent living programs.

Given that funding for independent living services is somewhat limited, states can likely benefit from learning about which services are the most effective. The research literature on independent living programs is scarce. However, pursuant to the law that established the CFCIP,[120] HHS has contracted with the Urban Institute and its partners to carry out evaluations at four independent living programs in California and Massachusetts—an employment services program in Kern County, CA; a one-on-one intensive, individualized life skills program in Massachusetts; and a classroom-based life skills training program and a tutoring/mentoring program, both in Los Angeles County. [121]

The 1,400 youth participating in the evaluation at the four sites were assigned to intervention and control groups, and have been surveyed at three points: baseline, one year after baseline, and two years after baseline. The results of the Los Angeles sites were made available in 2008 and the results of the other two sites are forthcoming. The evaluation of the Los Angeles programs found no statistically significant impact as a result of the life skills training and tutoring interventions. A limitation of the design for the evaluation is that some youth in the control group received life skills services or tutoring services through other programs, and some members in the treatment group did not receive the life skills or tutoring services as intended. Nonetheless, the evaluation team concluded that even if there were no challenges with the experimental design of the studies, the results would not likely change.

Preliminary results of the Kern County site found no statistically significant results. However, young people who received independent living services in the Massachusetts program were more likely than their similarly situated peers in foster care to have better educational and employment outcomes, including persistence in college. [122] The services in Massachusetts appear to be more intensive and holistic than services provided in the other programs. These findings suggest that more research is likely needed to determine which independent living services and supports are most effective for young people in care, and that more intensive programs may be needed to better ensure their success. However, whether funding and other resources are available for more intensive programs remains to be seen.

APPENDIX. DESCRIPTION OF EXTENDED FOSTER CARE PROGRAMS IN THREE STATES AND WASHINGTON, DC

At least three states—Illinois, New York, and Vermont—and Washington, DC, provide foster care to young people ages 18 to 21 through state maintenance payments or similar types of payments. These payments are made out of state or local dollars and without regard to prior Title IV-E eligibility status. The Congressional Research Service contacted the four jurisdictions to learn more about their maintenance payment programs for older youth. The jurisdictions provided varying levels of detail about their programs.[123] Note that this is not an exhaustive review of states that provide the payments to youth beyond their 18th birthdays.

Illinois

Illinois youth in foster care on their 18th birthday, regardless of their income or educational status, may stay in care (in a traditional foster care setting) until they are 19, and some continue in care until age 21. The majority of youth leave care at age 19. Until they age out of care, the Department of Child and Family Services (DCFS) continues to have guardianship of the youth and the courts retain jurisdiction of their cases. According to DCFS, Cook County, which includes the city of Chicago, tends to retain custody of youth for a longer period than other counties. (See Facilitating Youth Remaining in Care, above, for further information about Cook County's efforts to retain youth in care after age 18.)

Youth over the age of 18 are placed in foster care, an institution, or group home, or other setting. The court continues to hold six-month reviews and annual review hearings for the youth. Upon exiting foster care, youth remain under the guardianship of the state for six months, meaning that the court assigns DCFS the responsibility for the physical care and safety of the child, but does not make state foster care maintenance payments on their behalf. During and after the guardianship period, youth are eligible to receive transitional living services and housing through the state's independent living program. Youth attending college receive educational and other assistance from the state and remain in guardianship until age 21. This assistance is funded through state dollars, and not the federal Chafee Foster Care Independence program. As of March 2008, 815 youth ages 18 to 21 in guardianship lived in an independent living setting and 1,023 were in another setting, including college or a detention facility, or were on runaway status.

New York

New York enables youth to remain in foster care until age 21, provided the youth consents to remaining in care, if they are enrolled in a school, college, university, or vocational school, or if they lack the skills to live independently (generally due to cognitive and developmental deficiencies). Most youth who remain in care have a permanency planning goal of discharge to another planned permanent living arrangement (APPLA) with a permanency resource.[124]

The court continues to retain jurisdiction while the youth are in care (i.e., case hearings every six months and an annual permanency plan hearing) and the county provides the same case management services to youth (i.e., monthly case worker visits) as they received when they were under age 18. The county makes state foster care maintenance payments to foster parents for room and board, clothing, food, and other provisions, and youth continue to remain eligible for Medicaid. For youth who attend college and live on a college campus or in nearby housing, the local social services district pays the college directly for room and board.

Every youth who is discharged to APPLA with a permanency resource is first discharged on a trial basis, although youth can agree to be permanently discharged.[125] Trial discharge means the youth remains in the custody of the local social services district while living in the community. The same case planning and casework contact requirements apply as if the youth were still in a foster care placement, and permanency hearings are held. If a youth loses housing during the period of trial discharge, the district must assist the youth to find other appropriate housing or place the youth in a foster care setting. The trial discharge period may continue until a youth reaches the age of 21.

Vermont

Youth in Vermont generally remain in foster care until age 18. Effective July 1, 2007, Act 17 (2007) authorized funding for payments on behalf of former foster youth ages 18 through 22 under a program known as Extended Care, which includes the Adult Living program and the Housing Support and Incidental Grant program. [126] The Extended Care program is administered by the Vermont Department for Children and Families. Youth in the two programs are no longer in the custody of the state and the courts do not retain jurisdiction; youth voluntarily enroll in the program. A youth development coordinator contracted with the Vermont Department of Children and Family Services works with youth in both programs (The Department contracts for independent living services in its 12 service districts.)[127]

Adult Living Program

The purpose of the Adult Living program is for youth to live with caring adults, known as adult partners, after they reach age 18 through the age of 22. Any eligible youth may decide at any point, up to age 21.5, to enroll in the Adult Living program. Participants in the program live in an arrangement similar to a foster family in households that are certified for a foster care placement, or a caring adult at least age 25 who undergoes a background check.[128]

To be eligible for the program, youth who have aged out of foster care must sign a voluntary services agreement pledging to gain independent living skills and work toward self sufficiency, and they must assume responsibility for expenses other than room and board. They are also to develop a savings plan in which they gradually save money until they become self sufficient, where possible. Youth must be enrolled in school part- or full-time, working, or actively seeking work. These criteria may be waived by the Department for Children and Families Services Commissioner or designee based on an individual youth's circumstance. Furthermore, if a youth is unemployed or not enrolled in an educational program, the department will determine if the youth is meeting the criteria for "productive time." Enrolled youth may live in college dormitories, but return to a foster care arrangement during school breaks. Youth who exit the program before age 21.5 may reenter if they demonstrate a commitment to living within a homelike environment and working toward their goals of independent living.

For youth in the Adult Living program, the coordinator facilitates the youth working with their social worker and supportive adults to create and monitor a plan for life skills and self sufficiency; assists the youth in implementing the plan; calls and meets with him or her monthly; and submits monthly reports about the youth's status.

Payments are made on behalf of the youth to adult partners for the cost of (and the cost of providing) basic provisions, including shelter, clothing, food, and school supplies. In the case of youth attending college, adult partners receive the payments to provide provisions to youth over their school breaks.

Housing Support Program

The Housing Support program provides financial support for youth ages 18 to 22 who live independently. Youth in the Housing Support program are also to sign the same voluntary services agreement that is signed by youth in the Adult Living program. The agreement includes information about how many hours they are to work and their budget. Youth may be asked to leave the program if they fail to fulfill the responsibilities outlined in the agreement; those who exit may return if they demonstrate a commitment to working toward their self-sufficiency goals. For youth in the Housing Support program, the coordinator assists the young person in preparing a housing contract; contacts the youth weekly in the first two months and monthly thereafter; assists with the young person's service coordination; and submits monthly reports about the status of the youth. Youth in the Housing Support program receive a grant of up to $5,000 to cover housing and related expenses; on a case-by-case basis, youth may also receive supplemental funds for educational expenses, such as books and lab fees.[129]

Washington, DC

The Washington, DC Child and Family Service Agency (CFSA) requires that all foster youth remain in care until age 21 unless they (1) are reunified with their families or adopted; (2) get married; (3) join the military; or (4) can demonstrate that they have secured employment and housing and are self sufficient. Youth in care continue to remain under the jurisdiction of the court and receive the same case support from CFSA, except that social workers from the agency's Office of Youth Development manage their cases. Further, youth may live in a variety of settings—foster homes, group homes, and transitional living settings in an independent living setting, or in institutional settings. CFSA dollars from the DC government fund the foster care maintenance payments made to the foster parent or appropriate agency. Reimbursement payments cover the cost of room and board, food, clothing, and a stipend, among other resources. Youth who are away at college receive housing payments and other assistance through DC's independent living program.

Author Contact Information

Adrienne L. Fernandes-Alcantara
Specialist in Social Policy
afernandes@crs.loc.gov, 7-9005

End Notes

[1] The CFCIP replaced the former Independent Living Program, originally established in 1985 (P.L. 99-272).

[2] For additional information about the law, see CRS Report RL34704, *Child Welfare: The Fostering Connections to Success and Increasing Adoptions Act of 2008*, by Emilie Stoltzfus.

[3] Through the federal foster care program authorized under Title IV-E of the Social Security Act.

[4] U.S. Department of Health and Human, Administration for Children and Families, Children's Bureau. *Adoption and Foster Care Analysis and Reporting System (AFCARS) Report #12 and #17,* http://www.acf.hhs.gov/programs/cb/ stats_research/index.htm#afcars. In FY2007, the number of children in care reached under half a million (496,000) for the first time. Data on the age and other characteristics of these children are not yet available.

[5] Congressional Research Service analysis of AFCARS data.

[6] Fred Wulczyn and Linda Collins, *A 5-Year Projection of the Number of Children Reaching Age 18 While in Foster Care*, University of Chicago, Chapin Hall Center for Children, 2010, http://chapinhall.org/research/report/5-yearprojection-number-children

[7] Iowa amended its child welfare statute in 2006 to create a program that provides continuing support to foster youth ages 18 to 21. The Iowa youth in the Midwest Evaluation were already too old to benefit from the program when it was implemented.

[8] Mark E. Courtney et al., *Midwest Evaluation of the Adult Functioning of Former Foster Youth: Outcomes at Ages 23 and 24*, Chapin Hall Center for Children, University of Chicago, 2010, http://www.chapinhall.org/research/report/ midwest-evaluation-adult-functioning-former-foster-youth.

[9] Section 475(1), Title IV-E of the Social Security Act.

[10] Section 475(5), Title IV-E of the Social Security Act.

[11] Section 475(1)(D), Title IV-E of the Social Security Act.

[12] Section 475(5)(C), Title IV-E of the Social Security Act.

[13] For additional information about the Title IV-E foster care program, see CRS Report RL3 1242, *Child Welfare: Federal Program Requirements for States*, by Emilie Stoltzfus.

[14] P.L. 110-351 gave tribal entities the same authority that states have to seek federal reimbursement of a part of all their eligible Title IV-E foster care, adoption, and kinship guardianship assistance costs.

[15] States may also seek reimbursement for related costs of administration, child placement (e.g., case planning), training, and data collection.

[16] Pursuant to the Personal Responsibility and Work Opportunity Reconciliation Act of 1996 (P.L. 104-193).

[17] The income and asset tests, as well as family structure/living arrangement rules, are identical to the federal /state rules that applied to the now-defunct cash aid program, Aid to Families with Dependent Children (AFDC), as they existed on July 16, 1996. Under the prior law AFDC program, states established specific AFDC income and asset rules (within some federal parameters). The federal AFDC asset limit was $1,000, however, P.L. 106-169 raised the allowable counted asset limit to $10,000 for purposes of determining Title IV-E eligibility. In addition to meeting the income/asset criteria in the home from which he/she was removed, a child must meet the AFDC family structure/living arrangement rules. Those rules granted eligibility primarily to children in single-parent families (parents are divorced, separated, or never-married and one spouse is not living with the child; or the parent is dead). In some cases a child in a two-parent family may be eligible (if one parent meets certain unemployment criteria).

[18] Alternatively, the parent or legal guardian may voluntarily relinquish custody to the child welfare agency through a voluntary placement agreement with the agency.

[19] Section 475(4), Title IV-E of the Social Security Act.

[20] Sec. 422, Title IV-B of the Social Security Act, requires states to submit a plan that details how they will carry out their child welfare services for all children.

[21] HHS advises that states have broad discretion in determining which youth are "likely to remain in foster care until age 18," and that states may serve youth ages 18 to 21 who were formerly in foster care but did not age out. U.S. Department of Health and Human Services, *Child Welfare Policy Manual*, Section 3. 1B, Question 1. According to the National Foster Care Coalition, many states have developed indicators to help determine the likelihood that a child will remain in care until his or her 18th birthday. As a result, in some states, youth who are later reunified with their guardian(s), adopted, or placed with relative guardians, may receive CFCIP services. National Foster Care Coalition (formerly National Foster Care Awareness Project), *Frequently Asked Questions II: About the Foster Care Independence Act of 1999 and the John H. Chafee Foster Care Independence Program*, December 2000, p16, at http://www.casey.org/NR/rdonlyres/E8E5EC9B-2C0B-496B-A165-5A55D2F793A5/194/ChafeeFAQII1.pdf.

[22] The Child and Family Services Plan is a document submitted by states to HHS that describes how they will carry out activities and programs under Title IV-B of the Social Security Act, Child Abuse Prevention and Treatment Act (CAPTA) state grants, and the CFCIP, including the ETV program. States are required to update the plan annually.

[23] Four states—Illinois, Iowa, Tennessee, and Virginia—received waivers (prior to the enactment of P.L. 110-351) to enable children who exited through guardianship and/or adoption at age 14, 15, or 16 (or older) to receive vouchers under the Chafee Education and Training Voucher (ETV) program. For further information, see U.S. Department of Health and Human Services, *Profiles of the Child Welfare Demonstration Projects*, James Bell Associates, May 2007, at http://www.acf.hhs.gov/programs/cb/programs_fund/cwwaiver/2007/profiles_ demo2007.pdf.

[24] U.S. Congress, House Ways and Means Committee, Income Security and Family Support Subcommittee, "Hearing on Disconnected and Disadvantaged Youth," June 19, 2007, available at http://waysandmeans.house.gov/hearings.asp? formmode=detail&hearing=569.

[25] Ibid. See testimony of Representative Michele Bachmann, who has been a foster parent, and of Dan Lips, an Education Analyst at the Heritage Foundation.

[26] U.S. Congress, House Ways and Means Committee, Income Security and Family Support Subcommittee, "Hearing on Children who 'Age Out' of the Foster Care System," July 12, 2007, available at http://waysandmeans.house.gov/ hearings.asp?formmode=detail&hearing=576. (Hereafter U.S. Congress, "Hearing on Children who 'Age Out' of the Foster Care System," July 12, 2007.) U.S. Congress, House Ways and Means Committee, Income Security and Family Support Subcommittee, "Hearing on Improving the Child Welfare System," February 27, 2008, available at http://waysandmeans.house.gov/hearings.asp?formmode= detail&hearing=612. (Hereafter U.S. Congress, "Hearing on Improving the Child Welfare System," February 27, 2008.)

[27] U.S. Congress, "Hearing on Children who 'Age Out' of the Foster Care System," July 12, 2007. See testimony of Sam Cobbs, Executive Director, First Place Fund for Youth.

[28] U.S. Congress, "Hearing on Children who 'Age Out' of the Foster Care System," July 12, 2007. See testimony of Nicole Dobbins, a former foster youth.

[29] U.S. Congress, "Hearing on Children who 'Age Out' of the Foster Care System," July 12, 2007. See testimony of Tyler Bacon, a former foster youth.

[30] Section 472(3)(c) of Title IV-E, Social Security Act.

[31] U.S. Department of Health and Human Services, Administration on Children, Youth and Families, Administration for Children and Families, Children's Bureau, *Program Instruction: Guidance on Fostering Connections to Success and Increasing Adoptions Act of 2008*, ACYF-CB-PI-10-1 1, July 9, 2010, http://www.acf.hhs.gov/programs/cb/ lawsjolicies/policy/pi/2010/pi101 1.htm.

[32] The state or tribe is to submit this description as part of their Title IV-E plan, which describes how they administer or supervise the administration of programs under Title IV-E. Funding under Title IV-E is contingent upon an approved plan.

[33] The instructions appear to allow these young people to enter care so long as they meet IV-E eligibility requirements. See issues section below for further discussion.

[34] Section 472(a)(3), Title IV-E of the Social Security Act.

[35] Presumably some young people who enter care after age 18 would not necessarily have been removed when they were under age 18.

[36] Section 472(a)(2)(A), Title IV-E of the Social Security Act.

[37] Section 472(a)(2)(B), Title IV-E of the Social Security Act.

[38] Under Section 475(5)(C), Title IV-E of the Social Security Act, states are directed to assign one or more permanency goals for a child or youth, none of which explicitly are emancipation. These goals are that the child or youth will be returned to his or her own home, placed for adoption, placed for adoption with a fit and willing relative or with a legal guardian, or placed in another planned permanent living arrangement (APPLA), which states sometimes use for children who are likely to age out of care.

[39] Amy Dworsky and Judy Havlicek, *Review of State Policies and Programs to Support Young People Transitioning Out of Foster Care*, University of Chicago, Chapin Hall Center for Children, 2009, pp. 7-8. At http://www.wsipp.wa.gov/pub.asp?docid=08-12-3903. (Hereafter referenced as Dworsky and Havlicek, *Review of State Policies and Programs to Support Young People Transitioning Out of Foster Care*.)

[40] A 2004 review of state laws by the American Bar Association found that just under half of states have laws that explicitly permit court jurisdiction to continue for foster children beyond the age of majority. Two states extend this jurisdiction to age 19, three states to age 20, and 17 states to age 21. Jane Kim and Kevin Sobczyk, *Continuing Court Jurisdiction in Support of 18 to 21 Year-Old Foster Youth*, American Bar Association, Center on Children and the Law, July 2004, p. 16, available at http://www.abanet.org/child/court-jurisdiction.doc.

[41] See for example, Child Welfare League of America, "National News Roundup," Children's Voice, vol. 16, no. 9 (November/December 2007), p. 9; and "States Trying to Extend Foster Care Benefits," Stateline.org, August 23, 2007, available at http://www.stateline.org/live/details/story?contentId=234381.

[42] This information was provided to the Congressional Research Service by the state or city's child welfare or independent living services staff in March and April 2008.

[43] Mark E. Courtney, Amy Dworsky, and Harold Pollack, *When Should the State Cease Parenting? Evidence from the Midwest Study*, Chapin Hall Center for Children, University of Chicago, Issue Brief no. 115, December 2007, available at http://www.chapinhall.org/article_abstract.aspx?ar=1355.

[44] Iowa amended its child welfare statute in 2006 to create a program that provides foster care to foster youth ages 18 to 21. The Iowa youth in the Midwest study were already too old to benefit from the program when it was implemented.

[45] Amy Dworsky and Mark Courtney, *Does Extending Foster Care Beyond Age 18 Promote Postsecondary Educational Attainment?*, University of Chicago, Chapin Hall Center for Children, and University of Washington, Partners for Our Children, March 2010, http://www.partnersforourchildren.org/pocweb/ userfiles/file/ MW%20Wave%204%20Education%20issue%20brief.pdf. (Hereafter, Dworsky and Courtney, *Does Extending Foster Care Beyond Age 18 Promote Postsecondary Educational Attainment?*) The researchers acknowledge that differences in the three states, such as social or educational policy, the characteristics of the child welfare populations, and socioeconomic conditions may influence outcomes for youth.

[46] For further information, see Thomas Packard et al., "A Cost-Benefit Analysis of Transitional Services for Emancipating Youth," *Children and Youth Services Review*, vol. 30, no. 11 (November 2008); Mark E. Courtney, Amy Dworsky, and Clark M. Peters, *California's Fostering Connections to Success Act and the Costs and Benefits of Extending Foster Care to 21*, University of Washington, Partners for Our Children, 2009; and Cutler Consulting, *Cost Avoidance: Bolstering the Economic Case for Investing in Youth Aging Out of Foster Care*, 2009.

[47] Clark M. Peters et al., *Extending Foster Care to Age 21: Weighing the Costs to Government Against the Benefits to Youth*, University of Chicago, Chapin Hall Issue Brief, June 2009, http://www.chapinhall.org/ sites/default/files/ publications/Issue_Brie f%2006_23_09.pdf.

[48] These factors assumed variations in the baseline rate of bachelor's degree completion (with an average of 10.2%) and the estimated dollars earned among individuals with a bachelor's degree over the course of their work-life.

[49] Practically speaking, however, placing such a child in an out-of-home setting without providing some reimbursement for the cost of that child is difficult, and in many circumstances might be considered a questionable exercise of the state's responsibility for the child. Accordingly, all states are believed to provide payments on behalf of children who are placed out of the home and under the responsibility of the state, regardless of the child's Title IV-E eligibility status. Some states currently pay lesser amounts to relative guardians who provide foster care for non-Title IV-E eligible children.

[50] Congressional Research Service analysis of administrative data provided by the U.S. Department of Health and Human Services, January 2009.

[51] Each state's FMAP is determined annually by a specified formula. For FY2009, the maximum FMAP for Title IV-E foster care purposes is just under 76% (Mississippi). For more information, see http://aspe.hhs.gov/health and CRS Report RL32950, *Medicaid: The Federal Medical Assistance Percentage (FMAP)*, by April Grady.

[52] Section 1902(a)(10)(A)(i)(I) of the Social Security Act.

[53] For further information, see CRS Report RS22849, *Medicaid Financing*, by April Grady.

[54] Youth will be eligible if they are not eligible or enrolled under existing (at the time P.L. 110-351 was passed) Medicaid mandatory eligibility groups (or described in any of the existing Medicaid mandatory eligibility groups), regardless of whether they have income that exceeds the upper income eligibility limit established under any such group; and they were enrolled in the Medicaid state plan or under a waiver while in foster care. Children in foster care who are not Title IV-E eligible generally still qualify for Medicaid coverage because all states have implemented one or more mandatory or optional Medicaid eligibility categories that allow them to cover children in care regardless of their IV-E eligibility status. Rob Geen, Anna Sommers, and Mindy Cohen, *Medicaid Spending on Foster Children*, The Urban Institute, August 2005, http://www.urban

[55] Clark Peters et al., *Continuing in Foster Care Beyond Age 18: How Courts Can Help*, Chapin Hall Center for Children, University of Chicago, Issue Brief No. 116, July 2008, available at http://www.chapinhall.org/article _abstract.aspx?ar=1472.

[56] Ibid. The data on youth who exited at age 21 was reported in a presentation sponsored by the National Governors Association (NGA). Clark Peters et al., *Continuing in Foster Care Beyond Age 18 in Illinois*, The NGA Center for Best Practices Conference on Youth Transitioning Out of Foster Care, December 2007, available at http://www.nga.org/
portal/site/nga/menuitem.9123e83a1f6786440ddcbeeb501010a0/?vgnextoid=e59e99da5ae771 10VgnVCM1000001a01010aRCRD.

[57] It is not clear from the study whether there were actually fewer foster care placements.

[58] Amy Dworsky and Judy Havlicek, *Review of State Policies and Programs to Support Young People Transitioning Out of Foster Care*.

[59] For further information, see http://www.dfps.state

[60] This information was provided to the Congressional Research Service by New York's independent living coordinator in April 2008.

[61] Such a system of care might resemble the federal Runaway and Homeless Youth program, which provides transitional housing and supports to young people ages 16 through 22, regardless of their child welfare history. For further information, see CRS Report RL33785, *Runaway and Homeless Youth: Demographics and Programs*, by Adrienne L. Fernandes-Alcantara.

[62] Under federal law, states must establish standards for the content and frequency of caseworker visits of children in foster care which, at a minimum, are to ensure that children are visited on a monthly basis. Within a specified time frame, 90% of children in foster care must be visited at least monthly and most of these visits must occur in the place where the child lives. Sec. 422(b)(17) and Section 424(e)(1), Title IV-B of the Social Security Act.

[63] U.S. Government Accountability Office, *Foster Youth: HHS Actions Could Improve Coordination of Services and Monitoring of States' Independent Living Programs*, GAO-05-25, November 2004, p. 20, available at http://www.gao.gov/new.items/d0525.pdf.

[64] U.S. Department of Health and Human Services, *Child Welfare Policy Manual*, Section 1.3, Question 2.

[65] U.S. Department of Health and Human Services, "Adoption and Foster Care Analysis and Reporting System; Proposed Rule," 73 Federal Register 2081, January 11, 2008.

[66] U.S. Department of Health and Human Services, "Request for Public Comment and Consultation Meetings on the Adoption and Foster Care Analysis and Reporting System (AFCARS)," 75 Federal Register 43187, July 23, 2010.

[67] See 45 C.F.R. Sec. 1355.31 through Sec. 1355.37 available at http://www.access 45cfr1355_02.html. HHS discussion of the regulations are included in the Federal Register announcement of Jan. 25, 2000 available at http://www.acf.dhhs.gov/programs/cb/laws

[68] U.S. Department of Health and Human Services, *Child and Family Services Review Stakeholder Interview Guide,* June 2008, available at http://www.acf.hhs.gov/programs/cb/cwmonitoring/tools_guide/stakeholder.htm.

[69] U.S. Department of Health and Human Services, *Child and Family Services Review Procedures Manual, Chapter 4* available at http://www.acf.hhs.gov/programs/cb/cwmonitoring/tools_guide/proce_manual.htm.

[70] U.S. Department of Health and Human Services, *Child and Family Services Review Onsite Review Instrument and Instructions,* July 2008, available at http://www.acf.hhs.gov/programs/cb/cwmonitoring/tools_guide/proce_manual.htm.

[71] P.L. 110-351 authorized, for the first time, payments for the relatives of children and youth who leave care for kinship guardianship.

[72] This change was made by adding a definition of "child" as it relates to eligible children and youth.

[73] HHS has also issued other guidance on kinship guardianship arrangements. See U.S. Department of Health and Human Services, Administration on Children, Youth and Families, Administration for Children and Families, Children's Bureau, *Program Instruction: Guidance on Fostering Connections to Success and Increasing Adoptions Act of 2008 Title IV-E Plan Amendment—Guardianship Assistance Program; Title IV-E Guardianship Demonstration Projects; Fostering Connections to Success and Increasing Adoptions Act of 2008,* ACYF-CB-PI-10-01, February 18, 2010, http://www.acf.hhs.gov/programs/cb/laws

[74] P.L. 110-351 gave tribal entities the same authority that states have to seek federal reimbursement of a part of all their eligible Title IV-E foster care, adoption, and kinship guardianship assistance costs.

[75] These program requirements pertain to the way states carry out their independent living programs and the certifications that states make about how the programs are carried out.

[76] Congressional Research Service analysis of AFCARS data on foster care exits provided by the U.S. Department of Health and Human Services, January 2009.

[77] U.S. Department of Health and Human Services, Administration on Children, Youth and Families, Administration for Children and Families, Children's Bureau, *Program Instruction: Public Law (P.L.) 111-148, the Patient Protection and Affordable Care Act*, June 7, 2010, ACYF-CB-PI-10-10, http://www.acf.hhs.gov/programs/cb/laws policy/pi/2010/pi1010.htm.

[78] The case plan requirements are specified under Section 475(1), Title IV-E of the Social Security Act.

[79] Some states have policies in place to ensure that youth participate in their case planning and the court review process. In addition, the CFCIP requires states to certify that they will ensure that youth participating in CFCIP-funded independent living programs "participate directly in designing their own program activities ... and that [they] accept personal responsibility for living up to their part of the program." See 477(3)(J).

[80] Based on data provided by the U.S. Department of Health and Human Services, Administration for Children and Families, January 2009.

[81] Ibid, pp. 12-13.

[82] For additional information about the need for permanency for current and former older foster youth, see Benjamin Kerman and Madelyn Freundlich, *Recommendations for Policy, Practice & Research*, Proceedings from the Research Roundtable at the 2006 National Convening on Youth Permanence, Annie E. Casey Foundation and Excal Consulting Partners, 2006, available at http://www.caseyfamilyservices.org/pdfs/permanency_proceedings_final.pdf; and Gina Miranda Samuels, *A Reason, A Season, or A Lifetime: Relational Permanence Among Young Adults with Foster Care Backgrounds*, Chapin Hall Center for Children, University of Chicago, 2008, available at http://www.chapinhall.org/ article_abstract.aspx?ar=1466&L2=61&L3=130.

[83] Mardith J. Louisell, *Model Programs for Youth Permanency*, California Permanency for Youth Project, 2004, available at http://www.cpyp.org/Files/ModelPrograms.pdf.

[84] National Governors Association, Center for Best Practices, *State Policies to Help Youth Transition Out of Foster Care*, Issue Brief, December 2007, pp. 4-7, available at http://www.nga.org/Files/pdf/0701YOUTH.PDF.

[85] Lauren Frey, *Merging Permanency and Independent Living: Lifelong Family Relationships and Life Skills for Older Youth*, National Resource Center for Youth Development, 2004, available at http://www.aecf.org/KnowledgeCenter/Publications.aspx?pubguid=%7B06615A04-00E3-4B7C-A714-D0BAEEF23EFA%7D.

[86] Lauren L. Frey, Sarah B. Greenblatt, and Jim Brown, *A Call to Action: An Integrated Approach to Youth Permanency and Preparation for Adulthood*, Casey Family Services, April 2005, p. 2, available at http://www.caseyfamilyservices.org/pdfs/casey_permanency_0505.pdf.

[87] State of Texas, Department of Family and Protective Services, *Child Protective Services Handbook,* Section 6437.4, available at http://www.dfps.state

[88] Foster Club, *Permanency Pact*, http://www.fosterclub.com/files/PermPact_0.pdf.

[89] Oklahoma Department of Human Services, Oklahoma Administrative Code (OAC) 340:75-6-3 1.

[90] U.S. Department of Health and Human Services, National Resource Center for Adoption, *Adoption Opportunities Grantees*, http://www.nrcadoption.org/youthpermanencycluster/intro.html.

[91] For additional information, see CRS Report RL34306, *Vulnerable Youth: Federal Mentoring Programs and Issues*, by Adrienne L. Fernandes-Alcantara.

[92] Mark E. Courtney, "The Difficult Transition to Adulthood for Foster Youth in the U.S.: Implications for the State as Corporate Parent," *Social Policy Report*, vol. XXIII, no. 1 (2009), pp. 15-16. (Hereafter referenced Mark E.

Courtney, "The Difficult Transition to Adulthood for Foster Youth in the U.S.: Implications for the State as Corporate Parent.")

[93] University of Oklahoma, National Child Welfare Resource Center for Youth Development, *The John H. Chafee Foster Care Independence Program: Aftercare Services*, 2003, available at http://www.nrcys.ou.edu/ yd/resources publications/monographs/aftercare.pdf. (Hereafter referenced as University of Oklahoma, National Resource Center for Youth Development, *Aftercare Services*).

[94] Peter J. Pecora et al., *Improving Foster Family Care: Findings from the Northwest Foster Care Alumni Study*, Casey Family Programs, 2005. At http://www.casey.org/Resources/Publications/NorthwestAlumniStudy.htm.

[95] Mark E. Courtney et al., Midwest Evaluation of the Adult Functioning of Former Foster Youth: Outcomes at Age 21, pp. 15-16.

[96] Miryam J. Choca et al. "Can't Do It Alone: Housing Collaborations to Improve Foster Youth Outcomes." In Ruth Anne White and Debra J. Rog, eds., *Child Welfare*, vol. LXXXIII, no. 5 (September/October 2004), pp. 469-474.

[97] Mark E. Courtney and Darcy Hughes Heuring. "The Transition to Adulthood for Youth "Aging Out" of the Foster Care System" in Osgood et al., eds., *On Your Own Without a Net*, 2005, p. 54.

[98] University of Oklahoma, National Resource Center for Youth Development, *Aftercare Services*, pp. 24-26.

[99] California Education Code Sec. 89342.

[100] Mark E. Courtney et al., *Midwest Evaluation of the Adult Functioning of Former Foster Youth: Outcomes at Age 19*, Chapin Hall Center for Children, University of Chicago, May 2005, p. 44, available at http://www.chapinhall.org/ article_abstract.aspx?ar=1355. Although Iowa is one of 17 states that have taken up the Chafee Medicaid option, some former foster youth do not appear to be covered, perhaps because they do not meet the eligibility criteria for coverage. To be eligible for Medicaid coverage in Iowa from age 18 to age 21, youth must have exited foster care at age 18 and have countable income under 200% of the federal poverty line.

[101] As part of P.L. 106-169, Congress encouraged states to provide Medicaid coverage to children who were aging out of the foster care system. The law created the optional Chafee Medicaid eligibility pathway for "independent foster care adolescents." The law defined these adolescents as individuals under the age of 21 who were in foster care under the responsibility of the state on their 1 8th birthday. Within this broadest category of independent foster care adolescents, the law permits states to restrict eligibility based on the youth's income or resources, and whether or not the youth had received Title IV-E funding.

[102] Dworsky and Havlicek, *Review of State Policies and Programs to Support Young People Transitioning Out of Foster Care*.

[103] The American Public Human Services Association (APHSA) surveyed states in 2006 to determine whether they provide Medicaid through this option; 17 states (Arizona, California, Florida, Kansas, Indiana, Iowa, Massachusetts, Mississippi, Nevada, New Jersey, Oklahoma, Rhode Island, South Carolina, South Dakota, Texas, Utah, and Wyoming) have extended Medicaid coverage to youth eligible under P.L. 106-169. APHSA also surveyed five states (California, Florida, Iowa, South Carolina, and Texas) on the cost of Medicaid coverage for youth who have aged out, and determined that the costs of the program vary depending on the type of program offered. According to the analysis, the cost of providing care—$350 per youth per month (South Carolina)—may be affordable. See Sonali Patel and Martha A. Roherty, *Medicaid Access for Youth Aging Out of Foster Care*, pp. 3-6.

[104] Youth will be eligible if they are not eligible or enrolled under existing (at the time P.L. 110-351 was passed) Medicaid mandatory eligibility groups (or described in any of the existing Medicaid mandatory eligibility groups), regardless of whether they have income that exceeds the upper income eligibility limit established under any such group; and were enrolled in the Medicaid state plan or under a waiver while in foster care. Children in foster care who are not Title IV-E eligible generally still qualify for Medicaid coverage because all states have implemented one or more mandatory or optional Medicaid eligibility categories that allow them to cover children in care regardless of their IV-E eligibility status. Rob Geen, Anna Sommers, and Mindy Cohen, *Medicaid Spending on Foster Children*, The Urban Institute, August 2005, http://www.urban

[105] U.S. Government Accountability Office, Disconnected Youth: Federal Action Could Address Some of the Challenges Faced by Local Programs That Reconnect Youth to Education and Employment, GAO-08-3 13, February 2008.

[106] Jennifer Ehrle McComber et al., *Coming of Age: Employment Outcomes for Youth Who Age Out of Foster Care Through Their Middle Twenties*, Urban Institute, April 1, 2008, http://www.urban

[107] Jennifer L. Hook and Mark Courtney, *Employment of Former Foster Youth as Young Adults: Evidence from the Midwest Study,* University of Chicago, Chapin Hall Center for Children and University of Washington, Partners for Our Children, March 2010.

[108] Casey Family Programs, *A Roadmap for Learning: Improving the Educational Outcomes in Foster Care*, 2007, http://www.casey.org/Resources/Publications/RoadMapForLearning.htm.

[109] Dworsky and Courtney, *Does Extending Foster Care Beyond Age 18 Promote Postsecondary Educational Attainment?*

[110] For information about the education and workforce programs currently available for current and former foster youth, see CRS Report RL34499, *Youth Transitioning from Foster Care: Background and Federal Programs*, by Adrienne L. Fernandes-Alcantara.

[111] P.L. 110-315 authorizes that services provided under each of the four Trio programs could specifically target current and former foster youth, homeless children and youth, as well as other youth defined as "disconnected" under the act. HEOA does not define the term "disconnected."

[112] For additional information about the programs in each state, see http://www.doleta.gov/ryf/Resources/TechnicalAssistanceForum.cfm.

[113] Mark E. Courtney, "The Difficult Transition to Adulthood for Foster Youth in the U.S.: Implications for the State as Corporate Parent."

[114] HHS has contracted with the Urban Institute and its partners to conduct the five-year Multi-Site Evaluation of Foster Youth Programs. The goal of the evaluation is to determine the effects of independent living programs funded by P.L. 106-169 in achieving key outcomes, including increased educational attainment, higher employment rates and stability, greater interpersonal and relationship skills, reduced non-marital pregnancy and births, and reduced delinquency and crime rates. The evaluation is underway, and has found that at one of the sites, in Los Angeles, there was no statistically significant impact of the life skills training and tutoring interventions. For further information, see CRS Report RL34499, *Youth Transitioning from Foster Care: Background and Federal Programs*, by Adrienne L. Fernandes-Alcantara.

[115] U. S. Department of Health and Human Services, Administration on Children, Youth and Families, Administration for Children and Families, Children's Bureau,. *Developing a System of Program Accountability under the John H. Chafee Foster Care Independence Program*. September 2001, available at http://www.acf.hhs.gov/programs/cb/ programs_fund/state_tribal/chafeereport.htm.

[116] U.S. Department of Health and Human Services, "Chafee National Youth in Transition Database," 73 *Federal Register* 10338, February 26, 2008.

[117] For a detailed overview of the database and issues related to its implementation, see CRS Memorandum, *The Chafee Foster Care Independence Act National Youth in Transition Database*, by Adrienne L. Fernandes-Alcantara. Available upon request.

[118] See CRS Report RL34499, *Youth Transitioning from Foster Care: Background and Federal Programs*, by Adrienne L. Fernandes-Alcantara.

[119] Dworsky and Havlicek, *Review of State Policies and Programs to Support Young People Transitioning Out of Foster Care.*

[120] The Foster Care Independence Act (P.L. 106-169) directs HHS to conduct evaluations of independent living programs funded by the CFCIP deemed to be innovative or of national significance. The law reserves 1.5% ($2.1 million) of total CFCIP funding annually for these evaluations, as well as CFCIP-related technical assistance, performance measurement, and data collection.

[121] The evaluation is known as the Multi-Site Evaluation of Foster Youth Programs. Additional information regarding the evaluation is available at http://www.acf.hhs.gov/programs/opre/abuse

[122] Presentation at the State Independent Living Coordinators Conference, U.S. Department of Health and Human Services, Administration on Children, Youth and Families, Administration for Children and Families, Children's Bureau, July 20, 2010.

[123] This information was provided to the Congressional Research Service by the state or city's child welfare or independent living services staff in March and April 2008.

[124] A permanency resource is a caring adult willing to help provide emotional support and guidance to a youth as a youth transitions to adulthood, and can be a foster parent, teacher, parent of a friend in the community.

[125] Youth in care ages 16 and 17 must be discharged on a trial basis if they have been in care for 12 of the last 36 months and if their case goal is "APPLA with a permanency resource." These youth may decline the trial discharge and opt instead for a final discharge; they may also return to care if they are discharged.

[126] A third component of the program, not discussed here, offers supports and services on behalf of youth who reach their 1 8th birthday while in custody and are attending high school.

[127] All youth who emancipate from foster care are eligible to work with the youth development coordinators and for other supports, such as housing and workforce training, through the state's independent living program.

[128] The Department for Children and Families plans to address the feasibility of this second option in its regulations.

[129] Youth may receive direct payment under the Housing Support and Incidental Living Grants program. Yet these youth might be rendered ineligible for Temporary Assistance for Needy Families (TANF) because the payment would count as direct income for TANF eligibility purposes. If, however, the payment is made directly to a youth's vendor (i.e., landlord or college) this assistance is considered a "subsidy."

In: Children and Youth Transitions from Foster Care
Editor: Joseph A. Ferrari
ISBN: 978-1-61209-705-3

Chapter 3

CHILD WELFARE: THE CHAFEE FOSTER CARE INDEPENDENCE PROGRAM (CFCIP)

Adrienne L. Fernandes-Alcantara

SUMMARY

While most young people have access to financial and emotional support systems throughout their early adult years, former foster care youth often lack assistance in developing independent living skills to ease the transition to adulthood. Recognizing the difficulties faced by older youth exiting foster care, Congress passed the Chafee Foster Care Independence Act (P.L. 106-169) to expand the population of youth eligible to receive independent living services and to give states greater flexibility in designing their independent living programs. Under P.L. 106-169, Congress doubled the mandatory funding available to states for independent living services from $70 million to $140 million. In 2002, Congress passed legislation (P.L. 107-133) to authorize discretionary funding to eligible current and former foster care youth for education and training vouchers worth up to $5,000 annually per youth. The Chafee Foster Care Independence Program (CFCIP) and voucher component are administered by the U.S. Department of Health and Human Services (HHS). Seven pending bills (H.R. 2188, H.R. 3409, H.R. 4208, H.R. 4133, S. 1512, and S. 1956/H.R. 4688) propose to amend the program. This report briefly describes the CFCIP and will be updated.

INTRODUCTION

Although about half of all states permit youth to remain in foster care beyond age 18, in practice, most foster youth "age out" upon reaching their 1 8th birthday.[1] The number of youth reported as emancipating from care rose from approximately 19,000 in FY2001 to over 24,000 in FY2005.[2] This increase in the number of emancipated youth has occurred concurrently with the overall decrease in the number of children in care, from 556,000 on the last day of FY2001 to 513,000 on the last day of FY2005. The majority of youth emancipating entered care as teenagers, although as many as 30% were 12 years or younger when they entered care.[3] This suggests that children who are leaving care without being formally reunified with a parent, adopted, or placed in guardianship are a growing concern of child welfare agencies and policymakers. Recently emancipated foster care youth are particularly vulnerable during the transition to adulthood. While many young people have access to financial and emotional support systems throughout their early adult years, former foster youth often lack assistance in developing independent living skills to ease the transition.[4] Studies indicate that youth who have "aged out" of foster care fare poorly relative to their counterparts in the general population on several outcome measures, including employment, education, homelessness, and mental health.[5]

Recognizing the difficulties faced by youth exiting foster care, Congress created a new Independent Living initiative (P.L. 99-272) in 1986 to assist foster youth ages 16 to 18 whose original families qualified for Aid to Families with Dependent Children (AFDC), in achieving independence. The legislation authorized mandatory funding to states under a new Section 477 of the Social Security Act. States were awarded a share of independent living funds based on the number of children receiving federal foster care payments in FY1984.[6] In 1987, legislation (P.L. 100-647) was enacted to expand the program to serve any foster care children age 16 or older (regardless of AFDC status) and to provide independent living services to certain youth for six months after leaving care. The Omnibus Reconciliation Act of 1990 (P.L. 101-508) gave states the option of providing independent living services to youth until age 21, and in 1993, Congress permanently authorized funding for the program at $70 million annually (P.L. 103-66).

JOHN H. CHAFEE FOSTER CARE INDEPENDENCE PROGRAM

The John H. Chafee Foster Care Independence Act of 1999 (P.L. 106-169) replaced the 1986 Independent Living Program with the Chafee Foster Care Independence Program (CFCIP) and doubled the annual funds available to states from $70 million to $140 million. To be eligible for funds, the act required states to expand the population of youth who receive independent living services to include those who have "aged out" of foster care (until their 21st birthday) and those of any age in foster care who are expected to leave care without placement in a permanent family. Services may consist of educational assistance, vocational training, mentoring, preventive health activities, and counseling. States may dedicate as much as 30% of their program funding toward room and board for youth ages 18 through 20.

In addition, the law removed a disincentive for youth to accumulate earnings or other resources to assist in their transition to independent living. Eligibility for foster care maintenance payments under Title IV-E of the Social Security Act is based on whether the children's original families would qualify for AFDC, as it was in effect on July 16, 1996. Under those rules, children could not remain eligible for Title IV-E services if they accumulate assets of more than $1,000. P.L. 106-169, however, changed this asset limit to $10,000. The act also encouraged states to provide Medicaid coverage to youth ages 18, 19, and 20 who have emancipated from foster care. In 2002 (P.L. 107-133), discretionary funds — up to $60 million annually — were authorized for eligible current and former foster care youth to receive education and training vouchers.

Medicaid Provisions

P.L. 106-169 encouraged states to provide Medicaid coverage to emancipating foster care youth and also amended the Medicaid program to permit states to make all youth who "age out" eligible until their 21st birthday. Based on a 2006 survey of state human service officials, 17 states (AZ, CA, FL, KS, IN, IA, MA, MS, NV, NJ, OK, RI, SC, SD, TX, UT, and WY) have extended Medicaid coverage to youth eligible under P.L. 106-169; Missouri took up the Chafee Medicaid pathway in 2007.[7] According to the report, four other states were considering adopting the option. States that take up the option may limit Medicaid coverage to youth who, before age 18, were in foster care or independent living programs funded through Title IV-E of the Social Security Act. In all states, youth age 19 or younger with family incomes at or below 100% of the federal poverty limit (or up to 250% in some states) are eligible for Medicaid or SCHIP. Youth ages 18 to 21 in foster care who do not qualify for Medicaid or SCHIP may be eligible for Medicaid coverage through the "Ribicoff" pathway, named for the late former senator, Abraham Ribicoff. Ribicoff youth must meet the income and resource requirements for the former AFDC program but do not meet other categorical requirements for AFDC. Over half of all states have opted to provide coverage to former foster care youth through this pathway, although length of eligibility for coverage varies.[8]

Education and Training Vouchers

From FY2004 to FY2008, states have received $45.8 million, on average, annually to provide education and training vouchers worth up to $5,000 for each youth eligible under the CFCIP and youth adopted from foster care after 16 years of age. The vouchers are available for the cost of attendance at an institution of higher education, as defined by the Higher Education Act of 1965.[9] Only youth receiving a voucher at age 21 may continue to participate in the voucher program until age 23. For FY2006 (the most recent year data are available), 37 states and the District of Columbia disbursed vouchers to 6,545 foster youth.[10]

State Requirements

To be eligible for CFCIP funds, a state must submit a five- year plan describing how the state intends to design and deliver its independent living program across all political subdivisions; serve a range of youth of various ages and stages of development; use objective criteria for determining eligibility for services under the programs; involve the public and private sectors in assisting adolescents in foster care achieve independence; and cooperate in national evaluations of the programs. States must also certify that, among other requirements, they are providing assistance and services to former foster care youth ages 18 to 21 and coordinating the independent living programs with other youth programs at the local, state, and federal levels.

A November 2004 report by the U.S. Government Accountability Office (GAO) found that while 40 states expanded existing independent living services to younger youth and 36 states reported serving youth older than they had previously served since the passage of P.L.

106-169, one-third of the states served less than half of all eligible youth.[11] GAO also found gaps in securing housing and the availability of mental health services and mentoring services. Further, while 49 states reported increased coordination with a number of programs that provide or supplement independent living services, child welfare administrators and youth said that they were unaware of these services. GAO concluded that the lack of uniformity among the states' five-year plans impedes the federal government from using the plans to monitor how well the programs serve youth.

Funding and Allotment

The Consolidated Appropriations Act of 2008 (P.L. 110-161) provides $140 million in mandatory funding for the CFCIP and $45.4 million for the ETV program. Table 1 at the end of this report provides the federal CFCIP and voucher allotments for each state in FY2007 and FY2008. To receive Chafee general funds and voucher funds, states must provide a 20% non-federal match. States have two fiscal years to spend their general and voucher funds. Funds not spent in that time frame revert to the federal treasury.[12] States may apply to receive mandatory funds for all purposes specified in the CFCIP. These funds are distributed to each state based on its proportion of the nation's children in foster care. However, the law's "hold harmless" clause precludes any state from receiving less than the amount of funds it received in FY1998 or $500,000, whichever is greater. Although the general funding for independent living services doubled nationally under P.L. 106-169, the percentage increase in funds received has varied across states, and two states (LA and NY) and the District of Columbia received nearly the same amount of funds allotted to them prior to the enactment of the CFCIP legislation. Like the CFCIP's mandatory funds, discretionary funds for the education and training vouchers are distributed based on a state's proportion of foster care children nationwide.

Data Reporting and Evaluation

P.L. 106-169 requires that HHS identify the data needed to track the characteristics and outcomes of children to assess the performance of states in operating independent living programs. A notice of proposed rulemaking, published on July 14, 2006, in the *Federal Register* (vol. 71, no. 35), establishes a data collection system, known as the National Youth in Transition Database, to track the characteristics and outcomes of current and former foster care youth receiving (or not receiving) independent living services.[13] The proposed rule outlines the data elements and the penalty structure for states' non-compliance with the regulations. The final rule for the database are expected to be published by mid-year 2008.[14]

P.L. 106-169 also provides that HHS must conduct evaluations of state independent living programs funded by the act and deemed to be innovative or of national significance. Of all the funds authorized for the CFCIP, 1.5% (approximately $2.1 million for FY2008) is reserved for HHS to conduct evaluations of innovative and potentially significant state CFCIPs. HHS has contracted with the Urban Institute and its partners to conduct a five- year evaluation of 1,400 youth participating in four independent living programs in California and

Massachusetts. The goal of the evaluation is to determine the effects of the programs in achieving key outcomes such as increased educational attainment.

LEGISLATION IN THE 110TH CONGRESS

Seven pending bills propose amending the CFCIP. Three bills (H.R. 2188, H.R. 3409, and H.R. 4208) would provide that a purpose of the CFCIP is for a state to identify youth expected to remain in foster care until at least their 14th birthday and to provide them with independent living services, among other changes. An unrelated bill (H.R. 4311) proposes to permit states to use program funds to provide vouchers to cover tuition costs at private schools, and transportation costs to and from public schools for foster children of any age. Two other bills (S. 1956/H.R. 4688) authorize eligible tribal entities to receive a part of a state's CFCIP and ETV funds to administer services or to permit these entities to enter into cooperative agreements with the state to ensure independent living services for tribal youth (as is currently practiced in some states). Finally, S. 1512, a bill to extend federal foster care to youth age 18 to 21, would make conforming amendments to the CFCIP.[15]

Table 1. Final FY2007 and Estimated FY2008 Federal CFCIP General and Voucher Allotments by State ($ in Thousands)

State	Final FY2007 Allotments			Estimated FY2008 Allotments		
	General	Vouchers	Total	General	Vouchers	Total
Alabama	1,784	612	2,396	1,784	601	2,386
Alaska	500	159	659	500	156	656
Arizona	2,601	892	3,492	2,601	877	3,477
Arkansas	834	286	1,120	834	281	1,115
California	20,953	7,185	28,138	20,954	7,060	28,013
Colorado	2,120	727	2,847	2,120	714	2,834
Connecticut	1,815	622	2,438	1,815	612	2,427
Delaware	500	85	585	500	84	584
District of Columbia	1,092	222	1,314	1,092	218	1,310
Florida	7,566	2,595	10,161	7,566	2,549	10,116
Georgia	3,605	1,236	4,841	3,605	1,215	4,819
Hawaii	714	245	959	714	241	955
Idaho	500	161	661	500	158	658
Illinois	5,016	1,720	6,736	5,016	1,690	6,706
Indiana	2,906	996	3,902	2,906	979	3,885

Table 1. (Continued)

State	Final FY2007 Allotments			Estimated FY2008 Allotments		
	General	Vouchers	Total	General	Vouchers	Total
Iowa	1,754	601	2,355	1,754	591	2,345
Kansas	1,506	516	2,023	1,506	507	2,014
Kentucky	1,881	645	2,526	1,881	634	2,515
Louisiana	1,358	428	1,786	1,358	420	1,778
Maine	596	204	800	596	201	797
Maryland	2,805	962	3,767	2,805	945	3,750
Massachusetts	3,161	1,084	4,244	3,160	1,065	4,225
Michigan	5,291	1,814	7,106	5,291	1,783	7,074
Minnesota	1,801	618	2,419	1,801	607	2,408
Mississippi	844	289	1,133	844	284	1,128
Missouri	2,928	1,004	3,932	2,928	987	3,915
Montana	574	197	770	574	193	767
Nebraska	1,608	552	2,160	1,608	542	2,150
Nevada	1,205	413	1,619	1,205	406	1,612
New Hampshire	500	104	604	500	102	602
New Jersey	3,108	1,066	4,174	3,108	1,047	4,156
New Mexico	591	203	794	591	199	791
New York	11,586	2,693	14,279	11,586	2,646	14,232
North Carolina	2,761	947	3,708	2,761	930	3,692
North Dakota	500	121	621	500	119	619
Ohio	4,502	1,544	6,046	4,502	1,517	6,019
Oklahoma	2,966	1,017	3,983	2,966	999	3,965
Oregon	2,845	976	3,820	2,845	958	3,803
Pennsylvania	5,599	1,920	7,519	5,599	1,887	7,486
Puerto Rico	1,752	601	3,503	1,752	590	2,342
Rhode Island	648	222	870	648	218	866
South Carolina	1,228	421	1,649	1,228	414	1,642
South Dakota	500	152	652	500	149	649
Tennessee	2,328	798	3,126	2,328	784	3,112
Texas	7,456	2,557	10,012	7,456	2,512	9,967
Utah	590	202	792	590	199	789
Vermont	500	127	627	500	125	625
Virginia	1,813	622	2,434	1,813	611	2,423
Washington	2,599	891	3,490	2,599	876	3,474
West Virginia	1,118	383	1,501	1,118	377	1,495
Wisconsin	2,093	718	2,810	2,093	705	2,798
Wyoming	500	112	612	500	110	610
Total Funding[a]	**137,900**	**46,616**	**183,364**	**137,900**	**44,671**	**182,571**

Source: U.S. Department Health and Human Services, Administration for Children and Families, Children's Bureau, January 2008.

a. Training and technical assistance, research/evaluation, and set asides are not included in the total funding.

End Notes

[1] June Kim and Kevin Sobczyk, *Continuing Court Jurisdiction in Support of 18 to 21 Year-Old Foster Youth,* American Bar Association, Center on Children and the Law, July 2004.

[2] U.S. Department of Health and Human Services, Administration for Children and Families, *AFCARS Report #12 and AFCARS Report #13*, available at [http://www.acf.hhs.gov/programs/ cb/stats_research/index.htm#afcars].

[3] U.S. Department of Health and Human Services, *Child Welfare Outcomes 2003: Annual Report to Congress*, Executive Summary, June 2006, p. 2.

[4] Mark E. Courtney and Darcy Hughes Heuring. *The Transition to Adulthood for Youth "Aging Out" of the Foster Care System* in Wayne G. Osgood et al., eds., *On Your Own Without a Net: The Transition to Adulthood for Vulnerable Populations* (Chicago: The University of Chicago Press, 2005), pp. 27-32.

[5] See, for example, Peter J. Pecora et al. *Improving Foster Family Care: Findings from the Northwest Foster Care Alumni Study*, Casey Family Programs, 2005, pp. 1-2.

[6] AFDC was the federal-state cash welfare program that was replaced by the Temporary Assistance for Needy Families (TANF) program in 1996.

[7] Sonali Patel and Martha A. Roherty, *Medicaid Access for Youth Aging Out of Foster Care,* American Public Human Services Association. Puerto Rico was not included in this analysis. For additional inforrmation about Missouri's coverage option, see [http://www.senate.mo.gov/07 info/BTS_Web/Bill.aspx?SessionType=R&BillID=28834].

[8] Abigail English, *Health Insurance for Older Adolescents and Young Adults: Policy Options to Expand Coverage*, Center for Adolescent Medicine and the Law, 2006, available at [http://www.cahl.org/PDF s/CAHLYoungAdultInsuranceIssueBrief.pdf].

[9] See Sections 102 and 472 of the Higher Education Act of 1965.

[10] The Orphan Foundation, which contracts with nine other states to administer their ETV programs, reported that approximately 2,400 youth received vouchers under the program for FY2007. Information provided by the U.S. Department of Health and Human Services, Children's Bureau and the Orphan Foundation of America in June 2007.

[11] U.S. Government Accountability Office. *HHS Actions Could Improve Coordination of Services and Monitoring of States' Independent Living Programs*, GAO-05-25, November 2004.

[12] In FY2004 (the most recent data available for returned funds), states returned less than 1% in CFCIP funds and 14.4% in ETV funds No states returned their full allotment of CFCIP or ETV dollars. Nine states (IN, MD, MA, NV, NC, ND, PA, TX, and WY) returned between 0.2% and 13.3% of their CFCIP allocations. Fourteen states (AK, CA, FL, HI, ID, ME, MN, NM, NY, OH, OK, PA, SD, and WI) and Puerto Rico returned between 0.3% and 30% of their ETV allotments; and ten states (KS, KY, MD, MI, MO, ND, OR, SD, TX, and VA) returned between 33% and 72% of their ETV allotments. Mississippi returned nearly all of its ETV funding.

[13] For additional information, see CRS Congressional Distribution Memorandum, *Notice of Proposed Rule Making To Implement the Chafee Foster Care Independence Act Database*, by Adrienne Fernandes (available upon request from CRS at 7-5700).

[14] Based on an announcement made by HHS, Administration for Children and Families, Children's Bureau, May 2007 at the National Pathways to Adulthood Conference.

[15] S. 1512, H.R. 3408, and H.R. 4208 would permit or require states to seek federal reimbursement under the federal foster care program for eligible youth who elect to remain in foster care, at state option, until their 1 9th , 20th , or 21st birthday. S. 1512 would also make conforming amendments to the CFCIP by changing all references to youth who aged out, or who are expected to age out of care at age 18, to reference instead any older age that the state chooses.

In: Children and Youth Transitions from Foster Care
Editor: Joseph A. Ferrari
ISBN: 978-1-61209-705-3

Chapter 4

Coming of Age: Employment Outcomes for Youth Who Age Out of Foster Care through their Middle Twenties

U.S. Department of Health and Human Services

Acknowledgments

We would like to thank the state of Minnesota's Department of Human Services for participating in this study and providing the child welfare and public assistance data. In particular, we are especially grateful for the efforts of Christeen Borsheim and Leslie Crichton in acquiring and constructing the data files for this analysis. We would also like to thank the Minnesota Department of Employment and Economic Development for providing Unemployment Insurance wage data.

We also thank Michael Armijo in California for his expert assistance in linking the data sources. We would also like to thank the California Department of Social Services for their support of this project.

We would like to thank the North Carolina Division of Social Services, particularly Sherry Bradsher and JoAnn Lamm, for their support on this study. We also thank Rachel Buchanan for her assistance early on in collating the results of the analysis.

We would also like to thank Urban Institute researchers Caroline Ratcliffe, Doug Wissoker, and Ajay Chaudry for their thoughtful review of our analyses and this report.

Executive Summary

A youth's departure from home marks the beginning of adulthood and a new stage in a young adult's life. This critical juncture and the surrounding years, often referred to as the transition to adulthood, is increasingly recognized as a distinct developmental stage between adolescence and adulthood (Arnett, 2004). Youth who reach this stage and are living in foster care are often at a significant disadvantage. In 2005, over 24,000 youths found themselves in this circumstance (DHHS, 2006). They "aged out" of the foster care system and entered into the world of adulthood relatively alone.

Studies of former foster youth who age out of care find that these youth generally experience high unemployment, unstable employment patterns, and earn very low incomes in the period between ages 18 and 21 (Cook, 1991; Courtney et al., 2001; Dworsky and Courtney, 2001; Go-erge, Bilaver, Lee, Needell, Brookhart and Jack-man, 2002). The Department of Health and Human Services (DHHS) Office of the Assistant Secretary for Planning and Evaluation (ASPE) requested this study to examine employment and earnings outcomes for youth, through their mid-twenties, who age out of foster care. The key question and focus of the study is whether foster youth catch up or continue to experience less employment and significantly lower earnings than their peers even into their mid-twenties.

The study linked child welfare, Unemployment Insurance (UI), and public assistance administrative data to assess employment outcomes and welfare receipt for youth who age out of foster care. Child welfare data allow researchers to identify youth who age out of foster care, while the UI data provide information on employment and earnings. Public assistance data reveal later welfare receipt. Information is linked between sources using youths' social security numbers. Analyses are conducted in three states: California, Minnesota, and North Carolina. The sample of interest is youth who were 17 years old and in foster care in one of the participating states on December 31,1998, and who eventually aged out of care. A comparison group of youth from low-income families is created using the public assistance data, and baseline national estimates are derived from the National Longitudinal Survey of Youth (NLSY97).

Descriptive, multivariate, and trajectory analysis techniques are employed. Youth outcomes are assessed from age 16 to the first quarter of age 24.

Key Findings

Youth who age out of foster care continue to experience poor employment outcomes at age 24

At age 24, youth who age out of foster care do not fare well on a variety of employment outcomes. Compared to youth nationally and even youth from low-income families, they are less likely to be employed or employed regularly, and, not surprisingly, they earn very little. At age 24, average monthly earnings for youth who age out of foster care who worked are $690 in California, $575 in Minnesota, and $450 in North Carolina, compared to $1,535 for youth nationally. Employment and earnings differences between youth who age out of foster care and youth from low-income families remain in California and Minnesota even when controlling for demographic factors. Case history factors do not appear to play an important role in influencing employment outcomes.

Youth who age out of foster care tend to follow one of four employment trajectories as they transition to adulthood

Youth who age out of foster care exhibit four distinct patterns in connecting to the workforce. Overall about one-third to one-half of these youth follows a path that leads to relatively positive employment outcomes by age 24. At the same time, the other half to two-thirds of these youth exhibit patterns leading to poorer outcomes at age 24.

Positive outcomes at age 24:

- *Consistently Connected*: These youth maintain relatively high probabilities of employment between the ages of 18 and 24, and their average earnings are comparable to youth nationally. This group appears to begin connecting to the workforce prior to age 18. This group represents one-sixth to one-quarter of the youth in the states (25 percent in California, 22 percent in Minnesota, and 16 percent in North Carolina).
- *Later Connected*: Youth in this group have a slow start, but steadily increase their probability of employment and earnings throughout their early twenties. Their average earnings do not reach levels comparable to youth nationally but do show an upward trend. This group does not appear connected to the workforce prior to age 18. These youth represent one-sixth to one-fifth of youth who age out of foster care in the study states (20 percent in California, 21 percent in Minnesota, and 16 percent in North Carolina).

Poor outcomes at age 24:

- *Never Connected*: These youth have very low probabilities of employment and hardly any earnings at any time between ages 18 and 24 or prior to age 18. This group represents one-fifth to one-third of the youth who age out of foster care in these states (33 percent in California, 29 percent in Minnesota, and 22 percent in North Carolina). Some portion of these youth may not be covered in the earnings data.
- *Initially Connected*: Youth in this group begin making connections to the workforce prior to adulthood and maintain a high probability of employment through their late teens. Their probabilities of employment then decline rapidly in their early twenties. The average earnings for this group never get very high, which might explain the drop in employment, if lower earnings result in less incentive to continue working. The drop-off in employment for some portion of these youth might also be explained by changes to jobs not covered by UI data, moves out of state, incarceration, or childbearing. This group represents one-fifth to almost one-half of the youth in these states (22 percent in California, 29 percent in Minnesota, and 46 percent in North Carolina).

Implications

Pathways to adult services

Extending services to youth after age 18 is the focus of many recent initiatives and efforts to support youth aging out of foster care. Findings from this report would suggest, however, that risk for these youth extend beyond even age 21. Working at age 21 does not appear to be a guarantee that youth will sustain employment through age 24. In fact, significant changes in employment trajectories appear to occur for many youth who age out of foster care right around age 21. Some portion of these youth may need additional assistance staying connected to the labor market or accessing adult service systems.

Importance of ages 16 to 18

Ages 16 to 18 are a period of significant employment activity for many youth aging out of foster care. Rapid increases in employment occur for *consistently connected* youth and *initially connected* youth between the ages of 16 and 18. Similarly, results show that employment prior to age 18 is associated with positive employment outcomes at age 24 for youth in California, Minnesota, and North Carolina. This evidence suggests that helping youth connect to the work-force prior to adulthood may have benefits later.

Tailoring programs

As programs to serve former foster youth continue to evolve, policymakers and practitioners might consider strategies for tailoring programs to best meet the needs of youth on different trajectories. For example, those youth *initially connected* to the labor market exhibit a desire to work early on, but may need additional training or education to find sustainable, long-term employment. Those who are *later connected* may require extra supports while they are in school or receiving training in preparation for later connection to the workforce. For those youth who are *never connected*, the challenge may be finding them and identifying their service needs. Are they homeless, disabled, incarcerated, or living with their biological parents or extended family? The Chafee National Youth in Transition Database (NYTD) could be an important tool to help states identify the types of youth that follow different paths and their service needs. This database is designed to identify the numbers and characteristics of youth receiving Independent Living services, track the type and quantity of those services, and develop outcome measures to assess state performance in serving these youth.

Future research

This study analyzed outcomes for youth who aged out of foster care in the late 1990s, prior to the passage of the Chafee Foster Care Independence Act, which strengthened independent living programs for youth in foster care and focused attention on this population. In the future, researchers may want to examine later cohorts of youth who age out of foster care that may have benefited from the Chafee Foster Care Independence programs. With each additional year of earnings data, another age cohort can be analyzed. Researchers could also examine the role of education and other service systems in supporting these youth. Further exploration is also needed to understand the different employment paths these youth follow. For example, what are the resiliency factors that enable youth to age out of foster care and connect consistently to the workforce? This group could provide insights into the factors that help youth aging out of foster care succeed.

Section 1. Introduction

A youth's departure from home marks the beginning of adulthood and a new stage in life. This critical juncture and the surrounding years, often referred to as the "transition to adulthood," is increasingly being recognized as a distinct developmental stage between adolescence and adulthood (Arnett, 2004). Youth who reach this stage and are living in foster care are often at a significant disadvantage. In 2005, over 24,000 youths found themselves in this circumstance (DHHS, 2006). They "aged out" of the foster care system and entered into the world of adulthood relatively alone.

Research suggests these youth do not fare well. Youth who age out of foster care often have bouts of homelessness, criminal activity, and incarceration (Courtney, Piliavin, and Grogan-Kaylor, 1998; Courtney, Piliavin, Grogan-Kaylor, and Nesmith, 2001). Many suffer from physical and mental health challenges as a result of past abuse or neglect.

A primary task in transitioning to adulthood, and the focus of this report, is finding and sustaining employment. Studies of former foster youth who age out of foster care find that these youth generally experience high unemployment, unstable employment patterns, and earn very low incomes in the period between ages 18 and 21 (Cook, 1991; Courtney et al., 2001; Dworsky and Courtney, 2001; Goerge, Bilaver, Lee, Needell, Brookhart and Jackman, 2002). Studies also document consistently low rates of high school completion and welfare receipt (Courtney et al., 1998; Courtney et al., 2001; Festinger, 1983; McMillen and Tucker, 1999; Pecora, Kessler, Williams, O'Brien, Downs, English, et al., 2003).

What is less known about these youth is how they fare in their mid-twenties, after they have made the initial transition into adulthood. It might be hypothesized that some would experience unstable employment in their initial attempts to connect to the workforce, but that these patterns would stabilize when youth reached their mid-twenties. If these patterns do not stabilize, however, addressing job readiness and educational needs early in the transition to adulthood may be important to shaping the future trajectories of these youth.

The Department of Health and Human Services (DHHS) Office of the Assistant Secretary for Planning and Evaluation (ASPE) requested this study to examine employment and earnings outcomes for youth, through their mid-twenties, who age out of foster care. Key findings suggest:

- ***Low rates of employment persist through age 24:*** About three out of five youth who age out of foster care are working at age 24 in all three states, a rate lower than that of youth nationally and youth from low-income families.
- ***Low earnings persist through age 24:*** Average monthly earnings for youth who age out of foster care remain low at age 24 in all three states ($690 in California, $575 in Minnesota, and $450 in North Carolina). These earnings are substantially lower than earnings for youth nationally, who earn $1,535 a month.
- ***Four patterns of connectedness to the workforce emerge:*** *Never connected* youth have a consistently low probability of employment between ages 18 and 24. *Consistently connected* youth maintain a high probability of employment during this period and achieve earnings comparable to national averages. *Initially connected* youth have a high probability of employment around ages 18 and 19, but this

probability declines sharply by age 22. *Later connected* youth have a slow start but steadily increase their probability of employment through age 24.

BASIC STUDY METHODS

Child welfare, unemployment insurance (UI), and TANF administrative data are linked to assess employment outcomes and welfare receipt for youth who age out of foster care. Child welfare data allow researchers to identify youth who age out of foster care, while the UI data provide information on employment and earnings. TANF data reveal later welfare receipt. Information is linked between sources using youths' social security numbers. A comparison group of youth from low-income families is created using TANF data, and baseline national estimates are derived from the National Longitudinal Survey of Youth (NLSY97). Analyses are conducted in three states: California, Minnesota, and North Carolina. Descriptive, multivariate, and trajectory analysis techniques are employed. Youth outcomes are assessed from age 16 to the first quarter of age 24.

SECTION 2. BACKGROUND

Since the mid-1980s federal legislators have focused increased attention on youth who age out of the foster care system in recognition of the unique challenges they face during their transition to adulthood and independence. The Independent Living Initiative in 1985 (Public Law 99-272) amended Title IV-E of the Social Security Act to provide federal funding to states to help foster youth develop independent living skills. This program was reauthorized indefinitely in 1993 (Public Law 103-66) as part of the Omnibus Budget Reconciliation Act. Most recently, the Foster Care Independence Act (FCIA) of 1999 (Public Law 106-169) amended Title IV-E to provide states with more funding and greater flexibility in designing services to help foster youth transition from foster care to self-sufficiency. This law, which included the John H. Chafee Foster Care Independence Program, doubled funding formerly provided through the Title IV-E Independent Living Program. It allowed states to assist youth ages 18 to 21 who may have left foster care, and to extend Medicaid coverage for foster care youth to age 21. The law also permits states to use funds to assist youth with room and board payments. It is within this policy context of additional federal support and heightened interest in how youth are faring that the current study, which examines the employment outcomes of former foster youth through their mid-twenties, was conducted.

Prior Research

Prior research indicates that youth who age out of foster care tend to have less stable employment and lower earnings than their same-age peers (Cook, 1991; Courtney, Dworsky, Keller, & Havlicek, 2005; Goerge et al., 2002; Pecora et al., 2006; Singer, 2006). Findings across studies are strikingly similar regardless of whether researchers survey the youth directly (Courtney et al., 2005; Pecora et al., 2006) or analyze employment data from administrative records (Dworsky, 2005; Goerge et al., 2002; Singer, 2006). The Midwest Evaluation of the Adult Functioning of Former Foster Youth surveyed youth from Illinois, Iowa, and Wisconsin and found that compared to a nationally representative sample of 19-year-olds who had participated in the National Longitudinal Study of Adolescent Health, foster youth were significantly less likely to be employed at age 19 (40 percent compared to 58 percent) (Courtney et al. 2005). Goerge et al. (2002) also found a similar pattern of lower employment among foster youth using administrative data and comparing them to a nationally representative sample of youth ages 16 to 19 from the Current Population Survey (CPS). Further, the study found that foster youth tend to have significantly lower earnings than a comparable sample of low-income youth.

Other studies using administrative data find that the majority of foster youth are employed at some point after they leave the system but have very low earnings. A recent report using Utah state administrative data found that 86 percent of youth who exited foster care between 1999 and 2003 were employed at some point within three years of leaving the system (Singer, 2006). Another study that used administrative data from Wisconsin examined employment outcomes two years after youth exited care between 1992 and 1998 and found that 80 percent were employed at some point during that time (Dworsky, 2005). In both studies, earnings were significantly low and remained below the poverty threshold.

Few studies have tracked employment outcomes for this group into adulthood. One exception is the Northwest Foster Care Alumni Study, which surveyed youth who had been in family foster care between 1988 and 1998. Although 24 was the average age of the sample, many were between ages 26 and 33. Like the aforementioned studies, former foster youth were less likely to have been employed than the national average for adults between the ages of 20 and 34 (80 percent compared to 95 percent) (Pecora et al., 2006).

Notably, with the exception of the Northwest Foster Care Alumni Study, most research to date has tracked foster youth employment outcomes one to three years after youth have discharged from care. This relatively short time period is due in large part to the fact that only recently have data from automated child welfare data systems become viable for analysis. Prior to 2006, data collected by states typically had limited research utility. Longer tracking periods have only become possible as more time has passed.

The current study builds most directly on prior work conducted by Goerge and colleagues (2002), who incorporated both child welfare administrative data and Unemployment Insurance Wage Reporting Data. While they were able to examine youth employment outcomes two years after leaving foster care in California, Illinois, and South Carolina, this report presents employment outcomes six years after care for former foster youth from California, Minnesota, and North Carolina. A key question and focus of this report is whether youth who age out of foster care catch up or continue to experience less employment and significantly lower earnings than their peers even into their mid-twenties.

This study, like prior research, includes comparison groups. It compares youth who age out of foster care to a nationally representative sample of similar-age youth from the NLSY97 and a low-income sample of youth from welfare caseloads in each of the three participating states. Researchers also considered a comparison group of foster youth who had left the child welfare system for reasons other than aging out (e.g., reunification, adoption) but ultimately decided not to use these comparison groups. The main drawback to using these child welfare comparison groups was that youth age 16 and older who are reunified or adopted before exiting foster care are not representative of most youth who exit for these reasons. Therefore, any differences found in the study between age-out youth and reunified or adopted youth would not necessarily have reflected the true differences between youth who age out of foster care and a more representative sample of reunified or adopted youth.

Methods for This Study

The following provides a brief overview of the methods employed in the study. A more detailed description of methods and procedures is provided in the technical appendix (beginning on page 35).

State Selection

Analyses were conducted in three states: California, Minnesota, and North Carolina. States were selected based on the availability of child welfare and employment data, prior experience linking administrative data sources, and willingness to participate in the study. Each of the three states is demographically diverse and uses a different approach to serving youth who age out of the foster care system.

Data

Data for the study come from three state administrative sources: child welfare, public assistance, and Unemployment Insurance. Additional data for the national comparison estimates come from the NLSY97.

- *State Child Welfare Administrative Data:* Child welfare data were used to identify a sample of foster youth in California, Minnesota, and North Carolina. Discharge information in each state was used to distinguish the study group of interest--youth who age out of foster care--from youth who had exited for other reasons (e.g., reunified with their families and adoption). This data source also provided information on important case characteristics such as the reason youth entered the system, their age at entry, and their foster care placement history.
- *Unemployment Insurance (UI) Wage Reporting Data*: In each state, employers who pay a payroll tax based on an employee's earnings are required to report those earnings quarterly. This data source was used to obtain quarterly earnings information for youth in the study and includes most but not all types of employment (important limitations are described on page 11). Outcome measures related to employment and earnings come from this source.
- *Public Assistance Data:* Each state collects statewide public assistance data on caregiv-ers and dependents who receive Temporary Assistance for Needy Families (TANF). These data contain information on the types of assistance and spells of that receipt. These data were used to create a comparison sample of low-income youth in all three states. In Minnesota and North Carolina, public assistance data were also used to track welfare receipt after youth left foster care. In California, welfare data for this purpose were not available.
- *National Longitudinal Survey of Youth 1997* (NLSY97): The NLSY97 is a national probability sample of approximately 9,000 youth born in the years 1980 through

1984. The youth were first interviewed in 1997 and have been interviewed on an annual basis since. The most recently available data were collected in 2003-2004, representing the seventh round of interviewing. For the purpose of this study, youth born in 1980 were selected, which makes them 18 as of December 31, 1998, a comparable age group to the child welfare population examined. The survey includes questions about employment, earnings, and TANF receipt. These data were used to provide a nationally representative baseline comparison.

Data Linking

Data from each of these sources were combined into one analysis file for each state. Researchers used social security numbers as the primary means to identify the same youth across data systems and to link youth's information into one dataset. In North Carolina researchers also used name and date of birth when linking child welfare and public assistance records. In Minnesota all three data sources were compiled and linked using social security numbers. Minnesota's Department of Human Services and the Department of Employment and Economic Development did the link and provided one dataset to the researchers.

Cases with Missing or Invalid Social Security Numbers

Child welfare and employment data in each of the states could only be linked for youth with valid social security numbers in the child welfare data systems.[1] Those without a valid social security number could not be included in the study. In California 13 percent of the original sample lacked valid social security numbers, in North Carolina 2 percent lacked valid numbers, and in Minnesota less than 1 percent lacked valid social security numbers.

In California, the only state with sufficient sample sizes to compare youth with and without valid social security numbers, youth were compared on demographic and child welfare case characteristics to determine whether there were any differences between them. Analyses revealed few substantive differences between youth with and without valid social security numbers.

Table 1. Sample Sizes*: Key Constructs

	Age-Out	Low- Income	NLSY
California	2,697	43,725	
Minnesota	320	4,786	
North Carolina	284	2,709	
National Sample			878

*Sample sizes are for working youth only. CA, MN, and NC samples include youth age 17 in 1998. The NLSY sample includes youth who were 18 in 1998.

Samples

The analyses included three different samples of youth, two of which serve as comparisons to the study group of interest, youth who age out of foster care. Table 1 shows the sample size for each group in each state. Tables A1-A6 in the Appendix provide detailed demographic information for the age-out and low-income samples, and also include case history information for the age-out sample.

- *Age-Out Sample (study group):* This group includes all youth age 17 and in the child welfare system on December 31, 1998, who have "emancipation" or "age of majority" as their exit reason, or who had missing exit reasons, but exited after their 18th birthday. Employment outcomes are tracked as these youth turn 18 through their first quarter of age 24.
- *Low-Income Comparison Sample:* This group includes all youth age 17 on December 31, 1998 listed as a dependent on a family TANF grant. Employment outcomes are tracked as these youth turn 18 through their first quarter of age 24.
- *National Comparison Sample:* This nationally representative sample includes all youth age 18 in 1998 in the NLSY97. The sample is on average one year older than the child welfare and low-income comparison groups due to the availability of the NLSY97 data. Employment, earnings, and TANF receipt for these youth through age 24 are gathered from the survey.

This report examines employment and earnings for youth in the three samples described above. In Minnesota and North Carolina it also includes TANF outcomes for the child welfare and low-income samples.

Outcomes are examined through the quarter of the youth's 24th birthday. As this gives the status of the youth on a particular outcome at age 24, this year is referred to as age 24 throughout this report. It should be noted that this year includes three quarters prior to the youth's 24th birthday as well as the quarter of his or her 24th birthday. The other age data points presented in the report use this same approach.

There are several different ways to measure employment and welfare experiences using UI and TANF data, and the following is a description of the key constructs used in the study.

- *Employment:* Earnings reported quarterly are used to indicate whether youth are employed (i.e., had earnings) at any time between ages 18 and 24 and at each age between 18 and 24.
- *Earnings:* Quarterly earnings also are used to estimate average monthly earnings between 18 and 24 and at each age between 18 and 24.[2] The data are also used to determine whether earnings reached a livable wage using data on fair market rents for each state.
- *Stability:* Two measures were constructed to approximate employment stability, defined as consecutive quarters of employment. One measure indicates whether youth have ever been employed for four consecutive quarters (i.e., a full year) by age 24 and what portion of youth achieve the outcome at each age. A significant limitation of this measure is that data are quarterly and not date-specific. This means that youth who worked only one month in each quarter would still be considered employed four consecutive quarters. While this measure suggests that some regular employment occurred, it does not guarantee that the employment was stable. A second measure of stability estimates the portion of quarters in a year youth worked at each age.
- *Connectedness:* This construct considers patterns of connection to the workforce. Analyses identified groups of youth with similar probabilities of employment at a

given age over time. These groups include youth who are consistently, initially, later, and never connected to the workforce.

- *TANF Receipt:* Researchers examine whether youth received TANF between ages 18 and 24 in North Carolina and Minnesota, and what portion were receiving TANF at each age.

Analyses

Statistical analyses include bivariate, multivariate, and trajectory models to characterize and assess the employment, earnings, and TANF outcomes for youth in the study.

- *Bivariate:* Researchers calculated and analyzed the sample means for all demographic factors, child welfare case characteristics, employment, earnings, and TANF outcomes for youth who aged out of foster care in each of the states. Similar estimates were produced for demographic, employment, earnings, and TANF outcomes for youth in the low-income and national samples. The analyses were used to examine sample characteristics and employment and TANF trends.
- *Multivariate:* Multivariate analyses included ordinary least squares and logistic regression, and Cox proportional hazard models. These analyses served several purposes. The primary purpose was to determine whether differences between comparison groups in employment, earnings, or stability were maintained after controlling for other factors. Another purpose was to determine which factors were significantly associated with employment, earnings, and stability outcomes for the population of youth who age out of foster care.
- *Trajectory:* Trajectory analyses were conducted on the sample of youth who age out of foster care in each state to identify distinct employment patterns over time. This method groups youth with similar employment patterns and tracks the probability of employment at each age. Researchers used the semi-parametric group-based approach employed by Nagin (1999).

Limitations

There are a few important limitations to this analysis. First, with regard to the UI data, it is important to note that unemployment insurance does not cover all workers. For example, individuals employed by the military and federal government are not included. Neither is informal work and employment that is "off the books". Unemployment Insurance data explicitly exclude much of the agricultural sector and domestic services, as well as the self-employed. Also, youth who moved out of state, work across state borders, or are incarcerated would not appear in the data. The net effect of this limitation is that the analyses are likely to underestimate employment and earnings within the study samples. Hotz and Scholz (2001) have also concluded that UI administrative data underreport earnings in a study comparing administrative earnings data with survey data on earnings. This finding may be of concern to the current study, but previous research on the employment outcomes of youth aging out of foster care find consistent differences between youth who age out of foster care and other youth regardless of whether they use survey or administrative earnings data.

Second, it is also important to point out that earnings may not perfectly reflect how a youth transitioning into adulthood is faring, or his or her future earning potential. The main reason is that measures of educational attainment, college enrollment, or degrees earned are not present in the data. One advantage of the study design, however, is that it is longitudinal and includes findings through age 24. Presumably many youth who may have been in school around age 17 may have completed high school or post-secondary schooling by then. Another reason these data may not capture fully how these youth are faring is that they only report individual earnings and do not account for earnings from a spouse, roommate, or family member who may also provide support for the youth.

A third limitation pertains to using quarterly, as opposed to date-specific, data. One consequence is that true employment stability cannot be measured. In essence, a youth who may have worked four consecutive quarters may not have had stable or consistent employment each month. With data that are calculated quarterly, such employment patterns cannot be assessed. However, consecutive quarters of employment are an approximation for consistency and reveal regular, if not stable, work. Despite the limitations of UI data, it is nevertheless regarded as one of the most comprehensive sources of earnings data available. In addition, it is a data source that is collected consistently across all states, which is essential for comparative studies such as this one.

A fourth limitation concerns child welfare data. It is important to note that the sample is drawn from youth who were of a particular age in 1998. This period occurs shortly after states implemented statewide automated information systems (SACWIS). While the selected states have noticeably reliable data, it is likely that further improvements to the system and data collection process were made in subsequent years.

A related limitation concerns unmeasured characteristics generally. While analyses adjust for demographic factors and child welfare case characteristics, additional information known to be related to employment outcomes are not available. Examples include family income, social support, educational attainment, and other youth characteristics (e.g., mental and physical health), which can contribute to employment outcomes. This limitation of unmeasured and in some cases unobservable characteristics is not uncommon in research of this nature and may be improved as information systems generally improve. This research, however, makes a substantial contribution to what is currently known using some of the best data available.

SECTION 3. EMPLOYMENT OUTCOMES OF YOUTH WHO AGE OUT OF FOSTER CARE

Youth who age out of foster care experience lower than average rates of employment and low earnings through age 24,[3] compared to similar age youth nationally and those from low-income families in their respective states. The majority of these youth, however, do work at some point between the ages of 18 and 24 in all three states. Only 15 percent of youth in California never worked during this period. Similarly, 13 percent of youth in Minnesota and 18 percent in North Carolina had no reported earnings. It is uncertain to what extent these youth worked in jobs that would not be included in the UI data, were incarcerated, or moved out of state.

The estimates that follow are based on the sample of youth who aged out of foster care and who worked at some point between the ages of 18 and 24. To include those who never worked in estimates of employment outcomes would weight the results heavily toward zero, either in terms of no employment or as zero earnings. Focusing on the working population offers a picture of employment levels for those youth who engaged in work. This population is referred to as "working youth."

Working Youth Who Age Out of Foster Care Are Less Likely to Be Employed than Other Youth at Age 24

Of youth who aged out of foster care and who ever worked during the study period, about three out of five work at age 24 in each of the three states studied (62 percent in California, 65 percent in Minnesota, and 61 percent in North Carolina) (see Figure 1). The portion of youth aging out of foster care who worked is lower than the portion of the comparison groups that worked. Nationally, 92 percent of youth with work histories work at age 24.[4] And, two-thirds to three-quarters of working youth from low-income families work at 24 (74 percent in California, 71 percent in work in Minnesota, and 68 percent in North Carolina).

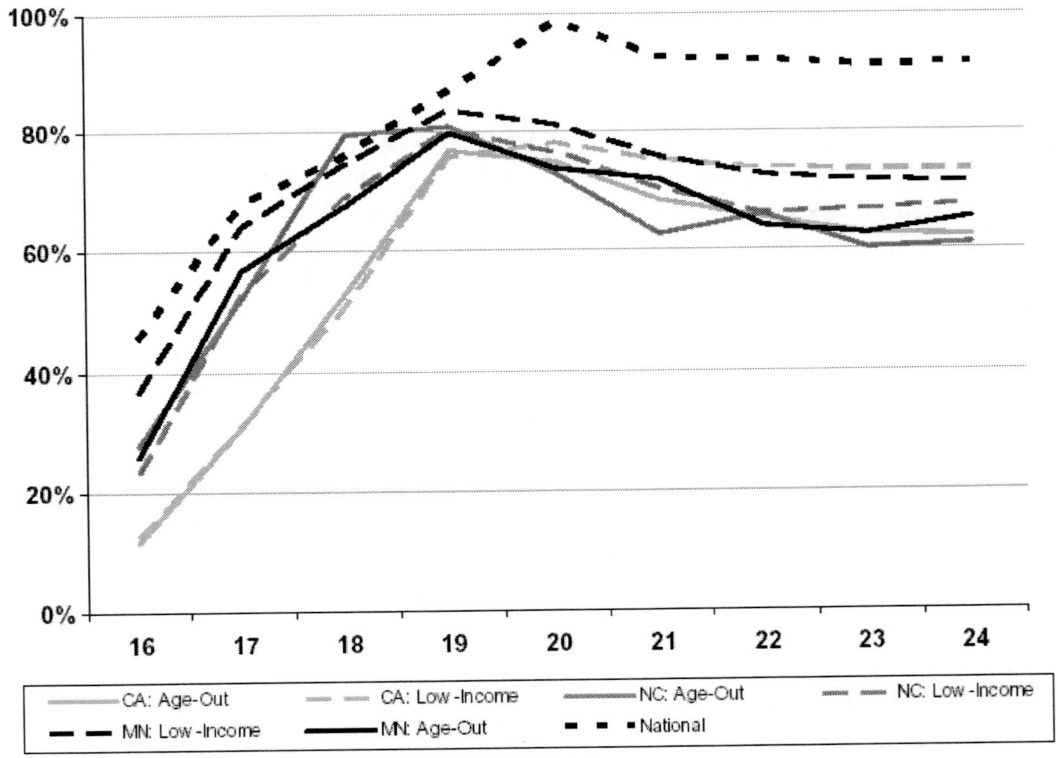

Notes: Each age is defined as the four quarters ending in that birthday.

Figure 1. Percent of Working Age-Out Youth Employed at Each Age Between 16 and 24.

Table 2. Comparing Youth Who Age Out of Foster Care to Low-Income Youth on Employment at Age 24

	Relative Odds of Being Employed at Age 24
Model Type	
	Logistic
Low-Income (age out is the reference group)	
CA	56% more likely to be employed***
MN	30% more likely to be employed**
NC	NS

Sample Size: CA: 46,094; MN: 4,915; NC: 2,993.

Notes: Age 24 is defined as three quarters prior to 24th birthday and quarter of 24th birthday.

Significance: NS = not significant; * significance at the 10% level; **significance at the 5 percent level; ***significance at the 1% level.

Models: adjust for the following factors: female, African American, other race/ethnicity (non-white) (MN & NC only), Native American (CA only), Asian (CA only), Hispanic (CA only), prior work experience, rural (MN & NC only), Los Angeles (CA only), and county unemployment rate at age 24.

Differences between working youth who age out of foster care and those from low-income families tend to persist in two of the study states when controlling for other factors like gender, race and ethnicity, prior work experience, unemployment rates, and urbanicity (see Table 2 and description of the full model in Tables A13–A15 in the Appendix).[5]

Specifically, controlling for these factors, low-income working youth in California and Minnesota have a higher likelihood of working at age 24 than do youth who age out of foster care (56 percent in California and 30 percent in Minnesota).

Trends over time suggest that rates of employment for working youth who age out of foster care decline after age 19. In all three states, 70 to 80 percent of these youth work at age 19. This portion then declines steadily through age 24—the last year of available data. This decline after age 19 is not observed for other populations. For youth nationally, rates of employment increase to a high of 99 percent around age 20, drop the next year, and then remain steady between 91 and 93 percent through age 24. Employment rates for low-income youth remain fairly steady through age 24 in California. In Minnesota and North Carolina, rates for low-income youth decline somewhat through age 24, but not as dramatically as do rates for youth who age out of foster care.

These differing patterns suggest that rates of employment for working youth who age out will diverge from other working youth nationally and those from low-income families. This divergence appears to begin around age 20 in all three states and becomes particularly pronounced by age 24.

Working Youth Who Age Out of Foster Care Increase Their Earnings with Age, but Few Earn a Livable Wage at Age 24

Working youth who age out of foster care in the three study states earn less than $700 a month on average at age 24 ($690 in California, $575 in Minnesota, and $450 in North Carolina) (see Appendix Tables 7–9). State differences in average earnings may be due to variation in the cost of living in each state. Regardless, these youth earn less than youth nationally and youth from low-income families in all three states. Nationally, at age 24, youth earn on average $1,535 per month, more than double the $700 per month on average earned by working youth who age out of foster care in California. Working youth who age out of foster care also earn less on average than youth from low-income families. At age 24, youth from low-income families in California earn $970 per month on average. These youth earn $865 in Minnesota and $570 in North Carolina.

Table 3. Comparing Youth Who Age Out to Low-Income Youth on Earnings at Age 24

	Mean Monthly Earnings at Age 24
Model Type	
	OLS
Low-Income (age out is the reference group)	
CA	11% higher earnings***
MN	17% higher earnings**
NC	NS

Sample Size: CA: 46,094; MN: 4,915; NC: 2,993.

Notes: Age 24 is defined as three quarters prior to 24th birthday and quarter of 24th birthday.

Significance: * significance at the 10% level; **significance at the 5 percent level; ***significance at the 1% level.

Models: adjust for the following factors: female, African American, other race/ethnicity (non-white) (MN & NC only), Native American (CA only), Asian (CA only), Hispanic (CA only), prior employment, rural (MN & NC only), Los Angeles (CA only), and unemployment rate at age 24.

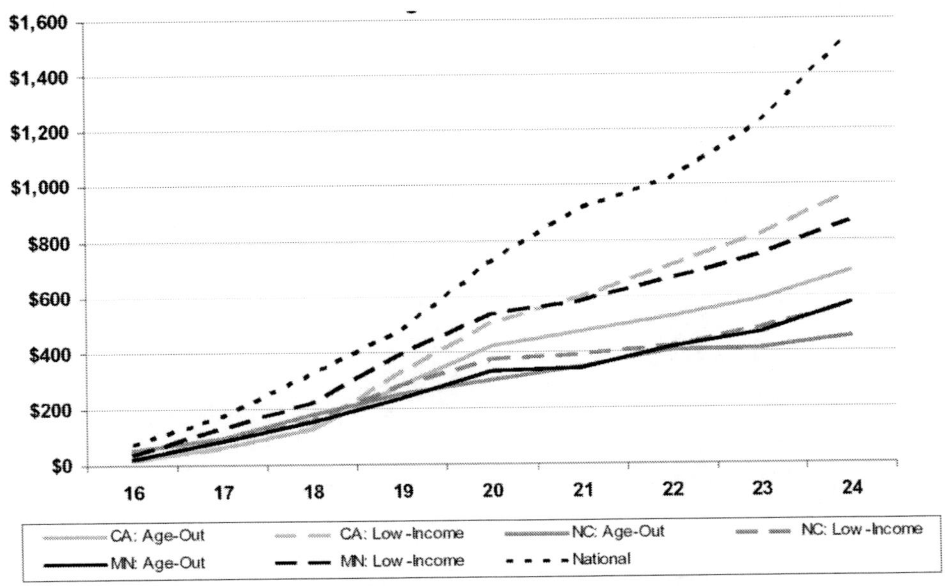

Notes: Each age is defined as the four quarters ending in the quarter with that birthday. Earnings are not adjusted for inflation.

Figure 2. Mean Monthly Earnings for Youth at Each Age Between 16 and 24.

Differences in earnings between working youth who age out of foster care and those from low-income families persist in two of the three study states when controlling for other factors like gender, race and ethnicity, prior work experience, unemployment rates, and urbanicity. Controlling for these factors, earnings of youth from low-income families are significantly higher in California (by 11 percent) and Minnesota (by 17 percent).

Looking at trends, youth who age out of foster care experience a steady increase in earnings over time, although earnings are not adjusted for inflation. In California, these youths' mean monthly earnings grew by $561 between ages 18 and 24. In Minnesota incomes grew by $421, and in North Carolina they grew by $275. It is important to note that although youth from North Carolina experienced the lowest growth in mean monthly income, they earned more at age 18 than youth from either California or Minnesota. Other youth also increase their earnings over time. The curve is generally steeper for low-income youth and much steeper for youth nationally (See Tables A7–A9).

Given their low earnings, it is not surprising that only a small portion of working youth who age out of foster care earn a livable wage at age 24[6] (7 percent in California, 17 percent in Minnesota, and 10 percent in North Carolina) (see Figure 3). Compared to other youth, far more working youth from low-income families in each state earn a livable wage: 13 percent in California, 23 percent in Minnesota, and 14 percent North Carolina.

Portions of working youth who age out of foster care and those from low-income families earning a livable wage generally increase with time in all three states. The increase is somewhat more substantial, however, for youth from low-income families (See Tables A7–A9).

Despite their low earnings, few working youth who age out of foster care receive benefits from TANF. In Minnesota and North Carolina, the states for which these data are available, only 2 percent and 7 percent, respectively, of youth who age out receive TANF at age 24 (see Figure 4). More youth from low-income families in each state receive TANF: 16 percent in Minnesota and 10 percent in North Carolina.

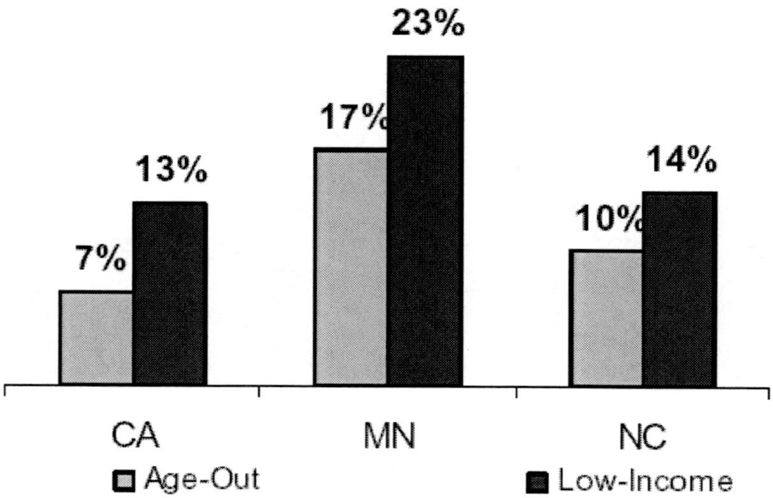

Notes: Age 24 is defined as three quarters prior to 24th birthday and quarter of 24th birthday.

Figure 3. Percent of Youth Earning a Livable Wage, Age 24.

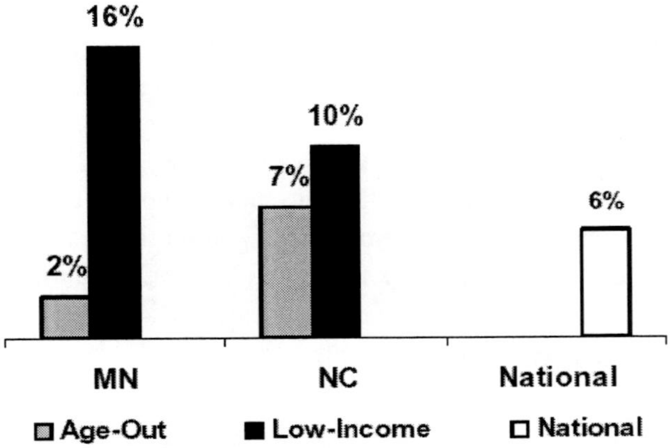

Notes: Age 24 is defined as three quarters prior to 24th birthday and quarter of 24th birthday.

Figure 4. Percent of Youth Receiving TANF at Age 24.

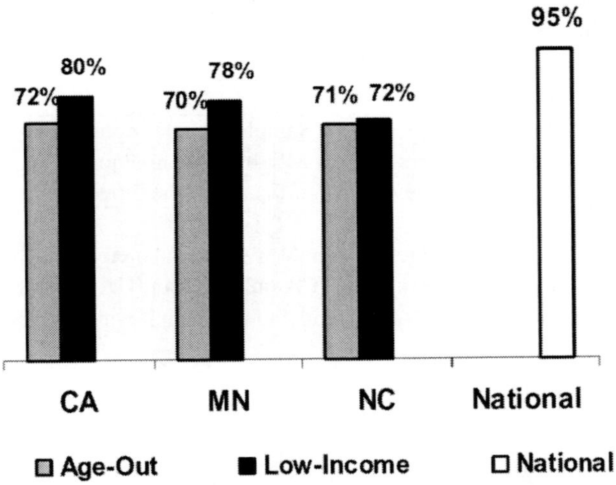

Notes: Age 24 is defined as three quarters prior to 24th birthday and quarter of 24th birthday.

Figure 5. Youth Employed Four Consecutive Quarters by Age 24.

This finding is consistent with Dworsky and Courtney (2000) who find that 2 percent of former foster youth in Wisconsin received AFDC two years after exiting from care. Looking out one to three years further, they find that about 12 percent of these youth receive TANF assistance. Given that these youth have such low earnings, it might be expected these rates would be higher. These youth, however, may not know how to access the benefits or might not have children.

Working Youth Who Age Out of Foster Care Continue to Experience Unstable Employment at Age 24

One way to look at stability of employment is to estimate the portion of youth who report employment for four consecutive quarters. The limitation of this measure is that youth may have worked for one day, week, or month of each quarter, rather than throughout the period. At minimum, this measure provides a sense of how frequently youth had regular, even if not entirely stable earnings. With this measure, about 7 out of 10 working youth who age out of foster care experience four consecutive quarters of employment at some time between ages 18 and 24 in all three states (72 percent in California, 70 percent in Minnesota, and 71 percent in North Carolina) (see Figure 5).

Other youth, however, are more likely to have been employed four consecutive quarters by age 24. Nationally, 95 percent of youth fall into this category. For youth from low-income families, portions are slightly higher than youth who age out in all three states (80 percent in California, 78 percent in Minnesota, and 72 percent in North Carolina).

Table 4. Comparing Age-Out to Low-Income Youth on Four Consecutive Quarters Employed by Age 24

	Relative Likelihood of Being Employed Four Consecutive Quarters by Age 24
Model Type	
	Hazard
Low-Income (age out is the reference group)	
CA	41% higher likelihood***
MN	45% higher likelihood***
NC	18% higher likelihood**

Sample Size: CA: 47,685; MN: 5,247; NC: 3,252. Sample includes non-employed as well.

Notes: Age 24 is defined as three quarters prior to 24th birthday and quarter of 24th birthday.

Significance: * significance at the 10% level; ** significance at the 5 percent level; *** significance at the 1% level.

Models: also adjust for the following factors: Female, African American, Other Race/Ethnicity (Non-White) (MN & NC only), Native American (CA only), Asian (CA only), Hispanic (CA only), rural (MN & NC only), Los Angeles (CA only), and county unemployment rate at Age 24.

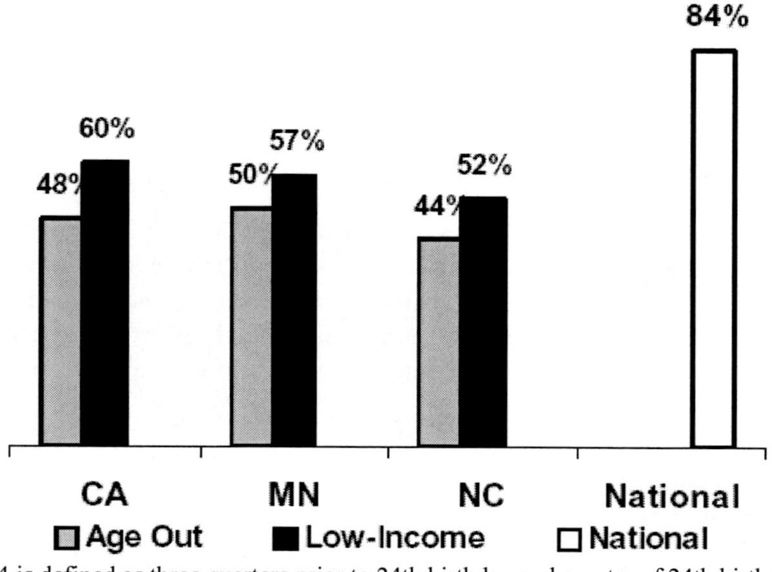

Notes: Age 24 is defined as three quarters prior to 24th birthday and quarter of 24th birthday.

Figure 6. Percent of Quarters Employed by Youth at Age 24.

These differences persist in all three states even when controlling for other factors like gender, race and ethnicity, prior work experience, unemployment rates, and urbanicity. After controlling for these factors, working youth from low-income families are more likely than youth who age out of foster care to have experienced four consecutive quarters of employment by age 24 in all three states (41 percent higher in California, 45 percent higher in Minnesota, and 18 percent higher in North Carolina) (see Table 4, Tables A13–A15 in the Appendix).

Another way to look at stability is to consider how many quarters in a year youth work. At age 24, youth who age out of foster care in all three study states work about half the quarters (see Figure 6). Working youth who age out of foster care in California work on average 48 percent of the quarters at age 24. Similarly, these youth in Minnesota work 50 percent of the quarters, and youth in North Carolina work 44 percent of the quarters. Youth nationally work far more often. They work 84 percent of the quarters at age 24. Generally, youth from low-income families in each of the three states also work slightly more quarters than youth who age out of foster care.

SECTION 4. EMPLOYMENT TRAJECTORIES OF YOUTH WHO AGE OUT OF FOSTER CARE

Looking at youth who age out of foster care in the aggregate masks the possibility that distinct groups of youth exhibit different patterns of connection to the workforce. This study uses group-based trajectory analysis to identify and differentiate patterns of "connectedness" to the work-force for youth who age out of foster care, through age 24. Trajectory analysis is a method that employs maximum likelihood estimation techniques to identify group patterns in longitudinal data as an alternative to calculating means from the entire sample, or making subjective group delineations.

Findings are very consistent across the three states in suggesting that youth who age out of foster care follow one of four distinct paths of connecting to the workforce as they transition into adulthood. These trajectories include all youth who age out of foster care, not just those who work at some point between ages 18 and 24. Analysis begins at age 16, to illustrate how employment prior to adulthood might be related to later employment for each trajectory. Four trajectories are identified:

- ***Never Connected:*** These are youth who are never or minimally connected to the workforce between the ages of 16 and 24. They represent as many as one-third of youth (33 percent) that age out in California, over a quarter of youth (29 percent) in Minnesota, and over one-fifth of youth (22 percent) in North Carolina (see Figure 7). It is important to note that some of these youth may be working, but in jobs not covered by UI data. They also might have moved to a different state and could be working there, could be in school, or could be incarcerated.
- ***Consistently Connected:*** These are youth who show consistent connections to the workforce as adults. This group represents a quarter of youth (25 percent) in California, just over one-fifth of youth (22 percent) in Minnesota, and about one-sixth of youth in North Carolina (16 percent).

- ***Initially Connected:*** These are youth who are connected to the labor market initially (i.e., in their late teens) but with time their probability of employment drops off. This group represents one-fifth of youth (22 percent) in California, 29 percent of youth in Minnesota, and almost half of youth in North Carolina (46 percent). In North Carolina, this group is composed of two subgroups, one with higher initial probabilities of employment (18 percent) and one with lower initial probabilities (28 percent).[7]
- ***Later Connected:*** These youth are not connected to the labor market initially but do begin working in their early twenties, perhaps because they were in school or in a training or apprenticeship program during their late teens. They also may have had earlier employment not covered in UI data but obtained employment with reported earnings later. This group represents one-fifth of youth in California (20 percent) and in Minnesota (21 percent), and about one-sixth of youth in North Carolina (16 percent).

It is striking that similar trajectories emerge in all three states, providing confidence that these patterns may be similar among youth who age out of foster care in other states or even nationally (see Figures 8–10). It is also notable that similar portions of youth follow each pattern. By age 24, one-third to almost half of youth who age out in all three states have high rates of employment (i.e., the consistent and later connectors). It is important to note, however, that despite their effort to work, the earnings for the later connectors to the workforce are still very low. At the same time, one-half to two-thirds of youth who age out of foster care are not connected to the workforce by age 24 (i.e., the never and initial connectors). These youth are either never connected to the labor market or are connected initially and then drop off.

While the patterns are similar overall, it is important to point out the few distinctions across the states. One distinction is seen in Minnesota where the later connectors exhibit a slight decline in their probability of employment at age 24 while the initial connectors who drop off show a rise in their probabilities of employment at this time. This pattern is not generally observed in the other states.

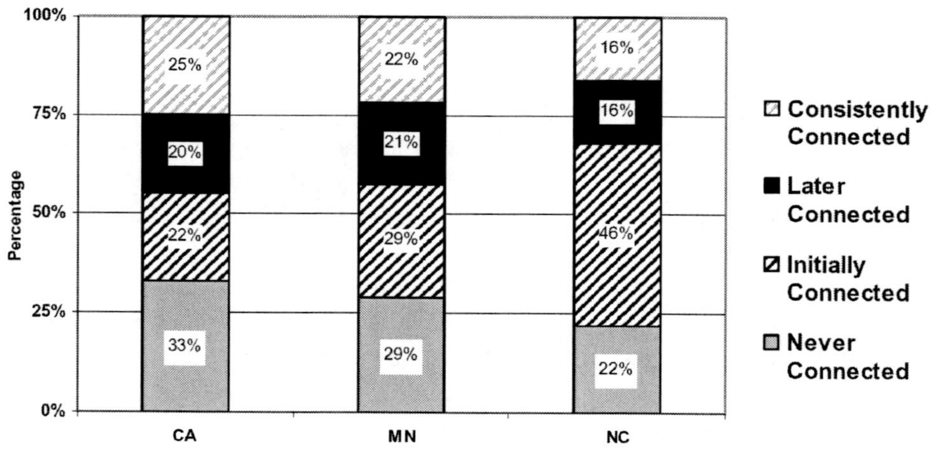

Figure 7. Trajectory Groups, by State.

Another distinction is seen in the later connector group. In California and North Carolina, their progress is more linear, while in Minnesota progress is more curvilinear with significant increases beginning around ages 18 and 19. It should also be noted that this group in Minnesota never reaches a probability of employment above 60 percent, whereas these youth in California and North Carolina reach probabilities around 70 to 80 percent, respectively.

Finally, as noted previously, in North Carolina there are two distinct groups of initial connectors, one with a high probability of initial employment nearing 80 percent and the other with initial probabilities of employment around 40 percent. Both groups, however, experience a drop in employment and have probabilities of employment around 20 percent by age 24.

In the pages that follow, the employment patterns of these four trajectories are described in greater detail. It should be noted, however, that sample sizes for these trajectory groups do get small, particularly in North Carolina and Minnesota. The trajectory lines of the probabilities of employment for these groups, however, are still distinct even after taking into account confidence intervals. A few other estimates of employment patterns are highlighted, but should be interpreted with caution due to small sample sizes. Estimates of case history and demographic characteristics are not highlighted in the text, but are included in the Appendix, with sample sizes and standard deviations noted.

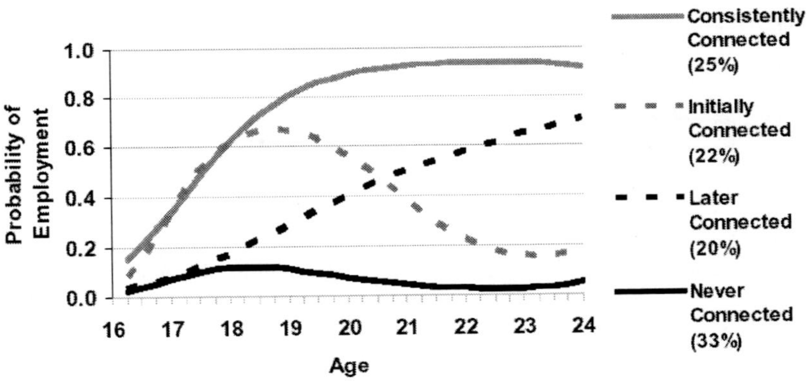

Figure 8. California Trajectories: Probability of Employment by Age.

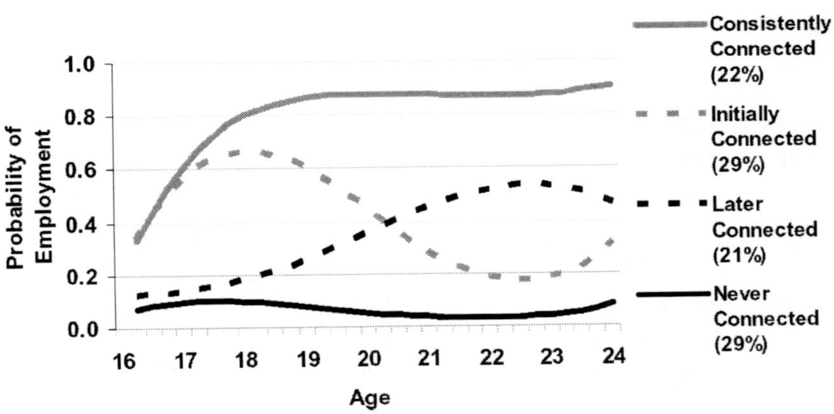

Figure 9. Minnesota Trajectories: Probability of Employment by Age.

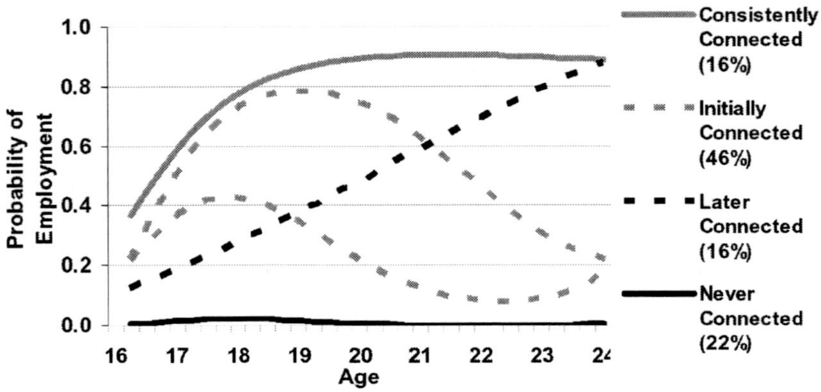

Figure 10. North Carolina Trajectories: Probability of Employment by Age.

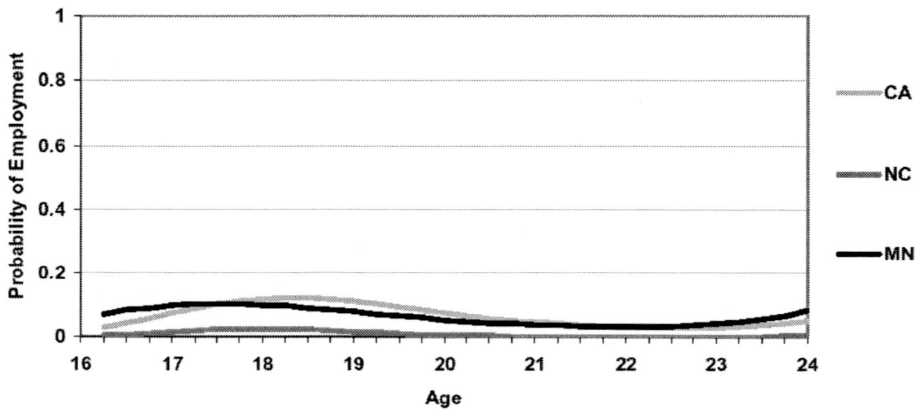

Figure 11. Never Connected Youth Trajectories by State: Probability of Employment by Age.

Trajectory 1. Never Connected

Of significant concern are the youth who age out of foster care and simply never connect to the workforce. They exhibit very low probabilities of employment and hardly any earnings between the ages of 16 and 24. The probability of employment for this group hovers between zero and 10 percent throughout this period. Even prior to adulthood, these youth have very low probabilities of employment (see Figure 11). This group includes the non-workers identified in the section 3 (15 percent of youth in California, 13 percent in Minnesota, and 18 percent in North Carolina) as well as those who work, but have very minimal employment. In California, 33 percent of youth are never connected, with 22 percent and 29 percent never connected in North Carolina and Minnesota, respectively.

The individual economic circumstances of these youth are poor (see Figure 12). They earn little to nothing each month and this is a steady pattern from ages 16 through 24. Average monthly earnings after age 18 for this group in California reach a high of $29 at age 19 and then drop to a low of $9 at age 23. Similarly, in Minnesota the highest average monthly earnings are $27 at age 24 and the lowest are $5 at age 22. In North Carolina the highest average monthly earnings are $5 at age 18 and the lowest are zero earnings at ages 22 and 23.

It is important to note, however, that some of these youth may be working in jobs not covered by UI data (such as the military), incarcerated, enrolled in school, or working in another state. Future research, perhaps with the data collected by state for the Chafee National Youth in Transi-tion Database (NYTD), can distinguish what portion of this group is truly never connected.

For those who are never connected, developing methods for identifying them, where they are, and how they are surviving will be vital to future policy and practice efforts. Specifically, researchers might examine to what extent these youth are homeless, disabled, or involved with the criminal justice system.

Trajectory 2. Consistently Connected

This trajectory is characterized by relatively high probabilities of employment after age 18 with earnings close to the national average in all three states (see Figure 14). The probability of employment for this group is close to 90 percent in all three states by age 20 and remains that high through age 24. It seems that connections to the workforce begin prior to adulthood for this group, as their probability of employment increases rapidly between ages 16 and 18 in all three states. Consistently connected youth include 25 percent of youth in California, 22 percent in Minnesota, and 16 percent in North Carolina.

What is most encouraging about this group is that their earnings are comparable to other youth nationally. At age 24, earnings for this group in California reach $1,575 a month on average. In Minnesota, average earnings reach a high at age 24 when youth make $1,325 per month. In North Carolina, average earnings for this group are the highest at age 23 when they earn $1,080 per month. Nationally, youth earn on average $1,525 a month at age 24 (see Figure 14).

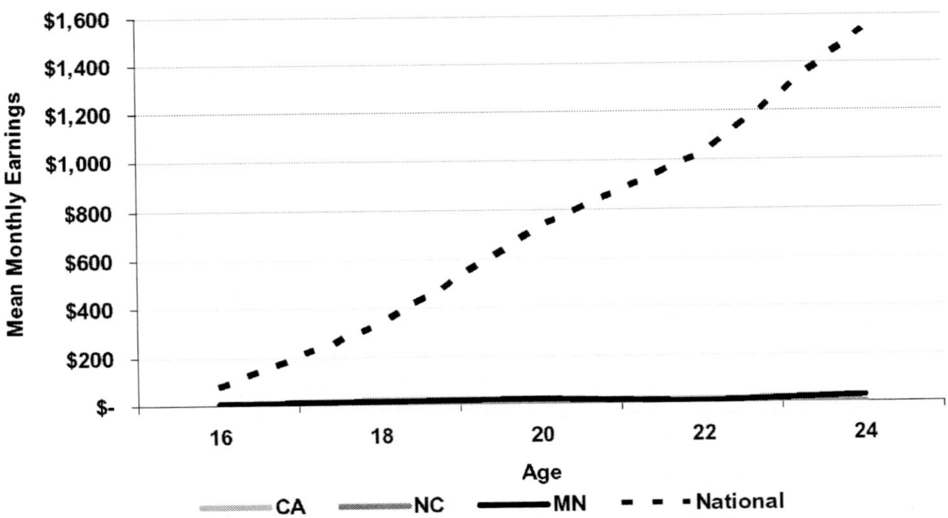

Figure 12. Never Connected Youth: Mean Monthly Earnings.

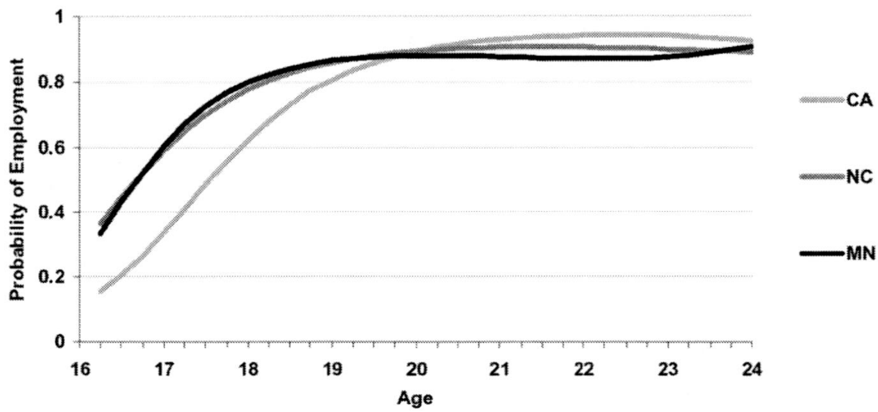

Figure 13. Consistently Connected Youth Trajectories by State: Probability of Employment by Age.

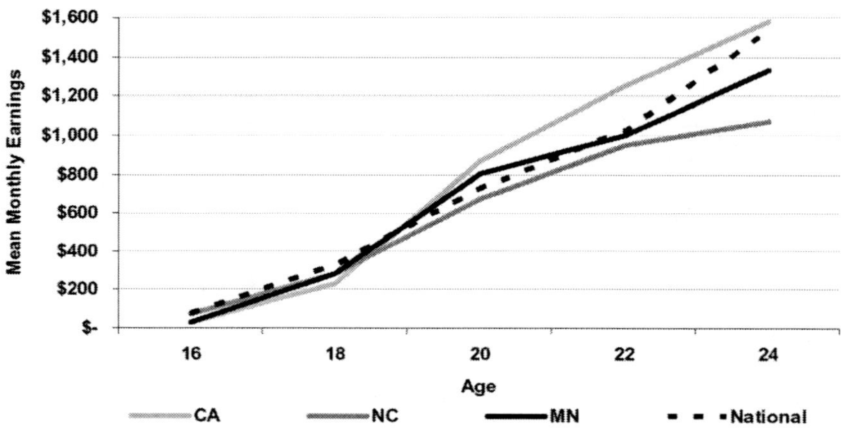

Figure 14. Consistently Connected Youth: Mean Monthly Earnings by Age.

Most of these youth, however, still do not earn a livable wage (see Figure 15). Only 17 percent of these youth earn a living wage in California at age 24. In Minnesota, however, almost half (42 percent) of these youth earn a livable wage at age 24, perhaps due to a lower cost of living. In North Carolina 23 percent of youth fall into this category at 24.

Trajectory 3. Initially Connected

Youth with this employment trajectory typically have higher probabilities of employment through their teens, with a drop in the probability of being employed occurring during their twenties (see Figure 16). In very early adulthood, around ages 18 and 19, these youth have initial probabilities of employment ranging from around 40 percent for North Carolina's low group to just over 80 percent for their high group. Percentages in California and Minnesota fall in between. By age 24, however, these probabilities hover around 20 to 30 percent in all three states. This drop may be the result of not working, returning to school, joining the military, or experiencing a major life event, job loss, or incarceration that causes them to disconnect from the workforce. Some of these youth may move to other states or start jobs not covered in UI data. Nationally, from 2005 to 2006, 5 percent of adults ages 20 to 24 moved out of state (U.S. Census Bureau, 2007). This may be especially true for North Carolina's high group, who appear strongly connected to the workforce between ages 18 and 21. The initial connectors appear to connect to the workforce prior to adulthood, as the probability of employment increases rapidly between ages 16 and 18 for these youth in all three states. In North Carolina, 46 percent of all youth are initially connected youth, compared to 22 percent in California and Minnesota.

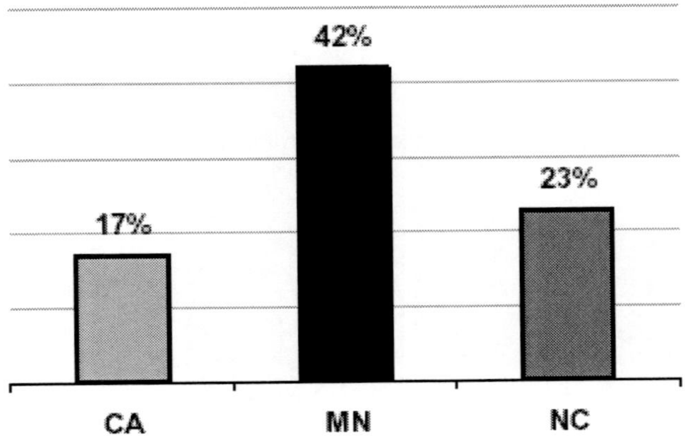

Figure 15. Consistently Connected Youth: Percent Earning a Living Wage at 24.

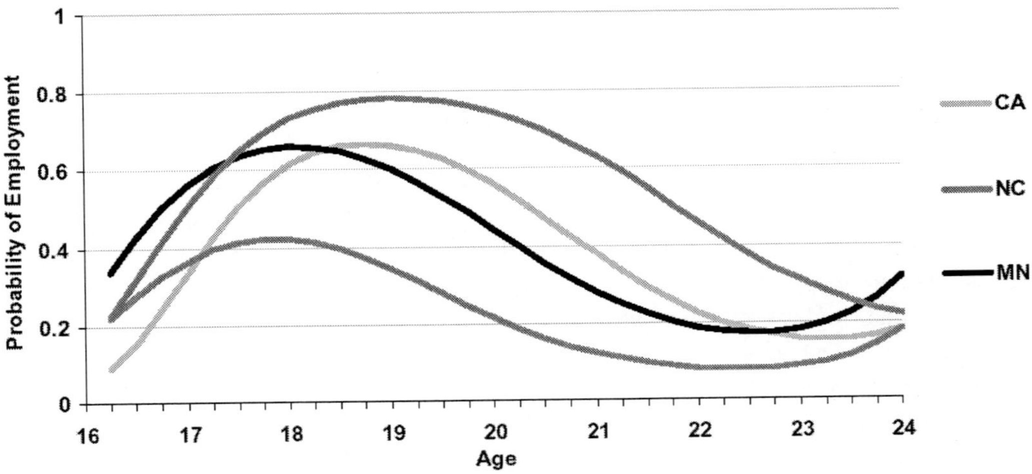

Figure 16. Initially Connected Youth Trajectories by State: Probability of Employment by Age.

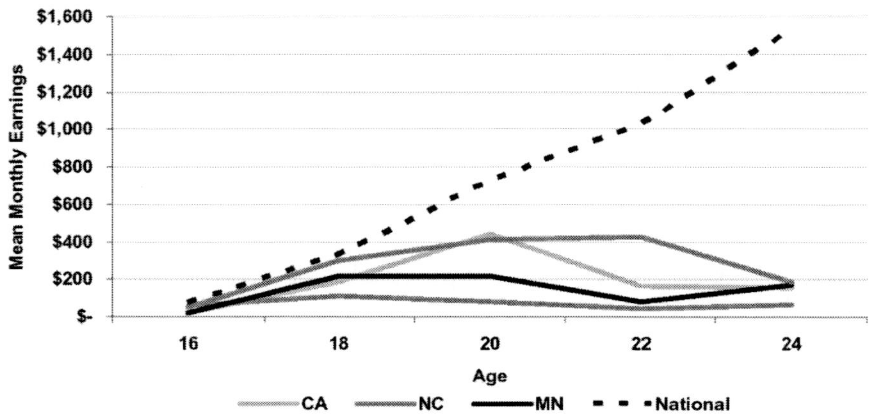

Figure 17. Initially Connected Youth Mean Monthly Earnings.

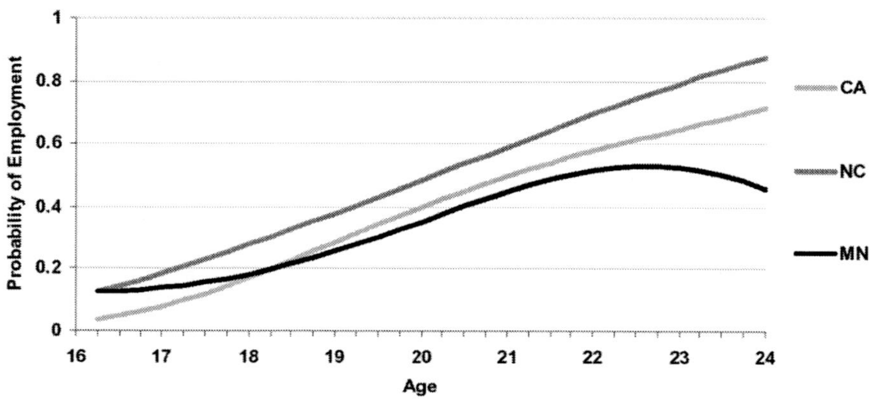

Figure 18. Later Connected Youth Trajectories by State: Probability of Employment by Age.

Earnings for this group reach a high between the ages of 18 and 21 and then decrease sub-stantially. Even at their peak, however, these youth earn very little. In California, these youth reach a high in average earnings at age 20 when they earn $450 a month. In Minnesota, highest average earnings occur for these youth at age 19 when they earn $250 a month. In North Carolina, highest average earnings are realized for the high group at age 21, and are $475 a month (see Figure 17). The relatively low earnings of this group might explain the drop off in employment if this creates a disincentive to continue working.

Few to none of these youth earn a living wage at any point during this period. In California, just 1 percent of these youth earn a living wage at age 24. None of North Carolina's low group is earning a livable wage at age 24. Sample sizes in Minnesota and North Carolina's high group are too small to report.

Trajectory 4. Later Connected

Youth in this trajectory have lower probabilities of employment until their early twenties but then see a steady increase in their probability of employment through age 24 (see Figure

18). In early adulthood their probabilities of employment are around or below 40 percent. Then in their twenties, these youth increase their probability of employment to highs above 70 percent in California and North Carolina and around 50 percent in Minnesota. In California, 20 percent of youth are later connected youth, compared with 21 percent in Minnesota and 16 percent in North Carolina.

Earnings start to increase for these youth through their twenties as well (see Figure 19).

Youth in California reach a high in average earnings at age 24 when they earn $750 a month. In Minnesota, highest average earnings occur for these youth at age 24 when they earn $700 a month. In North Carolina, highest average earnings are realized at age 24 when these youth earn $905 a month. Overall, these youth do not earn as much as the consistently connected youth at 24 but do exhibit a fairly steady rise in earnings in their twenties.

Most of these youth are not earning a livable wage at age 24 (see Figure 20). Only 5 percent of these youth earn a livable wage in California at age 24, perhaps due to a higher cost of living. In Minnesota, 19 percent of youth falls into this category. About a quarter (24 percent) of the later connectors in North Carolina earn a livable wage at age 24.

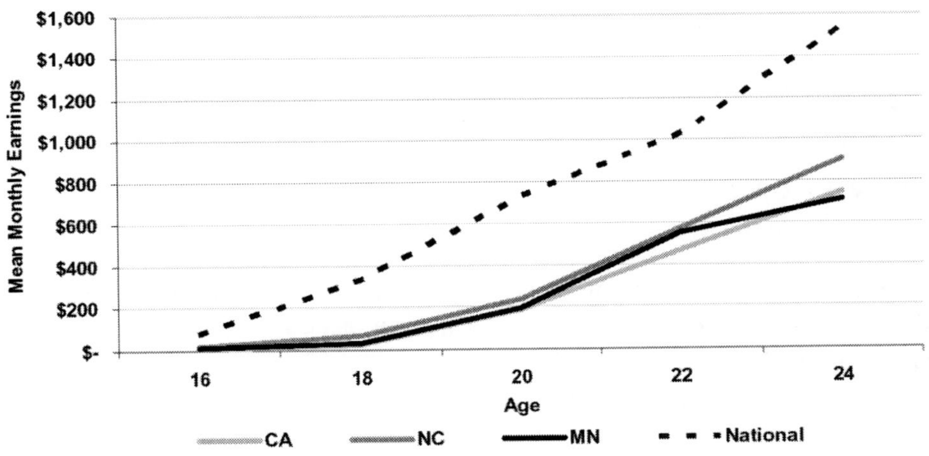

Figure 19. Later Connected Youth: Mean Monthly Earnings by Age.

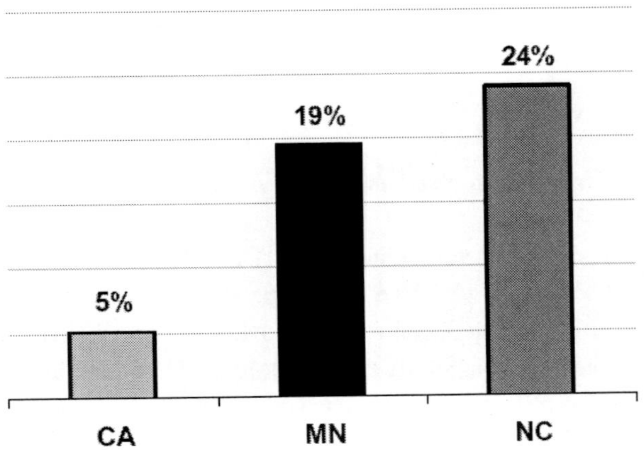

Figure 20. Later Connected Youth: Percent Earning a Livable Wage at 24.

SECTION 5. THE ROLE OF CHILD WELFARE FACTORS

This section focuses on the relationship between child welfare factors (i.e., age at exit, placement type, type of maltreatment, and time in care) and employment outcomes among youth who age out of foster care. Ordinary least squares regression, logistic regression, and Cox proportional hazard models were used to examine whether child welfare factors contribute significantly to employment, earnings, and employment stability outcomes (see Table 5).

Age at Exit: Youth who age out of foster care later are more likely to achieve four quarters of consecutive earnings

On the whole, a youth's age at exit is not significantly associated with employment and total earnings but has some relationship to stability. In Minnesota and North Carolina, youth who do not age out of foster care until they are one year older have greater odds of achieving four consecutive quarters of employment. That is, those who age out of foster care at 19 are more likely to achieve four consecutive quarters than those who age out of foster care at 18, who in turn are more likely than those aging out of foster care at 17. In Minnesota, aging out of foster care one year later is associated with a 22 percent increased likelihood of having four consecutive quarters of employment. In North Carolina, aging out of foster care one year later is associated with a24 percent increased likelihood. This relationship does not emerge in California.

Prior research has shown that youth who leave foster care later may have better employment outcomes (Courtney et al., 2005; Wade and Dixon, 2006). Also, youth who stay in care longer may be more likely to be in school, which might explain more "stable" or consecutive quarters of employment once they leave the system. These youth also may have received more training and employment-related skills than youth who exit foster care one year earlier, but further research is needed.

It is important to note that in 1999—the likely time that the majority of these youth exited care—youth typically remained in care only if they were disabled or in school. In North Carolina, to remain in care, youth had to be in school. Hence, it is difficult to distinguish whether some of the positive effects of aging out of care later may be due to being in school, receiving special assistance due to a disability, or staying involved with the system past age 18.

Placement Type

1) Youth in California who lived in group homes have lower relative odds of being employed at 24

A striking and consistent pattern emerges in California, but not in Minnesota or North Carolina, with respect to youth who live in group homes or institutions before aging out of care. In California youth who had been in group homes are significantly less likely to be employed at 24 than youth in non-relative foster homes. They also are less likely to have four consecutive quarters of employment, and earn significantly less than those in non-relative foster homes. At age 24 these youth have 31 percent lower odds of employment than youth in non-relative foster homes. The odds that they are employed four consecutive quarters at 24 is

47 percent lower than youth who had been in non-relative foster homes. They also earn 14 percent less than foster youth in non-relative placements at 24.

There is some support for this finding in prior research. Goerge and colleagues (2002) find that youth in group homes are significantly less likely than youth in relative foster care to be employed two years after exiting care in Illinois. This could be due to differences in employment services and support that youth receive in group homes versus foster home settings, or differences in youth characteristics, which should be explored further in future research.

2) Employment outcomes are similar for youth in relative versus non-relative foster care

On most employment outcomes, youth in relative foster homes did not differ significantly from those who had been in non-relative homes. In all three states they are equally likely to be employed at 24 and have similar earnings. In Minnesota and North Carolina they are also equally likely to have been employed four consecutive quarters at 24. In contrast, youth in relative foster homes in California are less likely to be employed four consecutive quarters at 24 than those who had been in non-relative foster care.

3) Youth whose placement prior to exit is undetermined or unspecified have less employment and earnings in California

For some youth in all three states, placement type at exit is unspecified in the administrative data.[8] In Minnesota and North Carolina, these youth do not have significantly different employment outcomes than youth in non-relative care. In California, however, they have decreased odds of employment and are less likely to have four consecutive quarters of employment than youth in non-relative care. Additional analyses in California reveal that many youth with unspecified placement at exit may have run away (i.e., their whereabouts are unknown). Researchers examined whether the last known placement type helped explain employment outcomes for youth with no placement information at the time they exited care. Youth whose last known placement status was "run away" are significantly less likely than youth in non-relative foster care to have four consecutive quarters of earnings. The findings suggest that youth with unspecified placement information, who have likely run away, are especially at-risk of poor employment outcomes.

Maltreatment Type: In general, type of maltreatment does not explain employment outcomes

For the most part, youth who experienced physical, sexual, or other forms of abuse are not significantly different from those who experienced neglect when it comes to employment outcomes. Type of maltreatment is not significantly related to any employment outcomes in California and North Carolina. The same is true in Minnesota except with respect to sexual abuse and employment at age 24. Youth who experienced sexual abuse have decreased odds of being employed at 24 compared with youth who had been neglected. This finding stands out as the only significant relationship between maltreatment type and employment at 24 and may be worth further investigation in future research.

Table 5. Role of Child Welfare and Demographic Factors in Predicting Employment Experiences Among Age-Out Youth*

	EMPLOYMENT			EARNINGS			STABILITY					
	A. Ever Employed at Age 24			B. Natural Logarithm of Mean Monthly Earnings at Age 24			C. 'Relative Risk' of Achieving 4 Consecutive Quarters of Employment by Age 24			D. Employed Four Consecutive Quarters at Age 24		
	CA	MN	NC	CA	MN	NC	CA	MN	NC	CA	MN	NC
Model Type	Logistic			OLS			Hazard			Logistic		
Sample Size	2,690	309	284	2,690	309	284	3,156	358	347	2,690	306	284
CASE HISTORY												
Age at Exit												
	NS	NS	NS	NS	NS	NS	NS	22% more likely**	24% more likely**	NS	NS	NS
Number of Placements												
	NS	13% lower odds**	NS	NS	NS	NS	NS	NS	NS	5% lower odds*	NS	NS
Placement Type (non-relative family foster care, reference)												
Foster Home, Relative	NS	NS	NS	NS	NS	NS	14% less likely**	NS	NS	26% lower odds**	NS	NS
Group Home/Institution	31% lower odds ***	NS	NS	14% lower**	NS	NS	36% less likely***	NS	NS	47% Lower Odds***	NS	NS
Supervised Independent Living		NS	NS		NS	NS		NS	NS		NS	NS
Unspecified Exit	32% lower odds ***	NS	NS	14% lower*	NS	NS	34% less likely***	NS	NS	50% lower odds***	NS	NS
Other	NS	NS	NS	21% lower***	89% lower***	NS	NS	53% less likely**	NS	NS	NS	NS

Table 5. (Continued)

	EMPLOYMENT			EARNINGS			STABILITY					
	A. Ever Employed at Age 24			B. Natural Logarithm of Mean Monthly Earnings at Age 24			C. 'Relative Risk' of Achieving 4 Consecutive Quarters of Employment by Age 24			D. Employed Four Consecutive Quarters at Age 24		
	CA	MN	NC	CA	MN	NC	CA	MN	NC	CA	MN	NC
Type of Abuse (neglect, reference)												
Physical Abuse	NS	NS	NS	NS	NS	NS	NS	NS	NS	31% higher odds*	NS	NS
Sexual Abuse	NS	75% lower odds ***	NS	NS	NS	NS	NS	NS	NS	NS	NS	NS
Other	NS		49% lower odds *	NS		NS	NS		NS	NS		NS
Total Number of Episodes												
	NS	NS	NS	NS	84% higher*	NS	NS	NS	NS	NS	NS	NS
Months in Care												
	NS	NS	NS	NS	NS	NS	NS	NS	NS	NS	NS	NS
DEMOGRAPHICS												
Gender (male, reference)												
Female	NS	71% higher odds**	NS	NS	38% lower***	NS	NS	NS	38% more likely**	NS	60% higher odds*	68% higher odds*
Race (white, reference)												
African American	NS	NS	NS	NS	45% higher**	NS	13% less likely**	NS	NS	18% lower odds*	NS	NS
Other Race (non-white		NS	NS		NS	NS		NS	59% more likely*		NS	NS
Native American	NS			NS			NS			NS		
Asian	NS			NS			34% more likely**			244% higher odds***		

Table 5. (Continued)

	EMPLOYMENT			EARNINGS			STABILITY					
	A. Ever Employed at Age 24			B. Natural Logarithm of Mean Monthly Earnings at Age 24			C. 'Relative Risk' of Achieving 4 Consecutive Quarters of Employment by Age 24			D. Employed Four Consecutive Quarters at Age 24		
	CA	MN	NC	CA	MN	NC	CA	MN	NC	CA	MN	NC
Hispanic	20% higher odds*			NS			NS			NS		
Urbanicity (non-rural, reference)												
		134% higher odds***	NS		NS	NS		NS	NS		72% higher odds*	NS
Los Angeles (not Los Angeles, reference)												
	36% higher odds***			NS			NS			NS		
Prior Work Experience (before age 18) (no prior work, reference)												
	42% higher odds***	NS	NS	NS	26% higher*	NS	78% more likely***	75% more likely***	27% more likely***	91% higher odds***	NS	NS

Notes: NS = Not Significant; * Significance at the 10% level; ** significance at the 5% level; *** significance at the 1% level.

*Models also adjust for the following factors: placements squared; models A, B, and D control for county unemployment rate at Age 24; and Model B controls for Number of Quarters Employed at Age 24 and Number of Quarters Employed between Ages 23 and 24.

Time in Care: Number of placements, total months in care, and total number of episodes (i.e., number of exits and re-entries into the foster care system) are not related to employment outcomes

Neither number of placements, total months in care, nor total number of episodes is significantly related to employment outcomes in California, Minnesota, or North Carolina at age 24. Relatively few case history factors distinguish employment outcomes among youth who age out of foster care.

The next section examines whether demographic characteristics like gender, and race and ethnicity, predict employment outcomes for the youth.

SECTION 6. THE ROLE OF DEMOGRAPHIC FACTORS

This section focuses on the role that factors such as gender, race and ethnicity, prior employment, and living in an urban or rural setting (i.e., urbanicity) play in predicting employment, earnings, and employment stability among youth who age out of foster care. Ordinary least squares regression, logistic regression, and Cox proportional hazard models were used to examine whether demographic factors contribute significantly to employment outcomes (see Table 5).

Gender: There is some evidence of gender differences, but not in all three states

Differences by gender are most apparent in Minnesota. Here, women have greater odds of being employed at 24 but earn significantly less than men. In North Carolina, women have a 38 percent greater likelihood of four consecutive quarters of employment than men. Similar gender differences in employment and earnings are observed in Illinois and South Carolina for youth who age out of foster care two years prior in the study by Goerge and colleagues (2002). In California, there are virtually no differences in employment outcomes by gender.

Race and Ethnicity: There are some racial and ethnic differences in employment outcomes

Racial differences in employment are seen among youth who age out of foster care. Compared to non-Hispanic white youth, African American youth show less favorable employment in California but more favorable earnings in Minnesota. In California, African Americans are significantly less likely to achieve four consecutive quarters of employment than non-Hispanic white youth. However, in Minnesota African Americans have 45 percent higher earnings at age 24 than non-Hispanic white youth. In North Carolina, no differences reach statistical significance.

In California, population size permits comparisons between Hispanic, Asian, Native American, and non-Hispanic white youth. Analyses reveal that Hispanic youth have increased odds of employment at 24 compared with non-Hispanic white youth but have no significant differences in earnings. In contrast, Asian youth do not differ significantly from non-Hispanic whites in employment and earnings but are 244 percent more likely to work four consecutive quarters at age 24.

Prior Employment: Youth with early work experience show more favorable employment at 24

In California, Minnesota, and North Carolina there is some evidence that youth with employment before age 18 have more favorable employment at 24. Youth in these states with early work experience are more likely to have four consecutive quarters of employment at 24. In California they are also likely to earn significantly more at age 24 than youth without early work experience. These findings should be interpreted with caution, however, as there may be unobserved characteristics of these youth that are correlated with both prior work and later employment. In this case, the coefficient on prior employment may be capturing the effects of these unobserved characteristics on later outcomes as well as the effects of working prior to age 18.

Urbanicity: Urbanicity has some relationship to employment in two states

Youth who had been in care in Los Angeles County were more likely to be employed at 24 than youth who had been in care in other counties in California. In contrast, youth who had been in care in rural counties in Minnesota have greater odds of being employed at 24 than youth who had been in care in other counties. In North Carolina there are no significant differences associated with having been in care in a rural versus non-rural county. These findings likely reflect regional differences in the employment opportunities in the counties examined.

SECTION 7. SUMMARY

This report describes employment outcomes for youth who age out of foster care, compared with youth nationally and a similar sample of youth from low-income families. A primary goal of the study is to extend prior research that finds that youth who age out of foster care exhibit poor employment outcomes two years after discharging from care and determine whether these patterns persist for youth through their mid-twenties. Findings reveal the following picture.

Youth who age out of foster care continue to experience poor employment outcomes at age 24

At age 24, youth who age out of foster care do not fare well on a variety of employment outcomes. Compared to youth nationally and even youth from low-income families, they are less likely to be employed or employed regularly, and, not surprisingly, they earn very little. At age 24, average monthly earnings for youth who age out of foster care are $690 in California, $575 in Minnesota, and $450 in North Carolina. Employment and earnings differences between youth who age out of foster care and youth from low-income families remain even when controlling for demographic factors in two of the three states.

Youth who age out of foster care tend to follow one of four employment trajectories as they transition to adulthood

Youth who age out of foster care exhibit four distinct patterns in connecting to the workforce. In all three states these four patterns emerge consistently, despite geographic, demographic, and labor market differences in the states. This suggests that similar patterns might emerge in other states or even nationally. Overall about one-third to one-half of youth follows a path that leads to relatively positive employment outcomes by age 24. At the same time, the other half to two-thirds of these youth exhibit patterns leading to poorer outcomes at age 24.

Positive outcomes at age 24:

- *Consistently Connected*: These youth maintain relatively high probabilities of employment between the ages of 18 and 24, and their average earnings are comparable to youth nationally. This group appears to begin connecting to the workforce prior to age 18. This group represents one-sixth to one-quarter of the youth in the states (25 percent in California, 22 percent in Minnesota, and 16 percent in North Carolina).
- *Later Connected*: Youth in this group have a slow start but steadily increase their probability of employment and earnings throughout their early twenties. Their average earnings do not reach levels comparable to youth nationally, but do show an upward trend. This group does not appear connected to the workforce prior to age 18. These youth represent one-sixth to one-fifth of the youth in the states (20 percent in California, 21 percent in Minnesota, and 16 percent in North Carolina).

Poor outcomes at age 24:

- *Never Connected*: These youth have very low probabilities of employment and hardly any earnings at any time between ages 18 and 24 or prior to age 18. This group represents one-fifth to one-third of the youth in these states (33 percent in California, 29 percent in Minnesota, and 22 percent in North Carolina). However, some portion of these youth may be working in jobs not covered by UI data, incarcerated, supported by other employed persons, or have moved out of state.
- *Initially Connected*: Youth in this group begin making connections to the workforce prior to adulthood and maintain a high probability of employment through their late teens. Their probabilities of employment then decline rapidly in their early twenties. The average earnings for this group never get very high, which might explain the drop off in employment if lower earnings result in less incentive to continue working. The drop-off in employment for some portion of these youth might also be explained by changes to jobs not covered by UI data, moves out of state, incarceration, or childbearing. This group represents one-fifth to almost half of the youth in these states (22 percent in California, 29 percent in Minnesota, and 46 percent in North Carolina).

Work prior to age 18 is associated with better outcomes at age 24, but individual or family characteristics may be playing a role

Working prior to age 18 is strongly associated with better employment outcomes at age 24. It is not possible to distinguish to what extent prior employment might be a proxy for characteristics of the family or the youth that cannot be controlled for in this analysis. Specifically, helping youth connect to the workforce prior to age 18 might not lead to better outcomes at age 24 if it is really family characteristics that affect prior work and also later outcomes. This finding therefore should be interpreted with caution. Looking at the four employment trajectories suggests that employment prior to age 18 also is no guarantee of positive or negative employment outcomes at age 24. For example, the initial connectors increase their probabilities of employment prior to age 18, but then their probabilities drop sharply by age 24. Their average earnings never increase substantially, however, which may suggest that prior work is most beneficial when it helps youth connect to better paying jobs. At the same time, the later connectors have low probabilities of employment prior to age 18 but substantially increase their probability of employment by age 24.

Case history factors do not play a significant role in influencing employment outcomes

Youth who age out of foster care do not fare well on employment outcomes regardless of how long they were in foster care, the number of placements they experienced, or the number of times they came into care. The factor that does appear to play a role in California is placement in group homes or institutions prior to exiting care. Youth placed in these settings prior to exit fare worse than youth in non-relative foster homes prior to exit on many of the employment outcomes. More research is needed to distin-guish whether it is placement in these settings that contributes to poor outcomes or character-istics of youth placed in them that are associated with worse outcomes.

SECTION 8. IMPLICATIONS

Key findings suggest that youth who age out of foster care do not fare well at age 24 compared to their peers. Groups of youth who age out of foster care, however, follow different patterns in connecting to the labor force. Some exhibit steady connections to the workforce (*consistently connected)*, and some never connect (*never connected*). Some connect initially but then see declines in employment (*initially connected*). Others get off to a slow start but connect to the workforce later (*later connected*). These findings suggest several potential implications for policy and future research.

Pathways to Adult Services

Extending services to age 21 is the focus of many recent initiatives and efforts to support youth aging out of foster care. Specifically, the FCIA allowed states to assist youth ages 18 to 21 who may have left foster care, and to extend Medicaid coverage for foster care youth to age 21. Many, but not all, states provide the FCIA independent living services to youth through age 21. Seventeen states have used the FCIA option to extend medical coverage to this group of youth, and another five states considered the option in 2007 legislative sessions. A large number of states (28) and the District of Columbia use other methods to extend Medicaid coverage to this population (Gever, 2007).

Findings from this report would suggest that risk for these youth extend beyond emancipation or even age 21. Working at age 21 does not appear to be a guarantee that youth will sustain employment through age 24. In fact, significant changes in employment trajectories appear to occur for foster youth who age out right around age 21. For example, the *initially connected* youth join the workforce prior to adulthood, sustain employment in their late teens, but by age 22, their probabilities of employment have substantially declined. Practitioners serving these youth in their late teens and early twenties might think these youth have successfully connected to the workforce, when in fact they may have difficulty sustaining their employment. It also might not be possible to fully detect the *never connected* youth until age 22 or 23 when a clear pattern of little to no employment has been established.

Some portion of these youth may need additional assistance staying connected to the labor market or accessing adult service systems. Poli-cymakers might consider strategies for serving young adults. For example, legislation to reauthorize the Workforce Investment Act (WIA) passed by the United States House of Representatives in 2005 changed the defined age for youth services from 16 to 21 to 16 to 24 to better reflect the age of transition for young adults. As Chafee programs move into their second decade, policymakers and practitioners might consider ways to use these programs to help identify youth who may need services beyond age 21, such as the *never connected* and *initially connected* youth.

Importance of Ages 16 to 18

Ages 16 to 18 are a period of significant employment activity for many youth aging out of foster care. Rapid increases in employment occur for *consistently connected* youth and *initially connected* youth between the ages of 16 and 18. Similarly, results show that employment prior to age 18 is associated with positive employment outcomes at age 24 for youth in California, Minnesota, and North Carolina, although it is important to note this estimate may be capturing the effects of unobserved individual and family characteristics as well. However, the results do suggest that helping youth connect to the workforce prior to adulthood may have benefits later.

Assisting them in accessing well-paying jobs and jobs with promising career paths might also be critical. Specifically, one hypothesis for why the *initially connected* youth do not sustain employment might be their low earnings. Youth who earn very little may not have an incentive to stay connected to the workforce. Job training, apprenticeships, and vocational education programs for youth in their late teens might be critical to helping these youth find better paying jobs. WIA-funded employment programs, such as Job Corps and Title I-B Youth Services, might target former foster youth who are able to work but have difficulty connecting to well-paying jobs. The 2005 WIA reauthorization legislation described above prioritized services for current and former foster youth.

Tailoring Programs

It is not surprising that different service approaches might be needed for different youth. This study suggests that there are likely four paths youth who age out of foster care will follow. As programs to serve former foster youth continue to evolve, policymakers and practitioners may want to consider strategies for tailoring programs to best meet the needs of youth on these different trajectories. For example, three of the four trajectories suggest the need for specific types of interventions:

- *Never Connected:* A significant challenge in serving this group is finding them. It is difficult to know if they are homeless, disabled, incarcerated, or living with their biological parents or extended family. Another challenge is figuring out how to help them access appropriate services. Youth with disabilities may benefit from assistance applying for Supplemental Security Income. Youth living with their families may need guidance to access programs that provide job training and housing, like Job Corps, to help them become self-sufficient. The Chafee NYTD could be an important tool to help states identify the types of youth that exhibit minimal connections to the workforce and determine which services they need.
- *Initially Connected:* This group may benefit from programs that help them connect to well-paying jobs that lead to self-sufficiency. This group exhibits a desire to work early on, but these youth may need additional training or education to find long-term and sustaining employment. In addition, to the extent practitioners can detect major life events, job losses, or involvement in criminal activity that may cause a youth to disconnect from the workforce, interventions might be put in place to help this group stay on a more positive trajectory. The connection that these youth initially had to the workforce may also be broken as a result of family formation. For these new parents, improved child care options may help youth who want to stay employed do so without compromising the healthy development of their children. Again, the Chafee NYTD could provide important information about the types of events that divert these youth and what services might help keep them on a positive path.
- *Later Connected:* These youth may require supports during the years that they are in school or receiving training in their preparation to later connect to the workforce. Youth who age out of foster care typically do not have the family supports their peers may enjoy during this period in their lives. To ensure these youth stay in school may require that they receive multiple supports during this period, including housing, food, clothing, transportation, and a stipend for other living expenses.

Future Research

This study uses administrative data to provide a first look at employment outcomes through age 24 for youth who have aged out of foster care in three states. Additional research in several areas could continue to build on and expand these results.

- *Youth Served by Chafee Programs:* The cohort of youth in this study was 17 in 1998 and likely aged out of care at age 18 in 1999. The FCIA that included the John H. Chafee Foster Care Independence Program (CFCIP) was enacted in 1999. While these programs would have been in their infancy at the time these youth aged out of foster care, the youth studied here may have been served by earlier generations of independent living programs. In the future, researchers may want to examine later cohorts of these youth that may have benefited from the CFCIP programs. With each additional year of employment data, another cohort of youth can be assessed through age 24. For example, with 2006 employment data, youth who age out in 2000 can be assessed through age 24. Another approach might be to compare youth who aged out in 1998 prior to CFCIP and youth who aged out in 2002 who would have experienced CFCIP to see how they fare at age 22. This type of approach was used by researchers in a study of youth aging out of foster care in Utah (Singer, 2006).

- *Education and Other Services:* Additional research could be done on the role of education and other service systems in supporting these youth. Education, in particular, is likely to have a significant effect on later success in the workforce and earnings po-tential. Knowing whether these youth enroll in school, when, for how long, and whether they obtain a degree would provide a major missing link to this story. Similarly, this study was able to look at TANF receipt for these youth, but these youth could have received other services like SSI, Social Security, Food Stamps, or other workforce develop-ment services. Understanding the full range of service receipt for this population is es-sential to understanding how these youth survive with such low earnings. Finally, ad-ditional research could help discern how often these youth become involved in the criminal justice system. Incarceration will affect youth employment and future earning potential.
- *Increased Understanding of the Trajectories*: Much more exploration could be done to understand the different employment paths these youth follow after aging out of foster care. Specifically, researchers might explore what factors are associated with youth taking a particular path. For example, what are the resiliency factors that enable youth to age out of foster care and connect consistently to the workforce? This group could provide valuable clues about what helps youth aging out of foster care suc-ceed. It will also be important to know more about what risk factors are associated with less encouraging outcomes for these youth. For example, what factors make it particu-larly difficult for some youth to connect? Or what factors or events derail youth who might otherwise have stayed consistently connected? In the future, researchers might also seek to better understand the heteroge-neity within each trajectory, as was ob-served for the initial connectors group in North Carolina. The two groups within this trajectory may benefit from different service responses. This additional information and answers to these questions would assist policymakers and practitioners in tailoring services to meet the varying needs of youth aging out of foster care as they come of age and begin their journey through adulthood.

TECHNICAL APPENDIX

This study employed multiple data sources to assess employment outcomes for youth between the ages of 16 and 24 who age out of foster care in three states: California, Minnesota, and North Carolina. The analysis also employed comparison groups of youth from low-income families and youth nationally. The primary sources of data for the study were administrative child welfare, public assistance, and Unemployment Insurance (UI) records. The study also used the National Longitudinal Survey of Youth 1997 to produce national estimates for comparison. Several analysis methods were employed including descriptive bivariate analyses, multivariate models, and trajectory analyses. Below the sources of data, sample and variable creation, and analysis methods are described in greater detail.

Data

The primary sources of data for this study were administrative child welfare, public assistance, and UI records. The study also employed survey data from the NLSY97. Some additional supplemental data on fair market rents and unemployment rates were also incorporated into the analysis. Each of these data sources are described below with information about how data were acquired and any potential limitations and biases when relevant.

Child Welfare Administrative Data

The child welfare administrative data had two primary purposes. First, these data were used to identify the sample of youth who age out of foster care. Second, these data also provided demographic and case history variables about the sample. This information was useful for describing the sample and also served as controls in the study's multivariate models. Child welfare administrative data were obtained in all three states.

- *California:* The California Child Welfare Services/Case Management System (CWS/ CMS) is California's automated child welfare data management system. CWS/CMS is a centralized statewide system that allows state or county child welfare workers to share information on child abuse cases. County conversion to CWS/CMS began in January 1997. On December 31, 1997, all 58 counties were online and accessing CWS/CMS. On a quarterly basis programming staff at the University of California, Berkeley, Center for Social Services Research (CSSR) refresh two aggregate longitudinal files, which are made available to CSSR researchers as well as California Department of Social Services (CDSS) staff. Currently, these include information for the period January 1, 1998, through December 31, 2005.
- *Minnesota:* The Minnesota child welfare data was provided by Minnesota's Department of Human Services (DHS). DHS was also able to provide data on youth participation in the Minnesota Family Investment Program (MFIP), the state's TANF grant program, through their AFDC/MFIP database. All cases were stripped of identifiers before being sent to the Urban Institute for analysis.
- *North Carolina*: The North Carolina child welfare data source is comprised of data extracts from the Service Information System (SIS), a state maintained data system. Basic SIS data for this study include demographic information on service recipients along with information on the services provided for these clients. Additional data from the Central Registry and Child Placement and Payment System (CPPS) have been combined with SIS data into a longitudinal dataset. The Jordan Institute updates this longitudinal dataset monthly using end of the month extracts from SIS and CPPS. Researchers at the Jordan Institute use this longitudinal file for research and

technical assistance to county and state staff. Data are available from 1992 until present.

Public Assistance Data

TANF records were used to create a low-income comparison sample for the analyses in all three states. In North Carolina and Minnesota, these TANF data were also linked to study youth by social security number to create TANF receipt histories into adulthood. North Carolina used approximate matching on social security number, date of birth, and name to link across the two systems. Minnesota linked the two data sources by social security number.

- *California*: The California low-income comparison group was drawn from the California AFDC/TANF MediCal Eligibility Data. These files include information on monthly aid participation between January 1993 and June 2007. Child-only cases were included in this file.
- *Minnesota*: The Minnesota low-income comparison group was constructed from data housed by the Minnesota Department of Human Services. These data were encrypted and sent to the Urban Institute for analysis. Cases were selected if they were 17 years old on December 31, 1998, and if they were classified as a child dependent (family status code C). Child-only cases were included in this file.
- *North Carolina*: In North Carolina, the low-income sample represents children who were part of a regular, monthly cash assistance grant from North Carolina's TANF program, Work First, who were born in 1981. This consists of all children who received Work First and were 17 in December 1998, and were classified as a child dependent (a family status code of C or D). Child only cases were included. Children who were classified only as a teen parent (a family status code of P) were not included. Also, children whose families only received diversion assistance, as opposed to a regular Work First grant, were not included. Information on these individuals was drawn from a set of longitudinal files that track the experiences of all families and individuals who have participated in the Aid to Families with Dependent Children (AFDC) or Work First program in North Carolina for one or more months since January 1995. These longitudinal files were constructed and are maintained using monthly extracts from state computer systems used in the administration of the program.

Unemployment Insurance (UI) Wage Reporting Data

UI administrative data were used in all three states to describe the earnings and employment histories of the youth who age out of foster care and the youth from low-income families.

- *California:* In California social security numbers from youth in the sample were used to select the appropriate employment records from the California Employment Development Department's Quarterly Wage Data files (EDD). Data were transformed into longitudinal format with two variables per quarter indicating quarter of receipt and quarterly wages between January 1, 1996, and December 31, 2005.

- *Minnesota:* Minnesota's UI data were obtained after linking social security numbers from youth in the sample with administrative data from the Minnesota Department of Employment and Economic Development.
- *North Carolina:* In North Carolina, these data were obtained by linking encrypted social security numbers from youth in the sample with a dataset composed of wage information obtained from North Carolina's Employment Security System. The Jordan Institute at the University of North Carolina receives quarterly updates of information on wage amount and sector of employment for the relevant individuals. The UI data used in the current analysis were last updated in August 2007, with data through March 2007.

There are some important limitations with the UI data to note. First, it may underestimate employment for the youth in this sample for a few reasons. For one, the Unemployment Insurance program does not cover all employment. For example, individuals employed by the military and federal government are not included. Neither is informal work and employment that is "off the books," which may be a job sector that former foster youth are more likely to occupy. Unemployment Insurance data explicitly exclude much of the agricultural sector and domestic services, as well as the self-employed. These exclusions suggest that earnings data derived from UI records will underestimate employment and earnings. Hotz and Scholz (2001) compare UI records to survey data and estimate that the gap in work covered by Unemployment Insurance is at least 13 percent, and that the understatement of reported wages may be 11 to 14 percent. This may account for a portion of the disparity between youth earnings in the state analyses, which are based on UI data, and youth earnings in the national analysis, which are based on NLSY survey data. In addition, since UI data is collected at the state level, employment for youth who move out of state or who live in a state but work across the border would not appear in the data. The net effect of this limitation is that the analyses are likely to underestimate employment and earnings among the study samples. This problem does not apply to youth who migrate across counties within a state, only for those who leave the state.

Another limitation of the UI data is that they report individual quarterly earnings, rather than wage rates or job histories. Researchers are therefore unable to distinguish between a high-paying job that lasts only a small portion of a quarter and a low-paying job that is held by a youth for the entire quarter. While this is a limitation, the models are still able to predict the total resources a youth has available at a given time. For this population, a measure of total resources available is likely to be more significant in determining well-being and labor market success than a measure of job quality, such as the wage rate.

Finally, the UI data do not provide information on other resources youth might have available to them. UI data only provide information on individual earnings. A youth may also benefit from the earnings of a spouse or other family member, or a roommate during the study period, although these resources will not be captured in the UI data. Youth also might receive income benefits from other service programs, like TANF, SSI, or Social Security.

National Longitudinal Survey of Youth 1997 (NLSY97)

The NLSY97 was used in this study to create baseline estimates of employment outcomes for all youth nationally. The NLSY97 is a national probability sample of approximately 9,000 youth born in the years 1980 through 1984. The youth were first interviewed in 1997 and have been interviewed on an annual basis since. The most recently available data were collected in 2004-2005, representing the eighth round of interviewing. The NLSY97 is available in public-use form via the Internet. For the purpose of this study, we selected youth born in 1980, making them age 18 as of December 31, 1998, a comparable age group to the child welfare population being examined. We restricted the sample to those youth who were interviewed in all eight rounds and were observed through their 24th birthday, using panel weights to account for non-response across the years. This resulted in a sample of 878 youth used for the analysis. The work histories in the NLSY97 were reconstructed on a quarterly basis, and used to construct employment and earnings outcomes.

Wage rates were constructed by multiplying the "usual" wage received at a given employer by the number weeks worked in the quarter for that employer. Wage rates across all employers during a given week were summed. The average wage across all jobs held in a given week was multiplied by the total number of "usual" hours worked for that week at all jobs generating weekly earnings. Weekly earnings were summed across the thirteen weeks of each quarter to create quarterly earnings. The distributions of earnings for each quarter were trimmed, deleting the top and bottom 1% of all positive earnings for that quarter.

Monthly histories of TANF receipt came from the income section of the NLSY97. Gender and race/ethnicity were assigned based on the first round interview data. Rural status was assigned based on the youth's location at the time of their 1997 interview.

Measurement error exists in the calculated earnings measures. Self-reported wages, hours, and weeks of employment are subject to various types of response error. In addition to the usual errors in survey data, our calculation method led to two other types of error. For one, NLSY97 respondents report their "usual" wage and "usual" weekly hours at the interview date. This information is updated at each interview, but interim changes in wage rates or hours worked are not captured. Most likely the wage rate is higher than was received over the entire interview period, leading to upward bias in wage rates. Varying hours worked or changes from part time to full time (or vice versa) could happen at any time, so the measurement error in hours worked may not be biased. Second, we used the average hourly wage for all jobs held in a given week. For youth with multiple jobs with a high degree of variance in their wage rates, the average wage will not be accurate if hours worked differ significantly across the different jobs. However, an inspection of the data indicated that (a) only a small percentage of youth held multiple jobs concurrently, and (b) variation in wage rates across multiple jobs was typically low. This type of measurement error may not be biased, though it is likely that higher wage concurrent jobs are associated with fewer hours, leading to upward bias in the earnings measure.

More jobs are covered by the NLSY97 than by the UI data, because the NLSY97 is not restricted to employment covered by the unemployment insurance program. However, retrospective reporting of job histories can be subject to various response errors. In addition to recall errors, respondents tend not to report short jobs, especially if they are sufficiently in the past. They also tend to merge two employment spells into one, reporting a longer time period with a given employer. While typically not a major source of error, these situations occur more with youth and anyone with a series of short-term jobs.

Supplemental Data

Several additional data sources were used to capture local labor market conditions, such as the local unemployment rate and cost of living. These data were linked with youth based on their county of residence.

- *Fair Market Rent:* The cost of living varies widely, not only across regions of the country, but also across communities within a state. Nationally measured income thresholds, such as the federal poverty level, cannot capture this variability and are often determined independently of market conditions. This study uses the Department of Housing and Urban Development's (HUD) annual fair market rent (FMR) for an efficiency apartment as a market-based, local, cost of living threshold. FMRs are set at the 40th percentile of the rent distribution for standard quality rental housing units in a county. HUD uses these FMRs to determine payment amounts for low-income housing vouchers, renewal rents for Section 8 housing, and to serve as a rental ceiling for the HOME rental assistance program. FMRs are reported annually at the county level, at http://www.huduser.org/datasets/fmr/fmrs/select_geography.odb.
  The FMR-based cost of living threshold used in this study for county i in year t is equal to (10/3) x (FMRit). This is the income level at which 30 percent of earnings will be spent on rent if that rent is at HUD's reported FMR level. This measure uses the 30 percent figure to scale monthly income, because many HUD housing assistance programs require that beneficiaries spend 30 percent of their income on rent before receiving assistance (Department of Housing and Urban Development, 2007). The FMR cost of living measure therefore reflects both local market heterogeneity, and income thresholds for important federal, means-tested assistance programs.
  This measure is used in this study in bivari-ate analyses to determine the portion of youth who age out of foster care and youth from low-income families that do not earn a living wage. FMR-based cost of living thresholds were not produced for the national, NLSY97 comparison sample because local geographic information is not available in the NLSY97. Calculating a national cost of living threshold from local FMRs to use with the national comparison sample would defeat the purpose of using a heterogeneous measure of the cost of living.
- *County Unemployment Rates:* County unemployment rates are used as a control variable in models predicting employment outcomes. These rates are produced monthly at the county level by the Bureau of Labor Statistics' Local Area Unemployment Statistics (LAUS) program. These monthly figures are combined to produce mean quarterly unemployment rates by county.

Both the FMRs and the local unemployment rates are county based, and they are linked to sample youth using indicators for county of removal (for the child welfare sample), or county where TANF grant was received (for low-income comparison sample). A small limitation of this data is that this linking will inaccurately represent local economic conditions if the youth moves out of the county over the course of the study.

Another limitation of the local unemployment rates is that they are produced using a different definition of unemployment than the employment indicators for the study youth. The

Bureau of Labor Statistics (BLS) considers an individual "unemployed" if they are not working and they are actively seeking employment. Individuals who are not seeking employment are considered to be out of the labor force, and are not included in the unemployment rate (BLS 2005). However, since there is no indication in the data of whether a study youth is seeking employment or not, all youth who are not employed are assumed to be "unemployed" for the purposes of the analysis. In other words, the employment variables in this study consider voluntary and involuntary unemployment to be the same phenomenon; the BLS data only counts involuntary unemployment.

Sample and Variable Creation

The sample of interest, youth aging out of foster care, was created, and comparable samples of youth from low-income families and youth nationally were also developed. Variables were created for the analyses to measure outcomes and provide information on demographic characteristics and case history characteristics.

Sample Creation

Comparable samples were created for youth who age out of foster care, youth from low-income families, and a national sample of youth.

- *Age Out Youth:* The sample includes all youth who were 17 years old and in a child welfare placement on December 31, 1998, who later age out of care or emancipate from care. Initially, all youth ages 16 through 18 who were in a child welfare placement on December 31, 1998, were selected. However, it was decided to only include youth who were 17 years old on December 31, 1998, for two reasons. First, most youth who age out leave care on or shortly after their 18th birthday. An 18-year-old cohort would disproportionately sample youth who stay in care for an extended period of time because these youth are in care in December, 1998, after their 18th birthday, by definition of the sample. By sampling 17-year-olds, the age out cohort will represent the correct distribution of youth who stay in care past their 18th birthday and youth who exit care on or soon after their birthday. Second, the 16-year-old cohort was not used because these youth would only be 23 in the latest year for which UI data was available. Given ASPE's interest in employment outcomes for youth in their mid-twenties, and that sample sizes for the 17-year-old cohort were sufficient, only 17-year-olds were used.

  One bias to be aware of with this sample is that youth in care for an extended period of time may be over-represented. Since the selection of the sample is anchored to a single point in time, December 31, 1998, youth who are in care for an extended period of time will be disproportionately selected, relative to youth who spend only a short time in care. The characteristics of youth who stay in the child welfare system for an extended period of time may be different from youth with shorter placement histories, and these may be correlated with the outcome variables. It is difficult to determine the direction of the potential bias. Findings might be biased in a negative direction as youth in care longer may fare worse on employment outcomes.

However, it might also be argued that youth in care longer receive more supports and may fare better, which would bias findings in the other direction.

Researchers also elected to anchor outcomes for these youth at particular ages rather than at a certain number of years post-discharge from care, as prior studies have done. Depending on when they discharge, youth could be different ages at five years after discharging from care. For example, youth who discharge at 18 would be 23, but youth who discharge at 20 would be 25, which could affect outcomes as a 25-year-old likely earns more on average than a 23-year-old. Hence, in the models, outcomes are assessed at particular ages and the age at discharge is included as a control.

Defining this sample also presented some challenges. In a very small number of cases, the case was never closed but the youth were presently 24 years old. In these cases a discharge age of 19 is used. Another issue in defining this population occurs when youth emancipate but go to live with their biological families. It is likely that most of these youth are classified in data systems as having aged out of care. There may be some cases, however, where the caseworker indicated the discharge reason was reunified because the youth was living with family. It is not possible to identify when this occurs, so samples for this study do not include these youth.

- *Low-Income Youth:* A comparable sample of youth from low-income families was created by selecting all youth age 17 on December 31, 1998, who were listed as a dependent on a family TANF grant.
- *National Youth:* This sample included youth age 18 in 1998 in the NLSY97. To follow youth for a sufficient number of years in the NLSY97, a cohort of 18-year-olds had to be used rather than 17-year-olds. These youth are not exiting from a system around age 18, so it is less important to pick them up prior to 18. It is also unlikely that there would be major differences in the economy in a one year span that would dramatically affect youth's labor market experiences. Specifically, when looking at earnings at age 20, it would be 2001 for the youth who age out and low-income youth but 2002 for the NLSY sample.

Researchers also attempted to compare youth who aged out of foster care to those who exited from foster care for other reasons. Specifically, a group of youth who had reunified was created as well as groups that had experienced a planned exit (i.e., adoption or guardianship) or unplanned exit (i.e., hospitalization, incarceration, or runaway). There were some significant limitations to using these groups, however. Most importantly, given the short observation period, they are not truly representative of youth that may have experienced a particular outcome. For example, reunified youth would not be representative of all reunified youth given only those who reunified after age 16 would be included in the sample. To say that reunified youth had better or worse employment outcomes than youth who age out would not be accurate, as the reunified group would be missing a substantial portion of the youth who had the outcome of reunification, but at an earlier age. This is not a problem for youth who age out of care, as that outcome only occurs at age 18 or later. Another limitation of the other child welfare groups is that to create a long enough observation period at all, the 16-year-old cohort has to be used. For these youth, employment data is only available through age 23.

Variable Creation

Variables were created to capture employment outcomes, case history, and demographic characteristics. For the most part, outliers were kept in the data and not adjusted. Analyses suggested that the results of the study were not sensitive to outliers in the data. In one exception, a youth had a very high number of placements, which appeared to be the result of rotating between placements. For this youth only, the number of unique placements was used as the total number of placements.

- *Employment Variables*: Three types of employment variables are created to measure employment, earnings, and stability (or the regularity of employment).
- *Employment*—UI data provide quarterly earnings information for sample youth. A youth is considered employed in a quarter if he or she has non-zero earnings during that quarter. When UI data are missing for a youth, it is assumed that the youth was not employed in that quarter.
- *Earnings*—Earnings from multiple jobs are aggregated, so all sources of wage income are included in a single earnings variable. Earnings are annualized from the quarterly UI data by summing the earnings of the four quarters subsequent to the quarter of the youth's birthday. For example, a youth's earnings in the year between age 18 and 19 are defined as the earnings in the first quarter subsequent to the quarter of the youth's 18th birthday, as well as the following three quarters. Average monthly earnings were calculated by dividing annual earnings by twelve. Quarters with zero earnings are included in the calculation of average monthly earnings, as well as quarters with zero earnings. Since periods of non-employment are included in the average monthly earnings measure, this measure does not provide information on time spent working. Furthermore, wage rates cannot be calculated from UI data because the data do not report how many hours were worked in a given quarter; they only report total earnings.
- *Stability*—Stability is measured using four consecutive quarters of employment or portion of quarters employed in a year. Time until four consecutive quarters of employment begins its count in the quarter subsequent to the quarter of the youth's 18th birthday.
- *Case History Variables:* Variables were created to capture age at exit, age at first removal from care, reasons for the most recent removal, total number of removals, number of placements total for all removals, cumulative months in care, and last known placement type. For some variables, discrepancies between the states had to be resolved. For example, placement types for children in care were collapsed into several major categories for the analyses (see Table 6). In addition, episodes were excluded from the construction of the case history variables if the episode lasted less than eight days. A single placement was excluded if it lasted less than twenty-four hours.
- *Demographic Variables:* Demographic information included gender, race/ethnicity, a measure of urbanicity, and employment prior to age 18. There were a few instances where state differences arose.

  Race/Ethnicity—In North Carolina and Minnesota, most racial categories had such a small sample size that they could not be included in the multivariate analysis. In these states, the racial categories were collapsed into "White, non-Hispanic," "African American," and "Other non-White."

Urbanicity—County of residence was derived from the county where a youth spent their most recent placement, in the case of the child welfare sample, and the county where a youth received their TANF grant for the low-income comparison sample. In North Carolina and Minnesota, these counties were classified as being "rural" or "not rural," based on their population size. Counties were considered rural if they have a population of less than 100,000. In California urbanicity is conceptualized as Los Angeles and other. Prior research using similar data in California suggests the importance of this differentiation.

Analyses

Bivariate analyses were conducted to describe the demographic and case history characteristics of the samples. These analyses were also used to profile the employment outcomes at each age for the different groups. Multivariate analyses were used 1) to look at differences between employment outcomes for the different groups, controlling for demographic factors and 2) to look at the demographic and case history factors that affect employment outcomes for youth aging out of foster care.

Bivariate Analysis

Means, medians, standard deviations, and frequencies were produced when relevant on all employment, case history, and demographic variables for the youth who age out of foster care, the low-income comparison sample, and the national comparison group.

The age-out youth and low-income youth samples were further sub-divided into youth who had worked at some point between age 18 and 24 and youth who had not worked between ages 18 and 24. These sub-divided samples were analyzed separately in the bivariate and multivariate analyses. Including the groups together would weight the samples heavily toward zero. The report focuses on the sample of youth who worked. Given the small sample sizes for the sample of youth that did not work, estimates for this group are not presented. This group is included in the trajectory analysis, however, which is described below.

Table 6. Placement Type Categories

Placement Type	Detailed Placements Included
Foster Family Home – Relative	Relative Home, Tribal Specified Home
Foster Family Home – Non-Relative	Agency Foster Family Home, Foster Family Agency Certified Home
Group Home	Small Family Home, Group Home, County Shelter
Other	Medical Facility, Adoptive Placement, Guardian Home, and Unspecified (child in open placement episode, but not out of home placement)
Supervised Independent Living	Supervised Independent Living (NC and MN only)

While youth may have worked at some point between ages 18 and 24, they might have no earnings for some extended period. When a youth has no earnings for an entire year, these years of non-employment are still included in the calculation of means and medians in the bivariate analysis. Since youth who age out and low-income youth may spend substantial portions of their early adulthood not employed, there is a strong positive skew to the distribution of the employment and earnings variables, with variable means typically exceeding medians.

Appendix tables A1 to A12 reporting bivariate results do not report categories with cell sizes smaller than 6 to protect the confidentiality of the sample youth. In these cases categories are collapsed to attain sufficient sample sizes. As a result, states may have different categories for some variables.

Multivariate Analysis

Two primary sets of multivariate models were run to assess differences on employment outcomes for youth who age out of foster care and low-income youth and to determine factors associated with employment outcomes for youth who aged out.

- *Comparing Youth Who Aged Out and Low-Income Youth:* A first set of models was developed to compare differences between employment outcomes at age 24 for youth who age out of foster care and youth from low-income families. These models controlled for demographic factors, prior employment, and the unemployment rate in the youth's county at the time of exit (see tables A12-A14 in the Appendix for more details on the model specifications). The universe for these models included the samples of youth who age out and youth from low-income families. A dummy variable for being from a low-income family was used to indicate differences between the two samples. Different model specifications were used depending on the particular outcome. Cox proportional hazard models were used to measure the effect of the independent variables on the relative risk of being employed for four consecutive quarters by age 24. Logit models were estimated to determine the effect of these independent variables on the likelihood of being employed at age 24. Ordinary least squares (OLS) regressions were used to predict the effect of the independent variables on the natural logarithm of average monthly earnings at age 24. By using the natural logarithm of average monthly earnings instead of level measures of earnings, the regressions are able to predict the percentage change in the earnings as a result of a change in the independent variables.
- *Determining Factors Associated with Employment Outcomes for Youth Who Aged Out*: A second set of models was estimated to look at the demographic and case history factors that affect employment outcomes for youth who age out of foster care. These models included case history and demographic factors to predict employment outcomes (see tables A16-A18 in the Appendix for more details on the model specifications). The models also controlled for prior employment and the unemployment rate in the youth's county at the time of exit. The universe for these models included just the sample of youth who age out of foster care. As with the first set of models, hazard models were used to predict four consecutive quarters of

employment by at 24, logit models were used to predict likelihood of being employed at age 24, and OLS models were used to predict earnings at age 24.

It is very likely that siblings may be in the child welfare and low-income comparison sample together, introducing autocorrelation into the error terms of the multivariate analyses. Unfortunately, sibling identifiers are not available in the child welfare administrative data, so the autocorrela-tion cannot be corrected in the analyses. The effect of the failure to correct for the inclusion of siblings in the data is that standard errors will be underestimated.

There are also likely to be many important omitted variables that are correlated with the outcome variables. It is not possible to control for a youth's history of education or incarceration, nor it is possible to identify the receipt of any social services besides TANF payments (even TANF grants are only included in the bivariate analyses, since they are not available in California). In addition, information is not available on pre-existing individual youth characteristics such as intelligence, motivation, and family background. In future research, these unobserved factors might be accounted for with the inclusion of child fixed effects in a longitudinal multivariate analysis. These fixed effects were not included in the analyses in this study because the employment outcomes are measured at age 24, rather than longitudinally. It is likely that our measure of work experience prior to age 18 may also control for a significant amount of unobserved, child-level characteristics that are correlated with employment from age 16 to 17 ("prior work experience"), as well as employment at age 24. To the extent that "prior work experience" is measuring these unobserved characteristics, readers should not interpret the effect of "prior work experience" in the model as a causal relationship between early employment and employment during the mid-twenties. It is possible that merely being employed between ages 16 and 17 has no effect on later employment at all, but that youth who typically find employment earlier in their lives have other, unobserved qualities that cannot be reproduced or induced but that do improve later prospects of working.

A final issue with the multivariate analyses is the potential for overlap between the sample of youth who age out and the sample of youth from low-income families. Generally, families with a child that has been placed in foster care often lose their eligibility for TANF. As a result, very few foster youth should also be dependents on a TANF grant. Researchers did in fact find that only a very small portion of these samples overlapped in North Carolina and California, and these cases were removed from the sample of youth from low-income families. Researchers suspect the overlap is likely due to cases moving in and out of child welfare. Specifically, in some instances, TANF cases may be kept open while parents try to reunify with their children. The Urban Institute did not have identifying information for the Minnesota samples, so it was not possible to check for overlap for this state.

Group Based Trajectory Analysis

In many cases, a population does not follow a single pattern of some type of behavior. Several distinct patterns may exist simultaneously in the population. By relying entirely on mean employment rates, or on models that predict individual deviations from these mean outcomes, an analysis may not accurately describe the heterogeneity of patterns in a population. To capture different employment patterns in the study, researchers used the group based trajectory analysis method developed by Nagin (1999) and his colleagues. Trajectory analysis uses maximum likelihood estimation to identify which distinct cubic functions of age are best suited to describe the actual employment trajectories of sample youth. Parameter estimates for these functions were produced using PROC TRAJ, a SAS macro developed by Bobby Jones (Jones, Nagin, and Roeder, 2001). The correct number of groups specified in the model is determined jointly with the Bayesian Information Criterion estimates (indicators of model fit produced by PROC TRAJ), and *a priori* theoretical knowledge of meaningful trajectory groups.

A major advantage of trajectory analysis over other methods of pattern recognition (such as cluster analysis) is that measures of statistical significance can be produced for parameters that describe the trajectory groups. Confidence intervals for the entire trajectory (as opposed a single parameter in the time function) were also derived using Taylor Series linearization, also known as the Delta Method. A four group solution to the group based trajectory analysis was used in California and Minnesota, and a five group solution was used in North Carolina.

TABLES APPENDIX

Note: Cell sizes less than 5 are not reported, with the exception of the missing category.

Table A1. CA: Demographic Characteristics

	Age-Out Age 17 on December 31, 1998, and employed between ages 18 & 24			**Low-Income Age 17 on December 31, 1998, and employed between ages 18 & 24**		
Sample Size	N			N		
	2,697			43,725		
Gender	n	p	sd	n	p	sd
Male	1,082	0.40	0.01	21,201	0.48	0.00
Female	1,614	0.60	0.01	22,524	0.52	0.00
Missing	1	0.00	0.00	0	0.00	0.00
Race/ Ethnicity	n	p	sd	n	p	sd
Black	1,036	0.38	0.01	7,782	0.18	0.00
White	874	0.32	0.01	10,041	0.23	0.00
Asian or Pacific Islander	66	0.02	0.00	9,251	0.21	0.00
Hispanic	697	0.26	0.01	16,070	0.37	0.00
Native American	22	0.01	0.00	260	0.01	0.00
Missing	2	0.00	0.00	321	0.01	0.00
Removed in Los Angeles? (CA Only)	n	p	sd	n	p	sd
Yes	1,078	0.40	0.01	15,528	0.36	0.00
Removed in a rural county?	n	p	sd	n	p	sd
Yes						

Table A2. MN: Demographic Characteristics

	Age-Out Age 17 on December 31, 1998, and employed between ages 18 & 24			Low-Income Age 17 on December 31, 1998, and employed between ages 18 & 24		
Sample Size		N			N	
		320			4,786	
Gender	n	p	sd	n	p	sd
Male	164	0.51	0.03	2,439	0.51	0.01
Female	156	0.49	0.03	2,347	0.49	0.01
Race/ Ethnicity	n	p	sd	n	p	sd
Black	45	0.14	0.02	1,179	0.25	0.01
White	219	0.68	0.03	2,018	0.42	0.01
Asian or Pacific Islander	26	0.08	0.02	849	0.18	0.01
Hispanic	10	0.03	0.01	316	0.07	0.00
Other	19	0.06	0.01	406	0.08	0.00
Missing	1	0.00	0.00	18	0.00	0.00
Removed in Los Angeles?	n	p	sd	n	p	sd
Yes						
Removed in a rural county?	n	p	sd	n	p	sd
Yes	163	0.51	0.03	1,631	0.34	0.01

Table A3. NC: Demographic Characteristics

	Age-Out Age 17 on December 31, 1998, and employed between ages 18 & 24			Low-Income Age 17 on December 31, 1998, and employed between ages 18 & 24		
Sample Size		N			N	
		284			2,709	
Gender	n	p	sd	n	p	sd
Male	135	0.48	0.03	1,217	0.45	0.01
Female	149	0.52	0.03	1,492	0.55	0.01
Race/ Ethnicity	n	p	sd	n	p	sd
Black	137	0.48	0.03	1,953	0.72	0.01
White	127	0.45	0.03	586	0.22	0.01
Other	20	0.07	0.02	170	0.06	0.00
Removed in Los Angeles?	n	p	sd	n	p	sd
Yes						
Removed in a rural county?	n	p	sd	n	p	sd
Yes	108	0.38	0.03	1,193	0.44	0.01

Table A4. CA: Case History

	Age-Out 17 years old on December 31, 1998, and employed between ages 18 & 24		
Sample Size	N		
	2,697		
Age at Exit	**n**	**p**	**sd**
17	408	0.15	0.01
18	1,807	0.67	0.01
19	403	0.15	0.01
20 and older	79	0.03	0.00
Age at First Removal	**n**	**p**	**sd**
Under 2	24	0.01	0.00
Ages 2-6	508	0.19	0.01
Ages 7-9	572	0.21	0.01
Ages 10 or 11	288	0.11	0.01
Ages 12 or 13	394	0.15	0.01
Ages 14 or 15	580	0.22	0.01
Ages 16 or 17	331	0.12	0.01
Reasons for Most Recent Removal	**n**	**p**	**sd**
Physical Abuse	321	0.12	0.01
Sexual Abuse	229	0.08	0.01
Neglect	1,546	0.57	0.01
Other	173	0.06	0.00
Missing	428	0.16	0.01
Total Number of Episodes (Removals)	**n**	**p**	**sd**
1	1791	0.66	0.01
2	539	0.20	0.01
3	179	0.07	0.00
4	96	0.04	0.00
5	35	0.01	0.00
6 or more	57	0.02	0.00
Number of Placements (All Episodes) (Continuous)	**mean**	**median**	**sd**
	5	3.00	4.06
Cumulative Months in Out of Home Care (Continuous)	**mean**	**median**	**sd**
	83	75.00	49.23
Last Known Placement Type	**n**	**p**	**sd**
Foster Family Home - Relative	1,022	0.38	0.01
Foster Family Home - Non-Relative	859	0.32	0.01
Group Home/Institution	606	0.22	0.01
Supervised Independent Living			
Other	210	0.08	0.01

Table A5. MN: Case History

	Age-Out 17 years old on December 31, 1998, and employed between ages 18 & 24		
Sample Size	**N**		
	320		
Age at Exit	**n**	**p**	**sd**
17	65	0.20	0.02
18	189	0.59	0.03
19	49	0.15	0.02
20 and older	17	0.05	0.01
Age at First Removal	**n**	**p**	**sd**
Under 2	8	0.03	0.01
Ages 2-6	33	0.10	0.02
Ages 7-9	31	0.10	0.02
Ages 10 or 11	39	0.12	0.02
Ages 12 or 13	59	0.18	0.02
Ages 14 or 15	77	0.24	0.02
Ages 16 or 17	73	0.23	0.02
Reasons for Most Recent Removal	**n**	**p**	**sd**
Physical Abuse	25	0.08	0.02
Sexual Abuse	20	0.06	0.01
Neglect	145	0.45	0.03
Other	126	0.39	0.03
Missing	4	0.01	0.01
Total Number of Episodes (Removals)	**n**	**p**	**sd**
1 or more*	320	1.00	0.00
Number of Placements (All Episodes) (Continuous)	**mean**	**median**	**sd**
	6	4	5.31
Cumulative Months in Out of Home Care (Continuous)	**mean**	**median**	**sd**
	59	45.66	45.53
Last Known Placement Type	**n**	**p**	**sd**
Foster Family Home – Relative	41	0.13	0.02
Foster Family Home – Non-Relative	169	0.53	0.03
Group Home/ Institution	39	0.12	0.02
Supervised Independent Living	31	0.10	0.02
Other	20	0.06	0.01
Missing	20	0.06	0.01

*Most youth had only one episode.

Table A6. NC: Case History

	Age-Out 17 years old on December 31, 1998, and employed between ages 18 & 24		
Sample Size	**N**		
	284		
Age at Exit	**n**	**p**	**sd**
17	16	0.06	0.01
18	222	0.78	0.02
19	21	0.07	0.02
20	11	0.04	0.01
21	14	0.05	0.01
Age at First Removal	**n**	**p**	**sd**
Ages 0-6	27	0.10	0.02
Ages 7-9	51	0.18	0.02
Ages 10 or 11	28	0.10	0.02
Ages 12 or 13	55	0.19	0.02
Ages 14 or 15	64	0.23	0.02
Ages 16 or 17	59	0.21	0.02
Reasons for Most Recent Removal	**n**	**p**	**sd**
Physical Abuse	29	0.10	0.02
Sexual Abuse	13	0.05	0.01
Neglect	200	0.70	0.03
Other	42	0.15	0.02
Total Number of Episodes (Removals)	**n**	**p**	**sd**
1	238	0.84	0.02
2	37	0.13	0.02
3	9	0.03	0.01
Number of Placements (All Episodes)	**mean**	**median**	**sd**
	8.43	6.00	6.62
Cumulative Months in Out of Home Care	**mean**	**median**	**sd**
	67	55.50	45.41
Last Known Placement Type	**n**	**p**	**sd**
Foster Family Home - Relative	27	0.10	0.02
Foster Family Home - Non-Relative	113	0.40	0.03
Group Home/ Institution	85	0.30	0.03
Supervised Independent Living	24	0.08	0.02
Other	35	0.12	0.02

Table A7. CA: Employment Characteristics

	Age-Out 17 years old on December 31, 1998, and employed between ages 18 & 24			Low-Income Age 17 on December 31, 1998, and employed between ages 18 & 24		
Sample Size	**N**			**N**		
	2,697			43,725		
Average monthly earnings at age (dollars):	**mean**	**median**	**sd**	**mean**	**median**	**sd**
16	16.95	0.00	129.24	18.54	0.00	137.84
17	64.39	0.00	500.50	57.12	0.00	180.71
18	127.21	9.58	403.44	130.02	3.83	258.43
19	283.49	125.13	445.44	332.35	171.90	436.75
20	420.52	191.55	705.63	504.62	302.46	594.34
21	470.11	153.80	895.98	599.16	342.67	718.86
22	523.31	141.84	953.76	705.63	408.56	848.15
23	584.96	118.74	928.57	819.31	488.48	998.40
24	687.64	166.63	1,075.82	971.97	602.28	1,131.04
Ever employed at age:	**n**	**p**	**sd**	**n**	**p**	**sd**
16	310	0.11	0.01	5,431	0.12	0.00
17	836	0.31	0.01	13,550	0.31	0.00
18	1,431	0.53	0.01	22,240	0.51	0.00
19	2,072	0.77	0.01	33,084	0.76	0.00
20	2,021	0.75	0.01	34,182	0.78	0.00
21	1,845	0.68	0.01	32,908	0.75	0.00
22	1,764	0.65	0.01	32,269	0.74	0.00
23	1,689	0.63	0.01	32,079	0.73	0.00
24	1,677	0.62	0.01	32,169	0.74	0.00
Number of quarters employed at age:	**mean**	**median**	**sd**	**mean**	**median**	**sd**
16	0.18	0.00	0.57	0.20	0.00	0.65
17	0.63	0.00	1.12	0.66	0.00	1.16
18	1.21	1.00	1.42	1.20	1.00	1.45
19	2.06	2.00	1.52	2.08	2.00	1.55
20	2.16	2.00	1.60	2.35	3.00	1.60
21	1.98	2.00	1.65	2.30	3.00	1.65
22	1.93	2.00	1.69	2.31	3.00	1.68
23	1.87	2.00	1.71	2.34	3.00	1.69
24	1.92	2.00	1.75	2.40	3.00	1.71
Age when first employed	**mean**	**median**	**sd**	**mean**	**median**	**sd**
	18.46	18.00	1.02	18.46	18.00	1.01

Table A7. (Continued)

	Age-Out 17 years old on December 31, 1998, and employed between ages 18 & 24			Low-Income Age 17 on December 31, 1998, and employed between ages 18 & 24		
Ever employed for four consecutive quarters as of age:	**n**	**p**	**sd**	**n**	**p**	**sd**
19	711	0.26	0.01	12,325	0.28	0.00
20	1,260	0.47	0.01	22,363	0.51	0.00
21	1,537	0.57	0.01	27,465	0.63	0.00
22	1,736	0.64	0.01	30,556	0.70	0.00
23	1,847	0.68	0.01	32,957	0.75	0.00
24	1,939	0.72	0.01	34,948	0.80	0.00
Receipt of TANF at age:	**n**	**p**	**sd**	**n**	**p**	**sd**
19						
20						
21						
22						
23						
24						
Total number of quarters received TANF:	**mean**	**median**	**sd**	**mean**	**median**	**sd**
Earned Fair Market Rent Income Level at age:	**n**	**p**	**sd**	**n**	**p**	**sd**
19	38	0.01	0.00	788	0.02	0.00
20	85	0.03	0.00	1,951	0.04	0.00
21	121	0.04	0.00	3,057	0.07	0.00
22	127	0.05	0.00	3,553	0.08	0.00
23	149	0.06	0.00	4,528	0.10	0.00
24	177	0.07	0.00	5,550	0.13	0.00

Table A8. MN: Employment Characteristics

	Age-Out 17 years old on December 31, 1998, and employed between ages 18 & 24			Low-Income Age 17 on December 31, 1998, and employed between ages 18 & 24		
Sample Size	**N**			**N**		
	320			4,786		
Average monthly earnings at age (dollars):	**mean**	**median**	**sd**	**mean**	**median**	**sd**
16	20.16	0.00	51.89	36.22	0.00	82.52
17	81.82	16.07	129.09	128.89	45.26	183.40
18	153.39	81.25	201.38	219.80	267.44	121.60
19	238.45	145.46	288.80	394.72	444.95	255.12
20	329.06	133.39	469.71	532.66	320.65	599.47

Table A8. (Continued)

	Age-Out 17 years old on December 31, 1998, and employed between ages 18 & 24			Low-Income Age 17 on December 31, 1998, and employed between ages 18 & 24		
Average monthly earnings at age (dollars):	**mean**	**median**	**sd**	**mean**	**median**	**sd**
21	339.54	132.77	489.05	584.66	300.88	700.10
22	412.59	83.88	614.18	659.74	321.72	790.51
23	465.49	706.06	84.15	743.28	381.07	880.21
24	573.52	163.84	814.00	863.37	463.14	1,180.16
Ever employed at age:	**n**	**p**	**sd**	**n**	**p**	**sd**
16	82	0.26	0.02	1,740	0.36	0.01
17	182	0.57	0.03	3,064	0.64	0.01
18	216	0.68	0.03	3,571	0.75	0.01
19	255	0.80	0.02	4,002	0.84	0.01
20	236	0.74	0.02	3,883	0.81	0.01
21	230	0.72	0.03	3,627	0.76	0.01
22	205	0.64	0.03	3,475	0.73	0.01
23	200	0.63	0.03	3,427	0.72	0.01
24	209	0.65	0.03	3,418	0.71	0.01
Number of quarters employed at age:	**mean**	**median**	**sd**	**mean**	**median**	**sd**
16	0.50	0.00	1.02	0.73	0.00	1.17
17	1.32	1.00	1.43	1.61	1.00	1.52
18	1.86	2.00	1.60	2.06	2.00	1.56
19	2.14	2.00	1.49	2.43	3.00	1.48
20	2.05	2.00	1.60	2.45	3.00	1.56
21	1.93	2.00	1.55	2.27	3.00	1.62
22	1.83	2.00	1.67	2.22	3.00	1.67
23	1.83	2.00	1.69	2.25	3.00	1.70
24	2.02	2.00	1.72	2.30	3.00	1.72
Age when first employed	**mean**	**median**	**sd**	**mean**	**median**	**sd**
	18.56	18.00	1.07	18.46	18.00	0.94
Ever employed for four consecutive quarters as of age:	**n**	**p**	**sd**	**n**	**p**	**sd**
19	85	0.27	0.02	1,685	0.35	0.01
20	143	0.45	0.03	2,677	0.56	0.01
21	173	0.54	0.03	3,089	0.65	0.01
22	197	0.62	0.03	3,376	0.71	0.01
23	205	0.64	0.03	3,567	0.75	0.01
24	224	0.70	0.03	3,747	0.78	0.01

Table A8. (Continued)

	Age-Out 17 years old on December 31, 1998, and employed between ages 18 & 24			Low-Income Age 17 on December 31, 1998, and employed between ages 18 & 24		
Receipt of TANF at age:	**n**	**p**	**sd**	**n**	**p**	**sd**
19-20	7	0.02	0.01	1,357	0.28	0.01
21	6	0.02	0.01	844	0.18	0.01
22	8	0.03	0.01	914	0.19	0.01
23	6	0.02	0.01	898	0.19	0.01
24	7	0.02	0.01	749	0.16	0.01
Total number of quarters received TANF:	**mean**	**median**	**sd**	**mean**	**median**	**sd**
	0.28	0.00	1.94	2.87	0.00	5.76
Earned Fair Market Rent Income Level at age:	**n**	**p**	**sd**	**n**	**p**	**sd**
19-20	24	0.08	0.01	970	0.20	0.01
21	23	0.07	0.01	807	0.17	0.01
22	37	0.12	0.02	844	0.18	0.01
23	42	0.13	0.02	936	0.20	0.01
24	53	0.17	0.02	1,103	0.23	0.01

Table A9. NC: Employment Characteristics

	Age-Out 17 years old on December 31, 1998, and employed between ages 18 & 24			Low-Income Age 17 on December 31, 1998, and employed between ages 18 & 24		
Sample Size	**N**			**N**		
	284			2,709		
Average monthly earnings at age (dollars):	**mean**	**median**	**sd**	**mean**	**median**	**sd**
16	50.45	0.00	162.86	22.58	0.00	103.06
17	94.56	7.74	191.21	88.87	8.67	166.10
18	175.87	97.70	267.15	159.39	62.28	287.47
19	253.43	114.89	337.21	280.77	155.29	345.30
20	298.66	103.41	407.37	372.18	192.19	460.17
21	347.12	70.28	494.46	388.83	156.52	510.17
22	406.40	130.40	624.34	420.67	138.51	592.95
23	409.74	48.42	669.07	484.70	163.40	667.01
24	451.31	65.05	724.28	568.01	225.84	749.34
Ever employed at age:	**n**	**p**	**sd**	**n**	**p**	**sd**
16	78	0.27	0.03	621	0.23	0.01
17	148	0.52	0.03	1,432	0.53	0.01
18	226	0.80	0.02	1,863	0.69	0.01

Table A9. (Continued)

	Age-Out 17 years old on December 31, 1998, and employed between ages 18 & 24			Low-Income Age 17 on December 31, 1998, and employed between ages 18 & 24		
Ever employed at age:	**n**	**p**	**sd**	**n**	**p**	**sd**
19	230	0.81	0.02	2,176	0.80	0.01
20	207	0.73	0.03	2,074	0.77	0.01
21	178	0.63	0.03	1,905	0.70	0.01
22	187	0.66	0.03	1,791	0.66	0.01
23	171	0.60	0.03	1,807	0.67	0.01
24	173	0.61	0.03	1,831	0.68	0.01
Number of quarters employed at age:	**mean**	**median**	**sd**	**mean**	**median**	**sd**
16	0.56	0.00	1.10	0.38	0.00	0.82
17	1.18	1.00	1.39	1.24	1.00	1.43
18	1.98	2.00	1.37	1.73	2.00	1.51
19	2.26	2.00	1.49	2.22	2.00	1.50
20	2.07	2.00	1.60	2.22	2.00	1.58
21	1.85	2.00	1.70	2.02	2.00	1.65
22	1.86	2.00	1.64	1.95	2.00	1.68
23	1.78	1.50	1.71	2.00	2.00	1.70
24	1.75	1.00	1.68	2.09	2.00	1.71
Age when first employed	**mean**	**median**	**sd**	**mean**	**median**	**sd**
	18.34	18.00	0.83	18.43	18.00	1.00
Ever employed for four consecutive quarters as of age:	**n**	**p**	**sd**	**n**	**p**	**sd**
19	128	0.45	0.03	1,202	0.44	0.01
20	159	0.56	0.03	1,525	0.56	0.01
21	175	0.62	0.03	1,701	0.63	0.01
22	193	0.68	0.03	1,817	0.67	0.01
23	201	0.71	0.03	1,927	0.71	0.01
24	202	0.71	0.03	1,952	0.72	0.01
Receipt of TANF at age:	**n**	**p**	**sd**	**n**	**p**	**sd**
19	11	0.04	0.01	364	0.13	0.01
20	22	0.08	0.02	363	0.13	0.01
21	24	0.08	0.02	356	0.13	0.01
22	25	0.09	0.02	381	0.14	0.01
23	21	0.07	0.02	342	0.13	0.01
24	20	0.07	0.02	279	0.10	0.01
Total number of quarters received TANF:	**mean**	**median**	**sd**	**mean**	**median**	**sd**
	1.05	0.00	3.05	1.98	0.00	4.24

Table A9. (Continued)

	Age-Out 17 years old on December 31, 1998, and employed between ages 18 & 24			Low-Income Age 17 on December 31, 1998, and employed between ages 18 & 24		
Earned Fair Market Rent Income Level at age:	**n**	**p**	**sd**	**n**	**p**	**sd**
19	6	0.02	0.01	61	0.02	0.00
20	10	0.04	0.01	144	0.05	0.00
21	13	0.05	0.01	193	0.07	0.00
22	15	0.05	0.01	236	0.09	0.01
23	24	0.08	0.02	321	0.12	0.01
24	27	0.10	0.02	367	0.14	0.01

Table A10. CA Trajectory Group Characteristics: Demographic, Case History, and Employment

	NEVER CONNECTED			LATER CONNECTED			CONSISTENTLY CONNECTED			INITIALLY CONNECTED		
Sample Size	**1,058**			**626**			**797**			**682**		
DEMOGRAPHICS												
Gender	**n**	**p**	**sd**	**n**	**p**	**sd**	**n**	**p**	**sd**	**n**	**p**	**sd**
Male	429	0.41	0.02	276	0.44	0.02	300	0.38	0.02	275	0.40	0.02
Female	628	0.59	0.02	350	0.56	0.02	497	0.62	0.02	407	0.60	0.02
Missing	1	0.00	0.00	0	0.00	0.00	0	0.00	0.00	0	0.00	0.00
Race/ Ethnicity	n	p	sd	n	p	sd	n	p	sd	n	p	sd
Black	447	0.42	0.02	264	0.42	0.02	261	0.33	0.02	258	0.38	0.02
White	341	0.32	0.01	173	0.28	0.02	275	0.35	0.02	242	0.35	0.02
Hispanic	240	0.23	0.01	168	0.27	0.02	231	0.29	0.02	156	0.23	0.02
Other	30	0.03	0.01	21	0.03	0.01	28	0.04	0.01	26	0.04	0.01
Missing	0	0.00	0.00	0	0.00	0.00	2	0.00	0.00	0	0.00	0.00
Removed in Los Angeles	**n**	**p**	**sd**	**n**	**p**	**sd**	**n**	**p**	**sd**	**n**	**p**	**sd**
Yes	445	0.42	0.02	282	0.45	0.02	318	0.40	0.02	230	0.34	0.02
Removed in a Rural County	**n**	**p**	**sd**	**n**	**p**	**sd**	**n**	**p**	**sd**	**n**	**p**	**sd**
Yes												
CASE HISTORY												
Age at Exit	**n**	**p**	**sd**	**n**	**p**	**sd**	**n**	**p**	**sd**	**n**	**p**	**sd**
17	153	0.14	0.01	71	0.11	0.01	128	0.16	0.01	130	0.19	0.02
18	708	0.67	0.01	414	0.66	0.02	549	0.69	0.02	447	0.66	0.02
19	157	0.15	0.01	114	0.18	0.02	105	0.13	0.01	89	0.13	0.01
20 and older	40	0.04	0.01	27	0.04	0.01	15	0.02	0.00	16	0.02	0.01

Table A10. (Continued)

	NEVER CONNECTED			LATER CONNECTED			CONSISTENTLY CONNECTED			INITIALLY CONNECTED		
Age at First Removal	**n**	**p**	**sd**	**n**	**p**	**sd**	**n**	**p**	**sd**	**n**	**p**	**sd**
Ages 0-6	233	0.22	0.01	143	0.23	0.02	131	0.16	0.01	140	0.21	0.02
Ages 7-9	218	0.21	0.01	128	0.20	0.02	187	0.23	0.02	135	0.20	0.02
Ages 10 or 11	134	0.13	0.01	68	0.11	0.01	94	0.12	0.01	59	0.09	0.01
Ages 12 or 13	140	0.13	0.01	95	0.15	0.01	109	0.14	0.01	106	0.16	0.01
Ages 14 or 15	195	0.18	0.01	128	0.20	0.02	167	0.21	0.01	160	0.23	0.02
Ages 16 or 17	138	0.13	0.01	64	0.10	0.01	109	0.14	0.01	82	0.12	0.01
Reasons for Most Recent Removal	**n**	**p**	**sd**	**n**	**p**	**sd**	**n**	**p**	**sd**	**n**	**p**	**sd**
Physical Abuse	132	0.12	0.01	79	0.13	0.01	86	0.11	0.01	88	0.13	0.01
Sexual Abuse	79	0.07	0.01	56	0.09	0.01	77	0.10	0.01	54	0.08	0.01
Neglect	623	0.59	0.02	356	0.57	0.02	451	0.57	0.02	392	0.57	0.02
Other	69	0.07	0.01	32	0.05	0.01	57	0.07	0.01	42	0.06	0.01
Missing	155	0.15	0.01	103	0.16	0.01	126	0.16	0.01	106	0.16	0.01
Total Number of Episodes (Removals)	**n**	**p**	**sd**	**n**	**p**	**sd**	**n**	**p**	**sd**	**n**	**p**	**sd**
1	653	0.62	0.01	419	0.67	0.02	575	0.72	0.02	443	0.65	0.02
2	212	0.20	0.01	126	0.20	0.02	134	0.17	0.01	150	0.22	0.02
3	91	0.09	0.01	40	0.06	0.01	46	0.06	0.01	43	0.06	0.01
4	43	0.04	0.01	26	0.04	0.01	24	0.03	0.01	22	0.03	0.01
5 or more	59	0.06	0.01	15	0.02	0.01	18	0.02	0.01	24	0.04	0.01
Number of Placements (All Episodes)	**mean**	**median**	**sd**	**mean**	**median**	**sd**	**mean**	**median**	**sd**	**mean**	**median**	**sd**
	5.50	4.00	4.92	4.38	3.00	3.66	3.83	3.00	3.29	4.74	3.00	4.15

Table A10. (Continued)

	NEVER CONNECTED			LATER CONNECTED			CONSISTENTLY CONNECTED			INITIALLY CONNECTED		
Cumulative Months in Out of Home Care	**mean**	**median**	**sd**	**mean**	**median**	**sd**	**mean**	**median**	**sd**	**mean**	**median**	**sd**
	84.82	79.00	49.19	87.59	79.00	49.62	81.61	76.00	49.19	82.14	70.00	49.88
Last Known Placement Type	**n**	**p**	**sd**	**n**	**p**	**sd**	**n**	**p**	**sd**	**n**	**p**	**sd**
Foster Family Home - Relative	350	0.33	0.01	256	0.41	0.02	314	0.39	0.02	253	0.37	0.02
Foster Family Home - Non-Relative	273	0.26	0.01	203	0.32	0.02	265	0.33	0.02	226	0.33	0.02
Group Home/ Institution	373	0.35	0.01	120	0.19	0.02	143	0.18	0.01	147	0.22	0.02
Other	62	0.06	0.01	47	0.08	0.01	75	0.09	0.01	56	0.08	0.01
EMPLOYMENT CHARACTERISTICS												
Average Monthly Earnings at Age	**mean**	**median**	**sd**	**mean**	**median**	**sd**	**mean**	**median**	**sd**	**mean**	**median**	**sd**
16	4.75	0.00	49.50	8.04	0.00	90.33	28.79	0.00	189.17	23.15	0.00	126.17
17	11.85	0.00	91.25	9.50	0.00	32.44	130.50	0.00	882.49	86.39	0.00	261.13
18	21.07	0.00	63.31	27.77	0.00	120.04	231.51	88.65	638.04	184.35	72.18	342.86
19	28.75	0.00	75.45	92.80	18.67	150.95	529.89	417.43	584.08	372.04	252.34	445.92
20	22.43	0.00	78.16	185.34	50.07	295.59	868.23	734.96	1,016.77	443.42	265.51	511.81
21	17.50	0.00	110.28	284.55	104.68	427.10	1,095.92	963.24	1,335.99	290.02	106.82	464.78
22	13.44	0.00	79.98	463.32	235.64	587.29	1,249.23	1,040.79	1,372.69	163.45	4.93	325.72
23	9.16	0.00	55.78	580.00	368.87	631.47	1,434.28	1,270.23	1,173.17	90.52	0.00	252.94
24	24.13	0.00	134.47	742.16	487.30	798.57	1,579.91	1,374.93	1,379.10	154.34	0.00	407.18

Table A10. (Continued)

	NEVER CONNECTED			LATER CONNECTED			CONSISTENTLY CONNECTED			INITIALLY CONNECTED		
Ever Employed for Four Consecutive Quarters as of Age	**n**	**p**	**sd**	**n**	**p**	**sd**	**n**	**p**	**sd**	**n**	**p**	**sd**
19	8	0.01	0.00	29	0.05	0.01	407	0.51	0.02	267	0.39	0.02
20	30	0.03	0.01	115	0.18	0.02	677	0.85	0.01	438	0.64	0.02
21	38	0.04	0.01	231	0.37	0.02	764	0.96	0.01	504	0.74	0.02
22	46	0.04	0.01	371	0.59	0.02	795	1.00	0.00	524	0.77	0.02
23	49	0.05	0.01	474	0.76	0.02	796	1.00	0.00	528	0.77	0.02
24	57	0.05	0.01	551	0.88	0.01	797	1.00	0.00	534	0.78	0.02
Total Number of Quarters Received TANF	**mean**	**median**	**sd**	**mean**	**median**	**sd**	**mean**	**median**	**sd**	**mean**	**median**	**sd**
Earned Fair Market Rent Income Level at Age	**n**	**p**	**sd**	**n**	**p**	**sd**	**n**	**p**	**sd**	**n**	**p**	**sd**
24	sample size too small to report			32	0.05	0.01	136	0.17	0.01	6	0.01	0.00
Probability of Employment at Age and Quarter	**Predicted probability**			**Predicted probability**			**Predicted probability**			**Predicted probability**		
Age 16-Q2	0.03			0.04			0.15			0.09		
Age 16-Q3	0.04			0.05			0.21			0.15		
Age 16-Q4	0.06			0.06			0.27			0.24		
Age 17-Q1	0.07			0.08			0.34			0.34		
Age 17-Q2	0.09			0.10			0.41			0.43		
Age 17-Q3	0.10			0.12			0.49			0.51		

Table A10. (Continued)

	NEVER CONNECTED	LATER CONNECTED	CONSISTENTLY CONNECTED	INITIALLY CONNECTED
Probability of Employment at Age and Quarter	**Predicted probability**	**Predicted probability**	**Predicted probability**	**Predicted probability**
Age 17-Q4	0.11	0.14	0.56	0.57
Age 18-Q1	0.12	0.17	0.62	0.61
Age 18-Q2	0.12	0.20	0.68	0.64
Age 18-Q3	0.12	0.22	0.73	0.66
Age 18-Q4	0.12	0.25	0.77	0.67
Age 19-Q1	0.11	0.28	0.81	0.66
Age 19-Q2	0.10	0.31	0.83	0.65
Age 19-Q3	0.09	0.34	0.86	0.63
Age 19-Q4	0.08	0.37	0.88	0.60
Age 20-Q1	0.07	0.40	0.89	0.56
Age 20-Q2	0.07	0.43	0.90	0.52
Age 20-Q3	0.06	0.45	0.91	0.48
Age 20-Q4	0.05	0.47	0.92	0.43
Age 21-Q1	0.04	0.50	0.93	0.38
Age 21-Q2	0.04	0.52	0.93	0.34
Age 21-Q3	0.04	0.54	0.94	0.29
Age 21-Q4	0.03	0.56	0.94	0.26
Age 22-Q1	0.03	0.58	0.94	0.23
Age 22-Q2	0.03	0.59	0.94	0.20
Age 22-Q3	0.03	0.61	0.94	0.18
Age 22-Q4	0.03	0.63	0.94	0.17
Age 23-Q1	0.03	0.65	0.94	0.16
Age 23-Q2	0.03	0.66	0.94	0.16

Table A10. (Continued)

	NEVER CONNECTED	LATER CONNECTED	CONSISTENTLY CONNECTED	INITIALLY CONNECTED
Probability of Employment at Age and Quarter	**Predicted probability**	**Predicted probability**	**Predicted probability**	**Predicted probability**
Age 23-Q3	0.04	0.68	0.93	0.16
Age 23-Q4	0.04	0.69	0.93	0.17
Age 24-Q1	0.05	0.71	0.92	0.18

Table A11. MN Trajectory Group Characiteristics: Demographic, Case History, and Employment

	NEVER CONNECTED			LATER CONNECTED			CONSISTENTLY CONNECTED			INITIALLY CONNECTED		
Sample Size	**106**			**77**			**81**			**106**		
						DEMOGRAPHICS						
Gender	**n**	**p**	**sd**	**n**	**P**	**sd**	**n**	**p**	**sd**	**n**	**p**	**sd**
Male	63	0.59	0.05	41	0.53	0.06	31	0.38	0.05	58	0.55	0.05
Female	43	0.41	0.05	36	0.47	0.06	50	0.62	0.05	48	0.45	0.05
Race/ Ethnicity	n	p	sd	n	P	sd	n	p	sd	n	p	sd
Black	9	0.08	0.03	9	0.12	0.04	6	0.07	0.03	24	0.23	0.04
White	78	0.74	0.04	49	0.64	0.05	62	0.77	0.05	69	0.65	0.05
Asian or Pacific Islander	12	0.11	0.03	7	0.09	0.03	6	0.07	0.03	6	0.06	0.02
Other	7	0.07	0.02	12	0.16	0.04	7	0.09	0.03	6	0.06	0.02
Missing	0	0.00	0.00	0	0.00	0.00	0	0.00	0.00	1	0.01	0.01
Removed in Los Angeles	**n**	**p**	**sd**	**n**	**P**	**sd**	**n**	**p**	**sd**	**n**	**p**	**sd**
Yes												
Removed in a Rural County	**n**	**p**	**sd**	**n**	**p**	**sd**	**n**	**p**	**sd**	**n**	**p**	**sd**
Yes	73	0.69	0.04	49	0.64	0.05	40	0.49	0.06	46	0.43	0.05
						CASE HISTORY						
Age at Exit	**n**	**p**	**sd**	**n**	**p**	**sd**	**n**	**p**	**sd**	**n**	**p**	**sd**
17	34	0.32	0.05	15	0.19	0.05	15	0.19	0.04	22	0.21	0.04
18	52	0.49	0.05	47	0.61	0.06	46	0.57	0.06	64	0.60	0.05
19 and older	20	0.19	0.04	15	0.19	0.05	20	0.25	0.05	20	0.19	0.04
Age at First Removal	n	p	sd	n	p	sd	n	p	sd	n	p	sd
Ages 0-9	22	0.21	0.04	18	0.23	0.05	22	0.27	0.05	25	0.24	0.04
Ages 10 or 11	22	0.21	0.04	9	0.12	0.04	7	0.09	0.03	8	0.08	0.03
Ages 12 or 13	19	0.18	0.04	11	0.14	0.04	17	0.21	0.05	20	0.19	0.04

Table A11. (Continued)

	NEVER CONNECTED			LATER CONNECTED			CONSISTENTLY CONNECTED			INITIALLY CONNECTED		
Ages 14 or 15	17	0.16	0.04	20	0.26	0.05	18	0.22	0.05	29	0.27	0.04
Ages 16 or 17	26	0.25	0.04	19	0.25	0.05	17	0.21	0.05	24	0.23	0.04
Reasons for Most Recent Removal	**n**	**p**	**sd**	**n**	**p**	**sd**	**n**	**p**	**sd**	**n**	**p**	**sd**
Physical or Sexual Abuse	9	0.08	0.03	11	0.14	0.04	17	0.21	0.05	10	0.09	0.03
Neglect	38	0.36	0.05	34	0.44	0.06	41	0.51	0.06	46	0.43	0.05
Other	57	0.54	0.05	31	0.40	0.06	23	0.28	0.05	48	0.45	0.05
Missing	2	0.02	0.01	1	0.01	0.01	0	0.00	0.00	2	0.02	0.01
Total Number of Episodes (Removals)	**n**	**p**	**sd**	**n**	**p**	**sd**	**n**	**p**	**sd**	**n**	**p**	**sd**
1 or more*	106	1.00	0.00	77	1.00	0.00	81	1.00	0.00	106	1.00	0.00
Number of Placem-ents (All Episodes)	mean	median	sd	mean	median	sd	mean	median	sd	mean	median	sd
	4.97	3.00	4.20	6.51	5.00	5.88	4.53	4.00	4.17	6.42	4.50	5.96
Cumulative Months in Out of Home Care	mean	median	sd	mean	median	sd	mean	median	sd	mean	median	sd
	61.31	50.35	47.77	56.11	41.32	46.93	64.44	50.26	47.21	59.47	44.61	47.26
Last Known Placement Type	**n**	**p**	**sd**	**n**	**p**	**sd**	**n**	**p**	**sd**	**n**	**p**	**sd**
Foster Family Home - Relative	12	0.11	0.03	11	0.14	0.04	11	0.14	0.04	12	0.11	0.03
Foster Family Home – Non-Relative	46	0.43	0.05	37	0.48	0.06	51	0.63	0.05	58	0.55	0.05
Other	43	0.41	0.05	24	0.31	0.05	16	0.20	0.04	27	0.25	0.04
Missing	5	0.05	0.02	5	0.06	0.03	3	0.04	0.02	9	0.08	0.03

Table A11. (Continued)

	NEVER CONNECTED			LATER CONNECTED			CONSISTENTLY CONNECTED			INITIALLY CONNECTED		
	EMPLOYMENT CHARACTERISTICS											
Average Monthly Earnings at Age	**mean**	**median**	**sd**	**mean**	**median**	**sd**	**mean**	**median**	**sd**	**mean**	**median**	**sd**
16	9.40	0.00	34.19	12.04	0.00	45.22	29.91	0.00	62.98	20.67	0.00	49.59
17	12.73	0.00	42.50	22.18	0.00	47.74	146.97	116.66	159.72	107.21	50.35	139.24
18	11.92	0.00	42.71	32.07	0.00	56.71	279.32	234.81	221.37	219.28	179.49	210.83
19	17.73	0.00	44.33	136.29	35.22	289.93	467.10	439.62	302.50	246.18	220.21	225.20
20	23.18	0.00	102.34	192.04	83.68	283.14	804.64	647.72	623.67	215.82	107.10	247.68
21	11.75	0.00	46.12	298.64	201.79	290.58	830.92	715.13	633.40	161.40	39.12	290.87
22	5.04	0.00	26.04	546.33	342.03	578.68	998.16	962.36	726.65	80.91	0.00	159.27
23	8.07	0.00	38.66	623.09	422.96	705.71	1,148.70	1,037.75	792.19	66.79	0.00	166.18
24	26.87	0.00	149.02	706.14	364.30	773.57	1,329.47	1,170.42	945.99	175.65	0.00	342.47
Ever Employed for Four Consecutive Quarters as of Age	**n**	**p**	**sd**	**n**	**p**	**sd**	**n**	**p**	**sd**	**n**	**p**	**sd**
24	sample size too small to report			70	0.91	0.03	81	1.00	0.00	68	0.64	0.05
Total Number of Quarters Received TANF	**mean**	**median**	**sd**	**mean**	**median**	**sd**	**mean**	**median**	**sd**	**mean**	**median**	**sd**
	0.11	0.00	1.17	0.27	0.00	1.70	0.23	0.00	1.65	0.36	0.00	2.42
Earned Fair Market Rent Income Level at Age	**n**	**p**	**sd**	**n**	**p**	**sd**	**n**	**p**	**sd**	**n**	**p**	**sd**
24	sample size too small to report			15	0.19	0.05	34	0.42	0.05	sample size too small to report		
Probability of Empl-oyment at Age and Quarter	**Predicted probability**			**Predicted probability**			**Predicted probability**			**Predicted probability**		
Age 16-Q2	0.07	0.12	0.33	0.34								

Table A11. (Continued)

	NEVER CONNECTED	LATER CONNECTED	CONSISTENTLY CONNECTED	INITIALLY CONNECTED
Probability of Empl-oyment at Age and Quarter	**Predicted probability**	**Predicted probability**	**Predicted probability**	**Predicted probability**
Age 16-Q3	0.08	0.13	0.43	0.43
Age 16-Q4	0.09	0.13	0.52	0.50
Age 17-Q1	0.10	0.14	0.60	0.56
Age 17-Q2	0.10	0.15	0.67	0.61
Age 17-Q3	0.10	0.16	0.73	0.64
Age 17-Q4	0.10	0.17	0.77	0.65
Age 18-Q1	0.10	0.18	0.80	0.66
Age 18-Q2	0.09	0.20	0.82	0.66
Age 18-Q3	0.09	0.21	0.84	0.65
Age 18-Q4	0.08	0.23	0.85	0.63
Age 19-Q1	0.08	0.25	0.86	0.60
Age 19-Q2	0.07	0.28	0.87	0.57
Age 19-Q3	0.06	0.30	0.88	0.53
Age 19-Q4	0.06	0.33	0.88	0.49
Age 20-Q1	0.05	0.35	0.88	0.45
Age 20-Q2	0.05	0.38	0.88	0.40
Age 20-Q3	0.04	0.40	0.88	0.36
Age 20-Q4	0.04	0.43	0.88	0.32
Age 21-Q1	0.04	0.45	0.88	0.28
Age 21-Q2	0.03	0.47	0.87	0.25
Age 21-Q3	0.03	0.49	0.87	0.22
Age 21-Q4	0.03	0.50	0.87	0.20
Age 22-Q1	0.03	0.52	0.87	0.19
Age 22-Q2	0.03	0.52	0.87	0.18
Age 22-Q3	0.03	0.53	0.87	0.17

Table A11. (Continued)

	NEVER CONNECTED	LATER CONNECTED	CONSISTENTLY CONNECTED	INITIALLY CONNECTED
Probability of Empl-oyment at Age and Quarter	**Predicted probability**	**Predicted probability**	**Predicted probability**	**Predicted probability**
Age 22-Q4	0.04	0.53	0.87	0.18
Age 23-Q1	0.04	0.53	0.88	0.18
Age 23-Q2	0.05	0.52	0.88	0.20
Age 23-Q3	0.05	0.50	0.89	0.22
Age 23-Q4	0.07	0.48	0.90	0.26
Age 24-Q1	0.08	0.46	0.91	0.32

Table A12. NC Trajectory Group Characteristics: Demographic, Case History, and Employment

	NEVER CONNECTED			LATER CONNECTED			CONSISTENTLY CONNECTED			INITIALLY CONNECTED-LOW			INITIALLY CONNECTED-HIGH		
Sample Size	76			54			57			97			63		
DEMOGRAPHICS															
Gender	**n**	**p**	**sd**	**n**	**p**	**sd**	**n**	**p**	**sd**	**n**	**p**	**sd**	**n**	**p**	**sd**
Male	47	0.62	0.06	28	0.52	0.07	15	0.26	0.06	52	0.54	0.05	32	0.51	0.06
Female	29	0.38	0.06	26	0.48	0.07	42	0.74	0.06	45	0.46	0.05	31	0.49	0.06
Race/ Ethnicity	n	p	sd	n	p	sd	ns	p	sd	n	p	sd	n	p	sd
White	37	0.49	0.06	22	0.41	0.07	29	0.51	0.07	44	0.45	0.05	28	0.44	0.06
Other	39	0.51	0.06	32	0.59	0.07	28	0.49	0.07	53	0.55	0.05	35	0.56	0.06
Removed in Los Angeles	n	p	sd	n	p	sd	n	p	sd	n	p	sd	n	p	sd
Yes															
Removed in a Rural County	n	p	sd	n	p	sd	n	p	sd	n	p	sd	n	p	sd
Yes	31	0.41	0.06	23	0.43	0.07	22	0.39	0.06	39	0.40	0.05	18	0.29	0.06
CASE HISTORY															
Age at Exit	n	p	sd	n	p	sd	n	p	sd	n	p	sd	n	p	sd
17-18	69	0.91	0.03	41	0.76	0.06	48	0.84	0.05	91	0.94	0.02	47	0.75	0.05
19-23	7	0.09	0.03	13	0.24	0.06	9	0.16	0.05	6	0.06	0.02	16	0.25	0.05
Age at First Removal	n	p	sd	n	p	sd	n	p	sd	n	p	sd	n	p	sd
Ages 0-9	30	0.39	0.06	19	0.35	0.06	11	0.19	0.05	23	0.24	0.04	21	0.33	0.06
Ages 14 or 15	12	0.16	0.04	7	0.13	0.05	14	0.25	0.06	27	0.28	0.05	15	0.24	0.05
Ages 16 or 17	10	0.13	0.04	7	0.13	0.05	14	0.25	0.06	22	0.23	0.04	10	0.16	0.05
Reasons for Most Recent Removal	**n**	**p**	**sd**	**n**	**p**	**sd**	**n**	**p**	**sd**	**n**	**p**	**sd**	**n**	**p**	**sd**
Physical Abuse and Sexual Abuse	10	0.13	0.04	9	0.17	0.05	13	0.23	0.06	14	0.14	0.04	3	0.05	0.03

Table A12. (Continued)

	NEVER CONNECTED			LATER CONNECTED			CONSISTENTLY CONNECTED			INITIALLY CONNECTED-LOW			INITIALLY CONNECTED-HIGH		
Neglect and Other	65	0.86	0.04	45	0.83	0.05	44	0.77	0.06	83	0.86	0.04	60	0.95	0.03
Missing	1	0.01	0.01	0	0.00	0.00	0	0.00	0.00	0	0.00	0.00	0	0.00	0.00
Total Number of Episodes (Removals)	**n**	**p**	**sd**	**n**	**p**	**sd**	**n**	**p**	**sd**	**n**	**p**	**sd**	**n**	**p**	**sd**
1	62	0.82	0.04	46	0.85	0.05	47	0.82	0.05	85	0.88	0.03	52	0.83	0.05
2 or more	14	0.18	0.04	8	0.15	0.05	10	0.18	0.05	12	0.12	0.03	11	0.17	0.05
Number of Placements (All Episodes)	mean	median	sd	mean	median	sd	mean	median	sd	mean	median	sd	mean	median	sd
	8.99	6.00	8.22	7.24	6.00	5.04	7.67	6.00	5.98	10.02	8.00	7.62	7.86	6.00	6.49
Cumulative Months in Out of Home Care	mean	median	sd	mean	median	sd	mean	median	sd	mean	median	sd	mean	median	sd
	75.26	67.00	42.40	88.00	83.50	52.79	60.26	49.00	38.57	59.55	47.00	42.30	70.52	61.00	43.71
Last Known Placement Type	n	p	sd	n	p	sd	n	p	sd	n	p	sd	n	p	sd
Foster Family Home – Relative and Non-Relative	38	0.50	0.06	33	0.61	0.07	28	0.49	0.07	45	0.46	0.05	26	0.41	0.06
Group Home/ Institution	20	0.26	0.05	11	0.20	0.05	18	0.32	0.06	33	0.34	0.05	20	0.32	0.06
Other	18	0.24	0.05	10	0.19	0.05	11	0.19	0.05	19	0.20	0.04	17	0.27	0.06

Table A12. (Continued)

	NEVER CONNECTED			**LATER CONNECTED**			**CONSISTENTLY CONNECTED**			**INITIALLY CONNECTED-LOW**			**INITIALLY CONNECTED-HIGH**		
Average Monthly Earn ings at Age (dollars):	mean	median	sd	mean	median	sd	mean	median	sd	mean	median	sd	mean	median	sd
16	2.94	0.00	22.36	18.11	0.00	61.70	72.93	0.00	206.35	58.70	0.00	185.89	55.06	0.00	154.43
17	0.73	0.00	4.64	36.69	0.00	75.47	173.71	85.65	277.84	92.25	5.03	204.11	95.63	36.50	131.24
18	5.35	0.00	24.39	71.91	28.55	113.77	280.20	255.03	251.43	109.86	71.33	157.37	302.05	186.12	414.61
19	2.84	0.00	15.59	145.25	42.50	206.18	519.70	425.02	387.77	119.90	50.67	186.79	359.71	253.24	407.55
20	2.18	0.00	16.38	234.12	63.16	367.11	671.97	554.75	484.53	78.86	9.33	165.32	413.65	292.73	386.92
21	0.09	0.00	0.82	316.44	100.66	407.93	860.27	793.04	573.87	28.48	0.00	92.90	471.28	382.14	469.36
22	0.00	0.00	0.00	571.05	423.37	535.01	946.02	789.24	660.11	41.56	0.00	105.99	422.64	242.68	767.53
23	0.00	0.00	0.00	751.37	571.21	709.27	1,079.19	844.61	816.40	21.73	0.00	108.99	193.20	39.60	401.04
24	1.69	0.00	14.75	905.27	805.56	803.23	1,071.04	868.27	876.49	67.48	0.00	191.94	183.54	17.41	463.64
Ever Emplo-yed for Four Consecutive Quarters as of Age	**n**	**p**	**sd**	**n**	**p**	**sd**	**n**	**p**	**sd**	**n**	**p**	**sd**	**n**	**p**	**sd**
19	0	0.00	0.00	14	0.26	0.06	45	0.79	0.05	25	0.26	0.04	44	0.70	0.06
20	0	0.00	0.00	27	0.50	0.07	52	0.91	0.04	26	0.27	0.04	54	0.86	0.04
21	0	0.00	0.00	35	0.65	0.06	56	0.98	0.02	27	0.28	0.05	57	0.90	0.04
22	0	0.00	0.00	46	0.85	0.05	57	1.00	0.00	31	0.32	0.05	59	0.94	0.03
23	0	0.00	0.00	53	0.98	0.02	57	1.00	0.00	32	0.33	0.05	59	0.94	0.03
24	0	0.00	0.00	53	0.98	0.02	57	1.00	0.00	33	0.34	0.05	59	0.94	0.03
Total Num-ber of Quar-ters Received TANF	mean	median	sd	mean	median	sd	mean	median	sd	mean	median	sd	mean	median	sd
	0.01	0.00	0.11	0.91	0.00	2.80	0.81	0.00	2.38	1.19	0.00	3.44	1.41	0.00	3.44

Table A12. (Continued)

	NEVER CONNECTED			LATER CONNECTED			CONSISTENTLY CONNECTED			INITIALLY CONNECTED-LOW			INITIALLY CONNECTED-HIGH		
Earned Fair Market Rent Income Level at Age	n	p	sd	n	p	sd	n	p	sd	n	p	sd	n	p	sd
24	0	0.00	0.00	13	0.24	0.06	13	0.23	0.06	0	0.00	0.00	sample size too small to	report	
Probability of Employment at Age and Quarter	**Predicted probability**			**Predicted probability**			**Predicted probability**			**Predicted probability**			**Predicted probability**		
Age 16-Q2	0.00			0.12			0.37			0.22			0.22		
Age 16-Q3	0.01			0.14			0.45			0.27			0.32		
Age 16-Q4	0.01			0.16			0.52			0.32			0.42		
Age 17-Q1	0.01			0.18			0.59			0.37			0.51		
Age 17-Q2	0.02			0.21			0.65			0.40			0.59		
Age 17-Q3	0.02			0.23			0.70			0.42			0.65		
Age 17-Q4	0.02			0.25			0.74			0.43			0.70		
Age 18-Q1	0.02			0.28			0.77			0.42			0.73		
Age 18-Q2	0.02			0.30			0.80			0.41			0.76		
Age 18-Q3	0.02			0.33			0.83			0.40			0.77		
Age 18-Q4	0.02			0.35			0.84			0.37			0.78		
Age 19-Q1	0.02			0.38			0.86			0.34			0.78		
Age 19-Q2	0.01			0.40			0.87			0.31			0.78		
Age 19-Q3	0.01			0.43			0.88			0.28			0.77		
Age 19-Q4	0.01			0.46			0.89			0.25			0.76		
Age 20-Q1	0.01			0.48			0.89			0.22			0.75		
Age 20-Q2	0.00			0.51			0.90			0.19			0.72		
Age 20-Q3	0.00			0.54			0.90			0.16			0.70		
Age 20-Q4	0.00			0.56			0.90			0.14			0.67		

Table A12. (Continued)

	NEVER CONNECTED	LATER CONNECTED	CONSISTENTLY CONNECTED	INITIALLY CONNECTED-LOW	INITIALLY CONNECTED-HIGH
Probability of Employment at Age and Quarter	**Predicted probability**	**Predicted probability**	**Predicted probability**	**Predicted probability**	**Predicted probability**
Age 21-Q1	0.00	0.59	0.91	0.12	0.63
Age 21-Q2	0.00	0.62	0.91	0.11	0.59
Age 21-Q3	0.00	0.64	0.91	0.10	0.55
Age 21-Q4	0.00	0.67	0.91	0.09	0.51
Age 22-Q1	0.00	0.69	0.90	0.08	0.46
Age 22-Q2	0.00	0.72	0.90	0.08	0.42
Age 22-Q3	0.00	0.74	0.90	0.08	0.38
Age 22-Q4	0.00	0.77	0.90	0.08	0.34
Age 23-Q1	0.00	0.79	0.90	0.09	0.31
Age 23-Q2	0.00	0.81	0.90	0.10	0.28
Age 23-Q3	0.00	0.84	0.89	0.12	0.25
Age 23-Q4	0.00	0.86	0.89	0.14	0.23
Age 24-Q1	0.01	0.87	0.89	0.18	0.22

Table A13. CA: Comparing Age-Out Youth and Low-Income Youth on Employment Outcomes

	Employment		Earnings		Stability			
	Ever Employed at Age 24		Natural Logarithm of Mean Monthly Earnings at Age 24		'Relative Risk' of Achieving 4 Consecutive Quarters of Employment by Age 24		Employed Four Consecutive Quarters at Age 24	
Model type	Logistic		OLS		Hazard		Logistic	
Sample Size	46,094		46,094		47,685		46,094	
Intercept	0.29	***	0.52	***			1.14	***
Female	1.10	***	-0.06	***	1.01		1.07	***
African American (white, reference)	0.97		-0.04	**	0.76	***	0.62	***
Native American (white, reference)	0.72	***	-0.17	***	0.78	***	0.66	***
Asian (white, reference)	1.49	***	0.09	***	0.97	**	1.15	***
Hispanic (white, reference)	1.32	***	0.02		1.07	***	1.19	***
Los Angeles	1.16	***	0.02	**	0.99		1.02	
Prior Work Experience (before age 18)	1.38	***	0.06	***	1.43	***	1.96	***
Unemployment Rate at Discharge Year					0.98	***		
Unemployment Rate at Age 23-24	0.99	*	-0.01	***			0.95	***
Number of Quarters Employed by Age 23			0.02	***				
Number of Quarters Employed Ages 23-24			1.68	***				
Low-Income (Age Out, reference)	1.56	***	0.11	***	1.41	***	1.39	***

Notes: Estimates reported in logistic regression and hazard models are odds ratios.
*Significance at the 10% level; ** significance at the 5% level; *** significance at the 1% level.

Table A14. MN: Comparing Age-Out Youth and Low-Income Youth on Employment Outcomes

	Employment		Earnings		Stability			
	Ever Employed at Age 24		Natural Logarithm of Mean Monthly Earnings at Age 24		'Relative Risk' of Achieving 4 Consecutive Quarters of mployment by Age 24		Employed Four Consecutive Quarters at Age 24	
Model Type	Logistic		OLS		Hazard		Logistic	
Sample Size	4,915		4,915		5,247		4,915	
Intercept	0.74	***	0.27	**			1.20	***

Table A14. (Continued)

	Employment		Earnings		Stability			
	Ever Employed at Age 24		Natural Logarithm of Mean Monthly Earnings at Age 24		'Relative Risk' of Achieving 4 Consecutive Quarters of mployment by Age 24		Employed Four Consecutive Quarters at Age 24	
Female	1.26	***	-0.10	***	1.13	***	1.36	***
African American (white, reference)	0.72	***	0.04		0.61	***	0.37	***
Other Race/Ethnicity (Non-White) (white, reference)	1.06		0.20	***	0.76	***	0.61	***
Rural	0.78	***	-0.04		0.82	***	0.68	***
Prior Work Experience (before age 18)	1.23	***	0.04		1.40	***	1.68	***
Unemployment Rate at Discharge Year					1.00			
Unemployment Rate at Age 23-24	0.96		0.00				0.93	
Number of Quarters Employed by Age 23			0.02	***				
Number of Quarters Employed Ages 23-24			1.69	***				
Low-Income (Age Out, reference)	1.30	**	0.17	***	1.45	***	1.66	***

Notes: Estimates reported in logistic regression and hazard models are odds ratios.
*Significance at the 10% level; ** significance at the 5% level; *** significance at the 1% level.

Table A15. NC: Comparing Age-Out Youth and Low-Income Youth on Employment Outcomes

	Employment		Earnings		Stability			
	Ever Employed at Age 24		Natural Logarithm of Mean Monthly Earnings at Age 24		'Relative Risk' of Achieving 4 Consecutive Quarters of Employment by Age 24		Employed Four Consecutive Quarters at Age 24	
Model Type	Logistic		OLS		Hazard		Logistic	
Sample Size	2,993		2,993		3,252		2,993	
Intercept	-0.56	**	0.42	***			-1.66	***
Female	1.81	***	-0.04		1.39	***	1.44	***
African American (white, reference)	1.17		-0.06		0.93		0.99	
Other Race/Ethnicity (Non-White) (white, reference)	0.97		-0.04		0.92		1.04	
Rural	1.01		-0.03		1.05		1.12	

Table A15. (Continued)

	Employment		Earnings		Stability			
	Ever Employed at Age 24		Natural Logarithm of Mean Monthly Earnings at Age 24		'Relative Risk' of Achieving 4 Consecutive Quarters of Employment by Age 24		Employed Four Consecutive Quarters at Age 24	
Prior Work Experience (before age 18)	1.19	***	-0.01		1.25	***	1.23	***
Unemployment Rate at Discharge Year					1.00			
Unemployment Rate at Age 23-24	1.08	**	0.01				1.04	
Number of Quarters Employed by Age 23			0.02	***				
Number of Quarters Employed Ages 23-24			1.66	***				
Low-Income (Age Out, reference)	1.24		0.04		1.18	**	1.43	**

Notes: Estimates reported in logistic regression and hazard models are odds ratios.
*Significance at the 10% level; ** significance at the 5% level; *** significance at the 1% level.

Table A16. CA: The Role of Child Welfare Factors in the Employment Experiences of Age-Out Youth

	Employment		Earnings		Stability			
	Ever Employed at Age 24		Natural Logarithm of Mean Monthly Earnings at Age 24		'Relative Risk' of Achieving 4 Consecutive Quarters of Employment by Age 24		Employed Four Consecutive Quarters at Age 24	
Model Type	Logistic		OLS		Hazard		Logistic	
Sample size	2,690		2,690		3,156		2,690	
Intercept	1.14		0.73				2.07	
Age at Discharge	0.98		-0.02		1.00		0.97	
Female	0.96		-0.04		0.97		0.88	
African American (white, reference)	1.05		0.01		0.87	**	0.82	*
Native American (white, reference)	1.06		-0.03		0.75		0.87	

Table A16. (Continued)

	Employment		Earnings		Stability			
	Ever Employed at Age 24		Natural Logarithm of Mean Monthly Earnings at Age 24		'Relative Risk' of Achieving 4 Consecutive Quarters of Employment by Age 24		Employed Four Consecutive Quarters at Age 24	
Asian (white reference)	1.25		0.10		1.34	**	3.44	***
Hispanic (white, reference)	1.20	*	0.01		1.07		1.18	
Los Angeles	1.36	***	0.07		0.98		1.03	
Physical Abuse (neglect, reference)	0.96		-0.06		1.07		1.31	*
Sexual Abuse (neglect, reference)	1.24		0.03		1.08		1.18	
Other Abuse (neglect, reference)	0.99		-0.07		1.01		0.97	
Foster Home – Relative (foster home—non-relative, reference)	1.02		-0.07		0.86	**	0.74	**
Group Home (foster home—non-relative, reference)	0.69	***	-0.14	**	0.64	***	0.53	***
Unspecified Exit (foster home—non-relative, reference)	0.68	***	-0.14	*	0.66	***	0.50	***
Other (foster home—non-relative, reference)	0.99		-0.21	***	1.05		1.15	
Total Number of Episodes	0.96		0.02		0.99		0.99	
Total Placements	0.96		-0.02		0.99		0.95	*
Total Placements, Squared	1.00		0.00		1.00		1.00	
Months in Care	1.00		0.00		1.00		1.00	
Prior Work Experience	1.42	***	0.03		1.78	***	1.91	***
Unemployment Rate at Discharge Year					0.98	**		
Unemployment Rate at Age 23-24	0.98		0.01				0.98	
Number of Quarters Employed by Age 23			0.02	***				
Number of Quarters Employed Ages 23-24			1.71	***				

Notes: Estimates reported in logistic regression and hazard models are odds ratios.
*Significance at the 10% level; ** significance at the 5% level; *** significance at the 1% level.

Table A17. MN: The Role of Child Welfare Factors in the Employment Experiences of Age-Out Youth

	Employment		Earnings		Stability			
	Ever Employed at Age 24		Natural Logarithm of Mean Monthly Earnings at Age 24		'Relative Risk' of Achieving 4 Consecutive Quarters of Employment by Age 24		Employed Four Consecutive Quarters at Age 24	
Model Type	Logistic		OLS		Hazard		Logistic	
Sample size	306		309		358		309	
Intercept	0.26		-2.82				-5.84	
Age at Discharge	1.01		0.10		1.22	**	1.38	
Female	1.71	**	-0.38	***	1.21		1.60	*
African American (white, reference)	1.06		0.45	**	0.83		0.85	
Other Race/Ethnicity (Non-White) (white, reference)	1.06		0.08		0.91		0.89	
Rural	2.34	***	0.23		0.84		1.72	*
Physical Abuse (neglect, reference)	1.39		0.03		1.32		1.19	
Sexual Abuse (neglect, reference)	0.25	***	-0.24		1.10		0.90	
Foster Home – Relative (foster home—non-relative, reference)	0.93		0.23		0.96		1.23	
Group Home (foster home—non-relative, reference)	0.57		-0.18		0.83		0.73	
Supervised Independent Living (foster home—non-relative, reference)	0.89		-0.24		1.01		0.94	
Unspecified Exit (foster home—non-relative, reference)	0.42		-0.12		1.00		0.86	
Other (foster home—non-relative, reference)	1.58		-0.89	***	0.47	**	0.52	
Total Number of Episodes			0.84	*	1.10		1.20	
Total Placements	0.87	**	-0.01		0.97		0.90	
Total Placements, Squared	1.00		0.00		1.00		1.00	
Months in Care	1.01		0.00		1.00		1.00	
Prior Work Experience	1.26		0.26	*	1.75	***	1.45	
Unemployment Rate at Discharge Year					1.07			
Unemployment Rate at Age 23-24	0.94		0.01				1.03	
Number of Quarters Employed by Age 23			0.08	***				
Number of Quarters Employed Ages 23-24			1.56	***				

Notes: Estimates reported in logistic regression and hazard models are odds ratios.
*Significance at the 10% level; ** significance at the 5% level; *** significance at the 1% level.

Table A18. NC: The Role of Child Welfare Factors in the Employment Experiences of Age-Out Youth

	Employment		Earnings		Stability			
	Ever Employed at Age 24		Natural Logarithm of Mean Monthly Earnings at Age 24		'Relative Risk' of Achieving 4 Consecutive Quarters of Employment by Age 24		Employed Four Consecutive Quarters At Age 24	
Model Type	Logistic		OLS		Hazard		Logistic	
Sample size	284		284		347		284	
Intercept	0.71		-0.50				-3.08	
Age at Discharge	0.98		0.04		1.24	**	1.15	
Female	1.44		-0.09		1.38	**	1.68	*
African American (white, reference)	0.97		-0.02		1.05		0.66	
Other Race/Ethnicity (Non-White) (white, reference)	0.80		0.02		1.59	*	1.16	
Rural	0.98		-0.08		0.95		0.88	
Physical Abuse (neglect, reference)	1.13		0.15		1.31		1.26	
Sexual Abuse (neglect, reference)	1.72		-0.34		0.75		1.14	
Other Abuse (neglect, reference)	0.51	*	-0.09		0.91		0.73	
Foster Home – Relative (foster home—non-relative, reference)	0.90		0.00		0.69		0.78	
Group Home (foster home—non-relative, reference)	0.72		-0.17		0.99		0.78	
Supervised Independent Living (foster home—non-relative, reference)	1.29		-0.02		1.04		0.73	
Unspecified Exit (foster home—non-relative, reference)	0.61		0.01		0.83		0.65	
Other (foster home—non-relative, reference)	0.94		0.01		0.81		0.51	
Total Number of Episodes	1.38		0.09		1.14		1.30	
Total Placements	0.97		-0.01		0.98		0.96	
Total Placements, Squared	1.00		0.00		1.00		1.00	
Months in Care	1.01		-0.00		1.00		1.01	
Prior Work Experience	1.14		0.03		1.27	***	1.13	
Unemployment Rate at Discharge Year					0.99			
Unemployment Rate at Age 23-24	0.92		0.04				0.86	

Table A18. (Continued)

	Employment		Earnings		Stability			
	Ever Employed at Age 24		Natural Logarithm of Mean Monthly Earnings at Age 24		'Relative Risk' of Achieving 4 Consecutive Quarters of Employment by Age 24		Employed Four Consecutive Quarters At Age 24	
Number of Quarters Employed by Age 23			0.02					
Number of Quarters Employed Ages 23-24			1.68	***				

Notes: Estimates reported in logistic regression and hazard models are odds ratios.
*Significance at the 10% level; ** significance at the 5% level; *** significance at the 1% level.

Table A19. NLSY97: Demographic & Employment Characteristics All youth age 18 in 1998 Observed Through their 24th Birthday (Weighted)

Sample Size	**878**		
DEMOGRAPHICS			
Gender	n	p	sd
Male	414	0.51	0.50
Female	464	0.49	0.50
Race/ Ethnicity	n	p	sd
Black	245	0.15	0.36
White	461	0.67	0.47
Native American	3	0.01	0.07
Asian or Pacific Islander	16	0.03	0.16
Hispanic	185	0.13	0.34
Other (includes multiracial)	8	0.01	0.11
EMPLOYMENT			
Average monthly earnings at age (dollars):	mean	median	sd
16	75	0	141
17	175	97	207
18	328	219	358
19	475	352	443
20	726	592	604
21	916	757	766
22	1024	854	869
23	1223	1107	997
24	1536	1398	1291

Table A19. (Continued)

Sample Size	878		
EMPLOYMENT			
Ever employed at age:	n	p	sd
16	354	0.46	0.50
17	542	0.68	0.47
18	625	0.76	0.43
19	742	0.87	0.34
20	862	0.99	0.12
21	805	0.93	0.26
22	794	0.92	0.27
23	790	0.91	0.28
24	792	0.92	0.28
Number of quarters employed at age:	mean	median	sd
16	1.09	0	1.46
17	1.94	2	1.63
18	2.37	3	1.65
19	2.83	4	1.44
20	3.35	4	1.04
21	3.29	4	1.21
22	3.3	4	1.25
23	3.31	4	1.29
24	3.36	4	1.25
Ever employed for four consecutive quarters as of age:	n	p	sd
19	386	0.48	0.50
20	597	0.71	0.46
21	729	0.85	0.36
22	769	0.89	0.31
23	797	0.92	0.27
24	822	0.95	0.23
Receipt of TANF at age:	n	p	sd
19	24	0.02	0.12
20	9	0.01	0.09
21	9	0.01	0.08
22	14	0.01	0.11
23	13	0.01	0.10
24	8	0.01	0.08

REFERENCES

Arnett, J. J. (2004). Adolescence and emerging adulthood: A cultural approach. Upper Saddle River, NJ: Prentice Hall.

Bureau of Labor Statistics. (2005). “BLS Glossary”,http://www.bls.gov/bls/glossary. htm#U.

Cook, R., Fleishman, E. & Grimes, V. (1991). A national evaluation of Title IV-E foster care independent living programs for youth: Phase 2. *Final report*, (Vol. *1*), Rockville, MD: Westat, Inc.

Courtney, M., Piliavin, I. & Grogan-Kaylor, A. (1998). The Wisconsin study of youth aging out of out-of-home care: A portrait of children about to leave care. (See an article covering this material in the Nov/ Dec 2001 issue of *Child Welfare*).

Courtney, M., Piliavin, I., Grogan–Kaylor, A. & Nesmith, A. (2001). Foster youth transitions to adulthood: A longitudinal view of youth leaving care. *Child Welfare, 80 (6)*, 685-715.

Courtney, M., Dworsky, A., Ruth, G., Keller, T., Havlicek, J. & Bost, N. (2005). *Midwest evaluation of the adult functioning of former foster youth: Outcomes at Age, 19*, Chapin Hall Working Paper.

Dworsky, A. (2005). The economic self-sufficiency of Wisconsin's former foster youth. *Children and Youth Services Review, 27*, 1085-1118.

Dworsky, A. & Courtney, M. E. (2001). Self-sufficiency of former foster youth in Wisconsin: Analysis of unemployment insurance wage data and public assistance data. Madison, WI: University of Wisconsin, Institute for Research on Poverty.

Festinger, T. (1983). No one ever asked us: *A postscript to foster care.* New York: Columbia University Press.

Gever, Matthew. (2007). *States Helping Foster Care Youth, After "Emancipation."* Washington, D.C.: National Conference of State Legislatures.

Goerge, R. M., Bilaver, L., Lee, B. J., Needell, B., Brookhart, A. & Jackman, W. (2002). Employment outcomes for youth aging out of foster care. Chicago, IL: Chapin Hall Center for Children at the University of Chicago.

Hotz, Joseph V. & Sholz, John Karl. (2001). "*Measuring Employment and Income for Low-Income Populations with Administrative and Survey Data*" Institute for Research on Poverty, Discussion Paper No. 1224-01.

Jones, B., Nagin, D. & Roeder, K. (2001). "A SAS Procedure Based on Mixture Models for Estimating Developmental Trajectories." *Sociological Method Research*, 29, 374-393.

McMillen, C. J. & Tucker, J. (1999). The status of older adolescents at exit from out-of-home care. *Child Welfare, 78*, 339-360.

Nagin, D., (1999). "Analyzing Developmental Trajectories: A Semi-parametric, Group-based Approach," *Psychological Methods*, *4*, 139-177.

Pecora, P., Kessler, R., Williams, J., O'Brien, K., Downs, A. & English, D., et al. (2003). *Improving family foster care: Findings from the Northwest Foster Care Alumni Study.* Seattle, WA: Casey Family Programs.

Pecora, P., Kessler, R., O'Brien, K., White, C., Williams, J., Hiripi, E., White, J. & Her-rick, M. A. (2006). Educational and employment outcomes of adults formerly placed in foster care: Results from the Northwest Foster Care Alumni Study. *Children and Youth Services Review, 28*(12), 1459-1481.

Singer, A. (2006). *Assessing outcomes of youth transitioning from foster care*. State of Utah: Department of Human Services. http://www.dhs.utah.gov/pdf/Assessing OutcomesofYouth_oct% 203.pdf

U.S. Census Bureau. (2007). "General Mobility, by Region, Sex, and Age: 2005 to 2006." http://www.census.gov/population/socdemo/migration/cps2006/tab01-1.xls

U.S. Department of Health and Human Ser-vices. (2006). Administration for Chil-dren and Families, Administration on Children Youth and Families, Children's Bureau, AFCARS Report.

U. S. Department of Housing and Urban Devel-opment. (2007). "Housing Choice Voucher Fact Sheet." http://www.hud.gov/offices/pih/programs/hcv/about/fact_sheet. cfm.

Wade, J. & Dixon, J. (2006). Making a home, finding a job: investigating early housing and employment outcomes for young people leaving care. *Child and Family Social Work, 11*, 199-208.

End Notes

[1] If a youth in the child welfare administrative data also appeared in the employment data, but with an invalid social security number, there was no way to distinguish whether that youth was unemployed or employed with an invalid number. These youth were included and considered unemployed.

[2] Average monthly earnings are calculated by dividing a youth's total annual earnings by 12. With this calculation, quarters in which a youth had zero earnings are included in this average. The average for the sample is the mean value of the monthly averages of all youth. Averaging quarterly earnings into a monthly measure assumes equal earnings each month, which may not be accurate. This, however, provides an approximation of a youth's monthly earnings.

[3] Each age is defined as the four quarters ending in the quarter with that birthday.

[4] Models include a measure of urbanicity. All national statistics are based on authors' calculations of the National Longitudinal Survey of Youth 1997.

[5] In North Carolina and Minnesota, counties were classified as being "rural" or "not rural" based on their population size. Counties are considered rural if they have a population of less than 100,000. In California urbanicity is conceptualized as Los Angeles and other. Prior research using similar data in California suggests the importance of this differentiation.

[6] This study defines a living wage using the Department of Housing and Urban Development's (HUD) annual fair market rent (FMR) as a market-based, local, cost of living threshold. The FMR-based cost of living threshold for county i in year t is equal to (10/3) x (FMRit). This is the income level at which 30 percent of earnings will be spent on rent if that rent is at HUD's reported FMR level. For context, the minimum wage in California increased from $5.15 to $5.75 on March 1, 1998, to $6.25 on January 1, 2001, and to $6.75 on January 1, 2002. In Minnesota, the minimum wage increased from $5.15 to $6.15 for large employers, and $5.25 for small employers in August 2005. In North Carolina, the minimum wage increased from $5.15 to $6.15 on January 1, 2007.

[7] In North Carolina a 5-group trajectory solution was used rather than a 4-group solution. This solution appeared to be a better fit with North Carolina's data. The classification of the five groups was similar to the other states, however, in that two of North Carolina's five groups exhibited the *initially connected* pattern.

[8] This may be due to several reasons, including that youth may have run away, been in a hospital, or been jail/detention. This included 17 percent of cases in California, 6 percent of cases in Minnesota, and 14 percent of cases in North Carolina.

In: Children and Youth Transitions from Foster Care
Editor: Joseph A. Ferrari
ISBN: 978-1-61209-705-3

Chapter 5

CHILD WELFARE: THE FOSTERING CONNECTIONS TO SUCCESS AND INCREASING ADOPTIONS ACT OF 2008

Emilie Stoltzfus

SUMMARY

The Fostering Connections to Success and Increasing Adoptions Act of 2008 (H.R. 6893) is an omnibus child welfare bill designed to ensure greater permanence and improve the well-being of children served by public child welfare agencies. The legislation received strong support in Congress and, beyond revising and extending the Adoption Incentives program, responds to a range of issues and concerns that have been raised (some for more than a decade) by public child welfare administrators; youth, adoption, tribal, and child welfare advocates; and by children and youth who have been (or still are) in foster care. The bill passed the House of Representatives, by voice vote (under suspension of the rules), on September 17, 2008, and the Senate, by unanimous consent, on September 22, 2008. It was signed into law by the President on October 7, 2008 (P.L. 110-351).

The final bill represented a compromise between earlier bills acted on in the House (H.R. 6307) and in the Senate Finance Committee (S. 3038). As enacted, it revises the Adoption Incentives program and extends its funding authorization for five years (FY2009-FY2013). It makes significant changes to federal funding for child welfare programs, which include authorizing new federal support for states that provide kinship guardianship assistance to eligible children leaving foster care; expanding eligibility for federal adoption assistance (by phasing out, over FY2010-FY2018, income and other eligibility criteria that are based on dated cash welfare program rules); extending, as of FY2011, eligibility for federal foster care assistance to youth who remain in care beyond their 18th birthday, up to age 21; and phasing in additional support to states for child welfare related training. Additionally, the bill authorizes tribal child welfare agencies, as of FY2010, to directly access federal funds for foster care, adoption, and guardianship assistance under the Title IV-E program, provided the tribes meet substantially the same requirements made of states. The bill also appropriates $15 million in annual funding, for five years, for a new competitive grant program, Family Connection Grants.

Apart from these financing changes, P.L. 110-351 establishes new requirements for receipt of federal child welfare funding by public child welfare agencies. These include several that focus exclusively on the health and education status of children in foster care and others intended to ensure, or enable, sibling and other kinship connections for children in, or entering, foster care, and those leaving to adoption or guardianship. The bill also requires states to make new efforts related to planning for the transition of older children leaving foster care for independent living and requires states to inform prospective adoptive parents of foster children of their potential eligibility for the adoption tax credit (under the federal tax code).

Many of the changes included in the new law are projected by the Congressional Budget Office (CBO) to increase federal spending for child welfare. However, the increases are projected to be fully offset (over the next five and ten years) by savings or increased revenues to the federal treasury that CBO expects to be produced by other changes in the bill (both related and unrelated to child welfare policy). This report may be updated if warranted by issues related to implementing the new law.

The Fostering Connections to Success and Increasing Adoptions Act of 2008 (H.R. 6893) is an omnibus child welfare bill designed to ensure greater permanence and improve the well-being of children served by public child welfare agencies —especially children in foster care, those who leave foster care in their later teens, and those who are Indian children. The legislation received strong support in Congress, and beyond revising and extending the Adoption Incentives program, it responds to a range of issues and concerns that have been variously raised (some for more than a decade) by public child welfare administrators; youth, adoption, tribal, and child welfare advocates; and by children and youth who have been (or still are) in foster care. The bill passed the House of Representatives, by voice vote (under suspension of the rules), on September 17 and the Senate, by unanimous consent, on September 22, 2008. It was signed into law by President George W. Bush on October 7, 2008. P.L. 110-351 represents a compromise between provisions that were included in the Improved Adoption Incentives and Relative Guardianship Support Act of 2008 (S. 3038, introduced by Senator Charles Grassley), as approved by the Senate Finance Committee on September 10, 2008 (S.Rept. 110-467), and the Fostering Connections to Success Act (H.R. 6307, introduced by Representative Jim McDermott with Representative Jerry Weller), as passed by the House on June 24, 2008.[1]

Overview of the Bill

The Fostering Connections to Success and Increasing Adoptions Act of 2008 (P.L. 110-351) revises and extends the Adoption Incentives program (under Section 473A of the Social Security Act) for five years, authorizes states to claim additional federal funds for certain child welfare purposes and adds new requirements for receipt of federal child welfare dollars. These changes are primarily designed to better ensure the well-being of children in foster care, to increase support for permanent living arrangements outside of foster care, to better support the transition of older foster youth to independent living, and to enable tribes to directly access federal support for foster care, kinship care, and adoption assistance provided to Indian children under their authority.

Financing Changes

P.L. 110-351 enacts the broadest changes to federal financial support for child welfare programs under Title IV-E of the Social Security Act, since that part of the law was created by the Adoption Assistance and Child Welfare Act of 1980 (P.L. 96-272). Among those changes, the bill

- permits states to claim open-ended federal reimbursement for a part of all eligible state costs related to providing kinship guardianship assistance;
- permits states to claim open-ended federal reimbursement for a part of the cost of making maintenance payments on behalf of eligible children who are in foster care beyond their 18th birthday (until their 21st birthday), provided those youths are in school, working, or engaged in a related activity (effective with FY2011);
- authorizes direct access for tribes to open-ended federal reimbursement for the costs of operating a foster care, adoption assistance, and kinship guardianship assistance program on behalf of children under tribal authority, provided those tribes meet substantially the same requirements made of states receiving these funds (effective with FY2010);
- expands federal support for adoption assistance by de-linking, over time (FY2010-FY2018), eligibility for that program from income and other criteria that were a part of the prior law cash welfare program, Aid to Families with Dependent Children (AFDC); and
- phases-in (FY2009-FY2013) authorization for states to claim open-ended federal reimbursement for a larger share of their short-term training costs for staff of state licensed or approved (private) child welfare agencies and to receive reimbursement, at this same increased rate, for eligible short-term training costs of current or prospective relative guardians and certain court or court-related personnel who handle child abuse and neglect cases.

In addition, P.L. 110-351 provides $15 million annually (FY2009-FY2013) for Family Connection Grants to support kinship navigator programs, family group decision making meetings, intensive family-finding efforts, and residential treatment centers for families (under Title IV-B of the Social Security Act). And it appropriates $3 million annually (FY2009 and every succeeding fiscal year) for technical assistance and implementation grants related to improving outcomes for Indian children (under Title IV-E).

New Requirements

Apart from expanding child welfare funding options for states, P.L. 110-351 establishes new requirements for receipt of federal child welfare funding by public child welfare agencies. The bill requires these agencies (under Title IV-E or Title IV-B) to

- provide assurance that each school-age child receiving federal foster care, adoption, or guardianship assistance is enrolled in school;
- work with other appropriate public agencies to reduce unnecessary school moves for all children in foster care and, separately, to coordinate and ensure access to health care for them, including mental health services and dental care;
- make "reasonable efforts" to place siblings together, whether in foster care, adoption, or guardianship;
- notify the adult relatives of children entering foster care of their options to participate in the care and placement of the child;
- no more than 90 days before a youth's exit from the foster care system (due to age rather than placement with a permanent family) develop with the youth a specific plan for his or her transition to independent living;
- negotiate "in good faith" with a tribe in the state that requests an agreement with the state to receive federal (Title IV-E) funds in return for that tribe's administration of some or all of the Title IV-E foster care, adoption assistance, and kinship guardianship assistance program for Indian children under its authority; and
- inform prospective adoptive parents of foster children of their potential eligibility for the federal adoption tax credit.

P.L. 110-351 makes additional child welfare financing, policy, or related program changes, which are detailed below. Finally, and unrelated to child welfare policy, it amends the federal tax code's uniform definition of child (for purposes of claiming a variety of credits or deductions) and it makes changes to certain investment rules for the Treasury Department. Those specific policy changes, together with savings projected from the implementation of guardianship assistance and the school enrollment requirement, are estimated by the Congressional Budget Office (CBO) to fully offset the federal cost of the increased spending authorized by the bill over the next 5 to 10 years. All of the child welfare policy changes in P.L. 110-351 are made to programs or parts of the law that are administered by the Administration for Children and Families (ACF), within the U.S. Department of Health and Human Services (HHS), and are expected to be implemented by ACF.[2]

This report begins with a more detailed and topical summary of the provisions of H.R. 6893, as enacted, including some legislative background and context. It continues by reviewing the cost estimates for the provisions, as projected by CBO, and then discusses the legislative origins of the enacted bill and Administration views of provisions included in related predecessor bills (H.R. 6307 and S. 3038). It closes with a section-by-section description of the bill's provisions.

New and Expanded Assistance or Activities Related to Permanence

The Fostering Connections to Success and Increasing Adoptions Act of 2008 (P.L. 110-351) makes a number of financing and policy changes that are designed to encourage and support children's placement in a permanent family — whether through strengthened or re-established connections with biological kin or through federal support and incentives to support children's adoption out of foster care.

Permanence via Family Connections

The enacted bill permits states to claim federal support for kinship guardianship assistance (under Title IV-E of the Social Security Act), makes other policy changes expected to promote or facilitate relative placement, authorizes and provides funding for Family Connection Grants, and requires states to make reasonable efforts to place siblings together.

Kinship Guardianship Assistance

The enacted bill permits states to claim open-ended reimbursement under Title IV-E for kinship guardianship assistance provided on behalf of eligible children who leave foster care for placement in a legal guardianship with a relative. As amended by the Adoption and Safe Families Act of 1997 (ASFA, P.L. 105-89), federal statute defines "legal guardianship" (for purposes of Title IV-E and Title IV-B of the Social Security Act) as "a judicially created relationship between child and caretaker which is intended to be permanent and self-sustaining as evidenced by the transfer to the caretaker of the following parental rights with respect to the child: protection, education, care and control of the person, custody of the person, and decisionmaking."[3] States are entitled to claim federal reimbursement for the cost of providing kinship guardianship assistance payments on behalf of eligible children at their Federal Medical Assistance Percentage (FMAP), which may range from a low of 50%, in states with higher per capita income, to 83%, in those with lower per capita income. States opting to provide such payments may also claim reimbursement of eligible general administrative costs at a 50% federal reimbursement rate, and for program-related training costs at 75% federal reimbursement, (although some of these eligible training costs will initially be reimbursed at a lower rate; see "Federal Support for Training and Other Changes" below).

Since the middle 1990s, close to 40 states have implemented some kind of subsidized guardianship program for children leaving foster care. However, many of those programs were not statewide and not all have been maintained.[4] Under child welfare "waivers," as many as 11 of those states have experimented with subsidized guardianship programs using federal Title IV-E funds.[5] Some of those earliest experiments found that providing guardianship subsidies increased exits to permanence for children in foster care and that on a range of safety and well-being measures, children placed in subsidized guardianship settings fared at least as well as did children placed in other permanent settings.[6]

In May 2004, the Pew Commission on Children in Foster Care recommended federal support of subsidized guardianship (under Title IV-E of the Social Security Act) as part of a broader package of child welfare financing reform measures. In July 2007, citing evidence that the subsidies "could help states increase the number of permanent homes available to African American and other children in foster care," the Government Accountability Office

(GAO) recommended that Congress consider authorizing federal subsidies for legal guardianship.[7] In its report approving guardianship assistance provisions similar to those that became a part of the final legislation, the Senate Finance Committee cited both the child welfare waivers and academic research to assert that children in kinship placements, including relative guardianships, have improved well-being; that guardianship is a good permanency option for children in foster care; and that provision of a state option to receive federal support for guardianship assistance under Title IV-E is expected to reduce federal costs under Title IV-E (by reducing the need for federal reimbursement of case planning and case review activities on behalf of children moved permanently from foster care to guardianship).[8]

Changes to Promote or Facilitate Relative Placement

The option to use federal Title IV-E funds to support children in kinship guardianship is only one of a number of changes included in P.L. 110-351 that seek to strengthen children's connections to their families and to create more opportunity for kinship placements (whether guardianship or otherwise).[9] These include

- a new plan requirement (under Title IV-E) that states "exercise due diligence" to identify grandparents and other adult relatives of a child, within 30 days of removing the child from the custody of his/her parents, and to notify those relatives of the child's removal and the relatives' options for participating in the care and placement of the child, including information about foster family home licensing and, as applicable, guardianship assistance;[10]
- codification of existing guidance (regarding a Title IV-E state plan requirement) that provides that when applying the state's foster family home licensing standards to the home of a relative caregiver, the state may — on a case-by-case basis and for a specific child only — waive any "non-safety"licensing requirement;
- a mandated study and report (by HHS) on the use of licensed and unlicensed relative foster family homes, including information on the frequency and kind of non-safety standards waived by states and recommendations for actions that might increase the number of children in foster care who are safely placed in licensed relative foster family homes; and
- authorization for HHS to make comparisons of names submitted by child welfare agencies to information in the Federal Parent Locator System (FPLS), which may aid in identifying or locating relatives.[11]

Family Connection Grants

Further, the bill establishes a new competitive grant program, under Title IV-B, Subpart 1 of the Social Security Act named Family Connection Grants. Under this program, public child welfare agencies (state, local or tribal), and non-profit private organizations may seek federal funding to help children — whether they are in foster care or at-risk of entering foster care — connect (or reconnect) with birth parents or other extended kin. Specifically, the funds must be used to establish or support one or more of the following:

- **kinship navigator programs,** which through information referral systems and other means, assist kinship caregivers in learning about, finding, and using programs and services to meet their own needs and those of the children they are raising;
- **intensive family-finding efforts** that use search technology to locate biological kin of children and then work to reestablish relationships and to explore permanent family placements for these children;
- **family group decision-making meetings** that enable families to develop plans that nurture children and protect them from abuse and neglect, and, when appropriate, must safely facilitate connecting children exposed to domestic violence to relevant services and reconnecting them with the abused parent; and
- **residential family treatment centers** that enable parents and children to live together in a safe environment for not less than six months and that provide, onsite or by referral, a full range of services to meet the needs of the family, including substance abuse treatment, early childhood intervention, family counseling, mental health services, medical care, and other services.

HHS is permitted to award up to 30 new Family Connection Grants each year and may not award a grant for a period of less than one year nor more than three years. Grantees are required to provide matching funds equal to no less than 25% of the total approved grant program costs in years one and two of a grant and no less than 50% in year three. The enacted bill appropriates $15 million for the Family Connection Grants in each of FY2009-FY2013, of which $5 million must be used annually to support kinship navigator programs.

Reasonable Efforts to Place Siblings Together

Finally, unless the state documents that doing so would be contrary to the safety or welfare of a sibling, the bill requires states (under the Title IV-E state plan) to make "reasonable efforts" to place siblings together, whether in foster care, kinship guardianship assistance, or adoption. It further stipulates that, whenever a joint placement is not made, the state must make "reasonable efforts" to provide for "frequent visitation or other ongoing interaction" between the siblings, unless the state documents that the facilitated contact is contrary to the safety or well-being of any one of the siblings.

Permanence via Adoption

P.L. 110-351 also expands eligibility for federal adoption assistance to children with special needs, revises and extends the Adoption Incentives program, and requires states to provide information to prospective adoptive parents concerning the adoption tax credit.

Phasing Out Income Eligibility and Related Rules for Adoption Assistance.

The enacted bill phases out (FY2010-FY2018) the use of income tests as part of determining eligibility for federal adoption assistance. This change will provide more *federal* support to special needs children who leave foster care for adoption. States must continue to pay a part of the cost of providing this support but are required to use any state funds that would be saved because of this expanded federal eligibility for adoption assistance on child welfare purposes.[12]

Federal adoption assistance was established in 1980 (P.L. 96-272) for children determined by their state to have "special needs."[13] The vast majority of these children, then and now, are children adopted out of foster care. The 1980 law also stipulated that to be eligible for federal adoption assistance a child must either be eligible for Supplemental Security Income (SSI) or have been removed from the home of birth parents in which he or she met the income and other eligibility criteria of the federal cash welfare program (Aid to Families with Dependent Children, AFDC).[14] AFDC was repealed in 1996 by the Personal Responsibility and Work Opportunity Reconciliation Act (PRWORA, P.L. 104-193). However, federal eligibility for Title IV-E assistance continues to be linked to AFDC eligibility rules as those rules existed (on July 16, 1996) prior to the program's repeal. Beginning in FY2010 (and continuing through FY2018), P.L. 110-351 will phase out this link for adoption assistance, which the Senate Finance Committee describes as "an inappropriate eligibility factor for Federal Adoption Assistance."[15] (As included in the enacted bill, the revised eligibility rules for federal adoption assistance also eliminate any income- or resource-related eligibility requirements that apply to special needs children who have physical or medical disabilities that qualify them for Supplemental Security Income, SSI.).

The revised eligibility rules will become effective in FY2010, but only for children who are age 16 or older when their adoption assistance agreement is finalized. With each new fiscal year, this age will be lowered (by two years) so that by FY2018 any child with special needs may qualify for federal adoption assistance under the revised rules. In addition, beginning in FY2010, any child who has been in foster care for 60 continuous months may qualify for federal adoption assistance under the revised eligibility rules (regardless of age) and any sibling of a child who is eligible under the revised rules (whether due to age or length of stay in care) may also qualify under those criteria. Throughout this eight-year phase-in period, the eligibility criteria that applied prior to the passage of H.R. 6893, including the link to AFDC eligibility, will continue to apply to any child who does not qualify for eligibility determination under the revised rules (at the time his or her adoption assistance agreement is finalized).

Reauthorization of the Adoption Incentives Program

Apart from the expanded support for federal adoption assistance, the Fostering Connections to Success and Increasing Adoptions Act of 2008 continues incentives to states for increased adoptions from foster care by revising and extending the Adoption Incentives program. This program was created by ASFA (P.L. 105-89) and was initially extended in 2003 by P.L. 108-145. A state earns a bonus for each eligible adoption out of foster care that is above its baseline number of adoptions. States earn an award for increases in total adoptions, increases in adoption of older children (age 9 and above) and, they may also receive an award for increases in the number of adoptions of children with special needs who are under the age of 9. For adoptions finalized in FY2007 (most recent year for which awards were made), 21states earned a total of $11.1 million in bonus funds.[16] States are permitted to spend this award money to provide any service to children or families, including post-adoption services, that is authorized by the major federal child welfare programs (under Title IV-B or Title IV-E of the Social Security Act).

P.L. 110-351 continues, through FY2013, the current annual funding authorization of $43 million for the Adoption Incentive program. It doubles the incentive amounts states may earn for each increase in the number of older children adopted from foster care (from $4,000 to

$8,000) and for children with special needs, under age 9, who are adopted from foster care (from $2,000 to $4,000). The incentive award for any increase in the total number of children adopted from foster care was not changed and remains at $4,000. The enacted bill also makes other changes to the incentive structure of the program, which are intended to ensure that states (even those with declining overall foster care caseloads) continue to have a fiscal incentive to increase adoptions. These changes include fixing each state's baseline adoption numbers at the numbers achieved in FY2007 and allowing (provided sufficient appropriations) a new incentive payment for states that increase the *rate* of children adopted from foster care.[17] To earn an award for an increased rate of adoptions, the state must increase the share of children adopted out of its foster care caseload (that is its foster child adoption rate) above the highest such rate it previously achieved, in any year, beginning with FY2002 and ending with the year just prior to the award year. The amount of the award is $1,000 times the increased number of adoptions achieved by the state that are attributed to the increased adoption rate.[18] The increased incentive payment amounts and the incentives for states increasin g the rate at which children are adopted out of their foster care caseload, will be used to calculate awards earned by states for adoptions finalized in FY2008. Those awards are expected to be announced in September 2009. Finally, P.L. 110-351 also ensures that states have a full 24 months to spend any adoption incentive funding awarded.

Information on Adoption Tax Credit

As part of supporting the goal of increasing permanence for foster children through adoption, P.L. 110-351 requires states (under Title IV-E), to provide notice to any individual who is adopting a child out of foster care (or who the state learns is considering such an adoption) of the individual's potential eligibility for the federal adoption tax credit. The credit is adjusted annually for inflation and for tax year 2008 equals $11,650 for individuals who adopt children with "special needs."[19]

Support for Older Foster Youth and Transition to Independent Living

The Fostering Connections to Success and Improving Adoptions Act of 2008 (P.L. 110-351) also seeks to strengthen support for children whose permanency outcome is "independent living." These are youth who "emancipate" from foster care; that is, they are released from state foster care custody because they have reached the state age of majority (typically age 18) rather than because they have been placed with a permanent family. At least since the middle 1980s (P.L. 99-272), Congress has sought to better aid the transition of these youth from foster care to independent living. With the Chafee Foster Care Independence Act of 1999 (P.L. 106-169), Congress significantly expanded support for services to youth both before and after they "age-out" and in 2001 (P.L. 107-133), it authorized funds for Education and Training Vouchers for these youth. Even so the number of children leaving foster care via emancipation continues to grow — reaching close to 27,000 youth in FY2006 — and, in general, their school, work, and other important life outcomes continue to be poor.[20]

Option to Extend Support for Youth Remaining in Care to Age 21

P.L. 110-351 takes a new tack in responding to this longstanding concern by permitting states, as of FY2011, to provide continued federal foster care maintenance payments on behalf of eligible children even after they have reached their 18th birthday. Under current law, federal Title IV-E assistance ends with a child's 18th birthday, (or, possibly, the 19th if the child is still completing high school). Specifically, the enacted bill permits states to continue to seek open-ended federal reimbursement for a part of the cost of providing maintenance payments to eligible children who remain in foster care after their 18th birthday, provided those children have not yet reached their 21st birthday and are either enrolled in school, employed at least 80 hours a month, or participating in an activity designed to promote or remove barriers to employment. States may exempt a youth from these requirements so long as the youth has a medical condition making him or her incapable of participating in the activity, and this incapacity is supported by regularly updated information in his or her case plan. P.L. 110-351 also permits continued support to youth in foster care (age 18 or older) who are living independently in a supervised setting and it stipulates that HHS must define, in regulation, what qualifies as such a setting.[21]

New Transition Planning Requirement

Separately, the bill requires each state (as part of its mandatory case review system) to have a procedure that ensures every child leaving foster care has a transition plan created on his or her behalf. The transition plan must be created with the youth by a caseworker and, as appropriate, other representative(s) of the child — no earlier than 90 days before the child's 18th birthday (or at whatever later age chosen by the state to end foster care assistance). It must address specific options for the youth with regard to housing, health insurance, education, local opportunities for mentors and continuing support services, as well as workforce supports and employment services.

Option to Extend Support for Youth Leaving Care for Permanent Home After Reaching Age 16

With limited exceptions, monthly federal (Title IV-E) assistance has not generally been available for a child who has reached his or her 18th birthday and who left foster care for a permanent family via adoption or kinship guardianship. However, P.L. 110-351 permits states, as of FY2011, to choose to continue federally supported subsidies on behalf of eligible children who leave foster care *after* their 16th birthday for adoption or kinship guardianship so long as those youth have not yet reached their *21st birthday*, and are enrolled in school, employed at least 80 hours a month, or participating in an activity designed to promote or remove barriers to employment. (States may exempt a child from these school, work or other engagement requirements if the child has a medical condition that makes him or her incapable of participating in the activity, and this incapacity is supported by regularly updated information in the child's case plan.) In addition, a state is allowed to continue federal adoption assistance *or kinship guardianship assistance* up to the 21st birthday on behalf of any child, regardless of the age at which the child left foster care, if the state determines that "the child has a mental or physical handicap that warrants the continuation of assistance." (This was and remains true with regard to adoption assistance; P.L. 110-351 will also extend it, as of FY2011, to kinship guardianship assistance.)

Services for Youth Leaving Foster Care after Reaching Age 16

Finally, the enacted bill expands the purposes of the Chafee Foster Care Independence Program to provide that any of the activities or services provided in support of independent living for youth who are expected to age out of foster care without a permanent family, may also be provided to youth who leave foster care at age 16 or older, to either adoption or guardianship. The bill also extends eligibility for Education and Training Vouchers (which are valued at \$5,000 annually and may be used for the cost of attending college or an equivalent training program) to youth who leave foster care for guardianship after their 16th birthday. (Children who leave foster care for adoption after their 16th birthday continue to be eligible for these vouchers as was true under prior law.)

Well-Being of Children in Foster Care

The Fostering Connections to Success and Increasing Adoptions Act of 2008 (P.L. 110-351) makes new requirements of states that focus on ensuring and enabling stable enrollment in school for children in foster care and on their access to needed and appropriate health care, including mental health services and dental care. For more then a decade, the primary goals of federal child welfare policy have commonly been expressed as achieving safety, permanency, and well-being for children. However, the health- and education-related requirements included in P.L. 110-351 are among the first federal *statutory* requirements of child welfare agencies that focus specifically on the well-being of children in foster care — as distinct from their need for safety and permanence.[22]

Education Stability and Enrollment

Specifically, P.L. 110-351 requires state child welfare agencies — as part of the Title IV-E case plan requirements that apply to each child in foster care — to work with relevant state and local education authorities to ensure that a child remains in the same school in which he or she is enrolled at the time of foster care placement, or, if this is not in the best interests of the child, to ensure immediate and appropriate enrollment for the child in a new school. To help support this requirement, the enacted bill permits states to claim federal funding for the cost of transporting children to their "school of origin" at the same reimbursement rate that is provided for foster care maintenance payments. (That rate ranges from 50%-83%, with states with higher per capita incomes receiving a lower federal reimbursement rate and vice versa.[23]) Separately (under the Title IV-E plan), P.L. 110-351 requires states to assure that children who have reached the minimum age for mandatory school attendance in their state, and who are receiving federal foster care maintenance payments, adoption assistance, or kinship guardianship assistance, are enrolled in school or have completed high school.

Health Care Oversight

Further (under Title IV-B, Subpart 1), the new law requires each state to develop a coordinated strategy and oversight plan to ensure access to health care, including mental health services and dental care, for all children in foster care. This coordinated strategy and oversight plan must be a collaborative effort between the state child welfare agency and the state agency that administers Medicaid (in consultation with pediatric and other health care experts, as well as experts in, or recipients of, child welfare services). Among other things, the strategy and plan must outline: a schedule for initial and follow-up health screens; how the health needs identified by those screens will be monitored and treated; how medical information for children in care will be updated and appropriately shared; steps to ensure continuity of health care services; and oversight of prescription medicines.

These new health- and education-related requirements are unique in federal child welfare policy because they look beyond the safety and permanence needs of children in foster care and focus instead on measures of well-being that are considered relevant to *any* child in the nation.[24] Safety and permanence are also critical to the well-being of all children. However, by definition, they are issues of immediate and special concern for children in foster care. Accordingly, federal child welfare policy has long focused on ways to better achieve and ensure them. Notably, the Adoption Assistance and Child Welfare Act of 1980 (P.L. 96-272) recognized the critical need for permanence by providing new incentives for case planning for each child in foster care and by authorizing federal support for adoption assistance to children leaving foster care. Further, more than a decade ago, ASFA (P.L. 105-89) asserted the primacy of safety in all child welfare decisions and reinvigorated attention to permanence for children in foster care by establishing new case planning and case review timetables and requirements, and by establishing the Adoption Incentives program.

Direct Federal Support to Tribal Programs

The Fostering Connections to Success and Increasing Adoptions Act of 2008 (P.L. 110-351) seeks to improve the child welfare services and supports available to Indian children by granting tribes (as of FY2010) the same authority that states have to seek federal reimbursement of a part of all their eligible foster care, adoption, and kinship guardianship assistance costs. Indian children may currently be eligible for Title IV-E assistance if they are in the care and placement responsibility of a state. However, children under the care and placement responsibility of a tribe may not receive this assistance *unless* the tribe's responsibility of the child is "supervised" by the state via a state-tribal cooperative agreement. Explaining their approval of direct tribal access to federal Title IV-E support — which has been a goal of tribal child welfare advocates for many years and has been proposed in every Congress since at least the 105th (1997) — the Senate Finance Committee stated that "tribes, tribal consortia, and tribal organizations may provide higher quality and more culturally appropriate care for Indian children."[25]

To receive Title IV-E funds, a tribe, tribal organization, or tribal consortium[26] must submit a plan for approval to HHS and, with specific and limited exceptions, must meet all the requirements for receipt of this funding "in the same manner" as they are required of states. The bill also permits tribes (as of FY2010) to apply to HHS and receive a direct federal allotment of Chafee Foster Care Independence and/or Education and Training Voucher funds. In addition, it stipulates that current "cooperative agreements" — agreements between a tribe and state, which permit a tribe to receive federal Title IV-E funds via the state — must continue unchanged, unless either party with the right to revoke or change the agreement elects to do so.

P.L. 110-351 provides for calculation of a tribe-specific federal matching rate for foster care maintenance payments, adoption assistance payments, and kinship guardianship assistance payments (a "tribal FMAP"). Tribes with an approved Title IV-E plan are to receive this reimbursement rate directly from the federal government. If a tribe has a cooperative agreement or contract with a state to administer Title IV-E payments, that state is to receive reimbursement at the tribal FMAP for the portion of its Title IV-E foster care maintenance, adoption assistance or kinship guardianship assistance payments that are made under the state-tribal agreement or contract. Further, as of FY2010, P.L. 110-351 requires a state to negotiate "in good faith" with any eligible tribal entity in the state if that tribal entity requests to enter into an agreement with the state under which the state would provide Title IV-E funds to the tribe for it to administer all or part of the program on behalf of children under tribal authority. A state will similarly be required to negotiate in good faith with any tribal entity in the state that is not receiving a direct federal allotment of Chafee Foster Care Independence Program and/or Education and Training Voucher funds and which requests an agreement or contract that would allow it to receive funds from the state to administer the program(s) on behalf of Indian children under its authority.

Finally, to help ensure these new provisions result in improved outcomes for Indian children, the bill appropriates $3 million (for FY2009 and every succeeding year) for technical assistance to tribes and states and for implementation grants to tribes that are preparing to submit a Title IV-E plan for approval to HHS. These implementation grants may be worth as much as $300,000. A tribal entity may receive this grant only once and it must agree to submit a Title IV-E plan to HHS for approval no later than 24 months after receiving the grant funding. If the plan is not submitted within 24 months the tribe must repay the entire grant amount. However, HHS must waive this repayment requirement if the tribe's failure to submit it within 24 months was a result of a "circumstances beyond the control" of the tribe.

Federal Support for Training and Other Changes

Over five years, P.L. 110-351 phases in an increased federal reimbursement rate for states that offer short-term training to workers at private, licensed child welfare agencies — provided this training is related to the Title IV-E foster care, adoption, and kinship guardianship program. The enacted bill also permit states to claim Title IV-E training reimbursement for certain short-term training of current and prospective relative guardians and for court and related personnel (including attorneys) who handle child abuse and neglect cases. The bill sets the federal matching rate for costs of providing short-term training to private agency workers, current and prospective relative guardians, and for certain court or court-related personnel handling abuse and neglect cases at 55% in FY2009, rising 5% annually until it reaches 75% in FY2013. (Title IV-E training costs that were reimbursed at 75% before passage of H.R. 6893 will continue to be reimbursed at that same level throughout this phase-in period.)

P.L. 110-351 makes several changes that are unrelated to child welfare policy. These include clarifying the uniform definition of child that is used for a variety of federal tax code purposes. It also amends the law to permit the Treasury Department to invest excess operating cash for 90 days in repurchase agreements. These non-child welfare-related provisions —

together with savings projected from the implementation of kinship guardianship assistance and the school enrollment requirement — are estimated by the Congressional Budget Office (CBO) to fully offset the cost of the bill to the federal treasury over the next five and 10 years.

Finally, the bill prohibits any interpretation of its provisions that would "alter" any current "prohibitions on Federal payments to individuals who are unlawfully present in the United States."

Effective Date

Unless otherwise stipulated, the provisions of the Fostering Connections to Success and Increasing Adoptions Act of 2008 became effective on its date of enactment (October 7, 2008). However, a state may have limited additional time to comply with any of the new requirements of the bill, if HHS determines that the state must enact legislation (other than legislation to appropriate funds) in order to meet that requirement(s). As discussed above, the bill stipulates delayed and/or phased in effective dates for its provisions related to removing income eligibility criteria from the federal adoption assistance program (i.e., de-link), extending Title IV-E assistance to eligible youth beyond age 18, providing direct access to tribal entities for federal Title IV-E funding, and providing new or increased federal reimbursement for certain short-term training costs.

Congressional Budget Office Estimates[27]

Although H.R. 6893, as enacted, authorizes significant expansions in federal support for state and tribal child welfare programs, CBO projects a combined change in federal spending and revenues from the overall bill that is roughly budget neutral over ten years (FY2009-FY2018). Specifically, CBO projects that the bill *will reduce* the federal budget deficit by $15 million over those ten years.[28] This positive effect (i.e. reduction in federal budget deficit) is projected to be much larger in the first five years of the bill's enactment ($449 million), in part because a number of the bill's provisions that are expected to increase federal spending are made effective a year or two after enactment and because the full effect of other provisions is phased in over five or more years.[29]

Projected Savings and Increased Revenue

As interpreted by CBO, four major provisions of the bill are projected to produce significant savings (and/or increase revenues) to the federal treasury over five (FY2009-FY2013) and 10 (FY2009-FY2018) years. These are as follows:

- authorization of federal Title IV-E support for kinship guardianship assistance (projected to save $60 million over five years and a total of $791 million over 10 years);[30]

- making school enrollment a condition of federal eligibility for foster care, adoption assistance, and kinship guardianship assistance under Title IV-E (projected to save $213 million over five years and a total of $484 million over 10 years);
- new authority to the Treasury Department related to investment of operating cash (projected to save $50 million over five years and a total of $100 million over 10 years); and
- changes to the tax code's uniform definition of qualifying child ($628 million in savings plus $123 million in increased revenue over five years and a total of $1.402 billion in savings plus a total of $307 million in increased revenue over 10 years).

Projected Increases in Federal Spending

As interpreted by CBO, seven major provisions of the bill are projected to have costs to the federal treasury over the next five (FY2009-FY2013) and 10 (FY2009-FY20018) years. A delayed or phased-in implementation of a number of these provisions helps to reduce their projected cost during these time periods. These provisions are as follows:

- annual appropriation of $15 million for Family Connection Grants (projected to increase federal spending by $59 million over five years and by a total of $75 million over 10 years);
- option for states to provide federal Title IV-E assistance up to age 21 for otherwise eligible children remaining in foster care after their 18th birthday and for those who left foster care for adoption after attaining age 16 (effective with FY2011 and projected to increase federal spending by $186 million between that year and FY2013 and by a total of $735 million between that year and FY2018);
- expanded child welfare training claims and/or increase in their federal reimbursement rate (the increased reimbursement rate is phased in over FY2009-FY2013 and is projected to increase federal spending by $138 million over those years and by a total of $412 million over the 10-year period);
- increased oversight of access to health care for children in foster care (projected to increase federal spending by $75 million over 5 years and by a total of $150 million over ten years;
- authority for tribes to apply for and receive direct federal Title IV-E funding (effective with FY2010 and expected to increase federal spending by $30 million between that year and FY2013 and by a total of $237 million through FY2018);
- annual appropriation of $3 million for technical assistance and implementation grants related to improving outcomes for Indian children generally, and implementing tribal access to Title IV-E, specifically (projected to increase federal spending by $12 million over 5 years and by a total of $27 million over 10 years); and
- phase out of income (and related) eligibility criteria for federal adoption assistance (phase-out begins with FY2010 and is expected to increase federal spending by $126 million between that year and FY2013 and by a total of $1.432 billion between that year and FY2018).

ORIGINS OF THE ENACTED BILL AND VIEWS

The Fostering Connections to Success and Increasing Adoptions Act of 2008 (H.R. 6893) was introduced by Representative Jim McDermott, with Representative Jerry Weller, on September 15, 2008, and passed the House (under suspension of the rules and by voice vote) on September 17, 2008. The bill then went to the Senate where it was passed (by unanimous consent) on September 22, 2008. Enacted on October 7, 2008 as P.L. 110-351, the final legislation represented a compromise between bills that were earlier acted on by the House and by the Senate Finance Committee. These bills are the Improved Adoption Incentives and Relative Guardianship Support Act of 2008 (S. 3038) and the Fostering Connections to Success Act (H.R. 6307). S. 3038 was introduced by Senator Grassley in May 2008, and the Senate Finance Committee approved the "Chairman's Mark" version of that bill on September 10, 2008 (S.Rept. 110-467).[31] H.R. 6307 was introduced by Representative McDermott with Representative Weller in June 2008, and it passed the House on June 24, 2008.[32] Both Representative McDermott and Representative Weller described the final bill, H.R. 6893, as the product of bipartisan and bicameral legislative work and they cited the importance of Senator Max Baucus and Senator Grassley in this effort.[33]

Congressional Activities

During the first session of the 110th Congress, the Income Security and Family Support Subcommittee of the House Ways and Means Committee held a number of hearings to review challenges facing the child welfare system overall, and, in particular, challenges faced by older youth leaving foster care without a permanent family. Following these hearings, in February 2008, Representative McDermott, who chairs that subcommittee, introduced the Invest in KIDS Act (H.R. 5466) to address a number of these challenges.[34]

Some of the provisions incorporated in H.R. 5466, as well as provisions subsequently included in S. 3038, H.R. 6307, and ultimately those that were included in H.R. 6893, were inspired by, or introduced in, other bills during this and earlier Congresses. From the 110th Congress, these bills include the Kinship Caregiver Support Act (S. 661, introduced by Senator Hillary Clinton with Senator Olympia Snowe / H.R. 2188, introduced by Representative Danny Davis); the Adoption Equality Act (S. 1462, introduced by Senator Jay Rockefeller / H.R. 4091, introduced by Representative Jim Cooper); the Tribal Foster Care and Adoption Access Act (S. 1956, introduced by Senator Max Baucus / H.R. 4688, introduced by Representative Earl Pomeroy); the Foster Care Continuing Opportunities Act (S. 1512, introduced by Senator Barbara Boxer); and a bill to increase reimbursement under Title IV-E for short-term training of private agency workers (H.R. 2314, by Representative Weller).[35]

HHS Views

In providing its view on aspects of earlier bills (H.R. 6307 and the Chairman's Mark of S. 3038), that were subsequently included in the final enrolled bill (H.R. 6893), the U.S.

Department of Health and Human Services (HHS) strongly supported revising and extending the Adoption Incentive program but disagreed with (1) the specific ways in which states will now be permitted to seek open-ended federal reimbursement for a part of the cost of providing guardianship subsidies to eligible children leaving foster care; (2) the creation of Family Connection grants; and (3) the approach taken in providing access to federal Title IV-E support for tribes.[36] In letters sent to Congress regarding H.R. 6307 and the Chairman's Mark of S. 3038, HHS, however, did not provide any specific comments related to the expansion of federal eligibility for Title IV-E adoption assistance, the option for states to continue providing federal Title IV-E foster care assistance to eligible youth after their 18th birthday, nor regarding the provisions related to increased federal reimbursement for certain child welfare training costs.

With regard to the state option to provide guardianship assistance under Title IV-E, HHS wrote: "Moving children to permanent homes as expeditiously as possible is an important goal. However, we oppose creating a new entitlement under the title IV-E program for subsidized relative guardians."[37] HHS noted that under the Child Welfare Program Option it has proposed, states would have the "flexibility to support guardianship agreements if they choose."[38] HHS also noted its support for direct federal support to tribes for child welfare programs but, again, it preferred the approach that would be provided to tribes under the Child Welfare Program Option. (The Bush Administration's proposed program option would permit federally recognized tribes to receive child welfare funds from a fixed sum that would be set aside for that purpose.) The Department wrote that it had "serious concerns" that the bills would "weaken [child protection] requirements placed on Tribes in comparison to those placed on States."[39] Finally, in the letter regarding H.R. 6307, HHS pointed out that the activities allowed under the Family Connection Grants could already be funded under existing Title IV-B programs (Child Welfare Services, and Promoting Safe and Stable Families) and also that the Department does not support any new "authorization of activities outside the President's Budget."[40]

Bill Advocates and Support

The act responds to a variety of issues that have been raised for many years (and some for more than a decade) by public child welfare administrators; child welfare, youth, adoption, and tribal advocates; and children and youth who have been (or still are) in foster care; and/or by public child welfare administrators. Enactment of the Fostering Connections to Success and Increasing Adoptions Act of 2008 was urged by many groups, including a coalition of 581 national, state, and local entities (representing organizations in all 50 states) that advocate on behalf of children and youth, as well as by the National Conference of State Legislators (NCSL) and the Conference of Chief Justices and Conference of State Court Administrators.[41]

SECTION-BY-SECTION DESCRIPTION OF THE BILL

The Fostering Connections to Success and Increasing Adoptions Act of 2008 (P.L. 110-351) is divided into six titles, most with multiple sections, and makes the following changes.

TITLE I. CONNECTING AND SUPPORTING RELATIVE CAREGIVERS

Section 101. Kinship Guardianship Assistance Payment for Children

- *Permits states to claim federal reimbursement* (under Title IV-E) *for a part of the cost of providing kinship guardianship assistance* to every eligible child who leaves foster care for placement with a grandparent or other relative who has chosen to become the child's legal guardian.
- Requires that *to be eligible* for federal kinship guardianship assistance *a child must have been eligible to receive federal foster care maintenance payments while living for no less then six consecutive months in the home of his or her prospective relative guardian* (this effectively requires that the prospective relative guardian has met the state foster family home licensing standards and prospective foster parent background checks).
- Stipulates the following additional conditions of federal eligibility for kinship guardianship assistance: The state must determine that (1) the child has been removed from his or her home through a voluntary placement agreement or because a judge found that home contrary to the child's welfare; (2) neither being reunited with his or her parents nor adoption are appropriate permanency options for the child; (3) the child demonstrates a strong attachment to the prospective relative guardian and the relative guardian has a strong commitment to caring permanently for the child; and (4) any child age 14 or older was consulted before being placed in the kinship guardianship arrangement.
- Provides also that the state must have specific background checks procedures for relative guardians, including fingerprint-based checks of national crime databases and child abuse and neglect registry checks, which must be conducted before a relative guardian may receive kinship guardianship assistance payments on behalf of an eligible child.
- Permits states to place a sibling(s) of an eligible child in the same kinship guardianship arrangement and to make kinship guardianship assistance payments on behalf of the sibling(s).
- Establishes that a *kinship guardianship assistance payment* made on behalf of an eligible child *must not be more than the amount the child would receive as a foster care maintenance payment* if he or she remained in a foster family home.
- *Ensures continued categorical Medicaid eligibility* for children receiving federal kinship guardianship assistance.
- Provides that *to receive federal reimbursement for kinship guardianship assistance payments, the state must enter into a written and binding kinship guardianship agreement with the prospective relative guardian*, which must stipulate that it will

remain in effect without regard to the state in which the relative guardian lives and must include (1) the amount of, and manner in which, the kinship guardianship assistance payments will be made on the child's behalf, including the manner in which the amount may, in consultation with the relative guardian, be adjusted periodically based on the circumstances of the relative and the needs of the child; and (2) the additional services and assistance the child and relative will be eligible for under the agreement, including the procedure the relative guardian may use to apply for additional services as needed.

- Entitles each state to claim federal reimbursement for the cost of providing kinship guardianship assistance payments on behalf of an eligible child at the same federal reimbursement rate that is provided for adoption assistance (i.e., ranges from 50%-83%, based on each state's Federal Medical Assistance Percentage, FMAP); and entitles state to claim federal reimbursement of 50% for (non-training) administrative costs related to providing kinship guardianship assistance to eligible children.
- Further stipulates that the kinship guardianship assistance agreement must provide that the state will pay the total nonrecurring expenses *associated with obtaining legal guardianship of the child, or $2,000 of those expenses, whichever is less*.
- For any child in foster care whose permanency plan is placement with a relative guardian and receipt of kinship guardianship assistance payments, requires states to describe in the child's written case plan the (1) steps the agency has taken to determine that it is not appropriate for the child to be returned home or adopted; (2) reasons why a permanent placement in a kinship guardianship assistance arrangement is in the child's best interests; (3) reasons for any separation from siblings during the placement; (4) efforts the state has made to discuss adoption with the relative foster parent, and, if adoption is not chosen by the relative foster parent, documentation of reasons why this is so; and (5) efforts made by the state to discuss with the child's parent or parents, the kinship guardianship arrangement or reasons why the efforts were not made; and (6) the ways in which the child meets the eligibility criteria for kinship guardianship assistance.
- At the termination of any state child welfare demonstration project (waiver) that is related to guardianship and was authorized by the U.S. Department of Health and Human Services (HHS) under Section 1130 of the Social Security Act, provides that the state's costs of providing assistance or services to any child being served under such a demonstration project, as of September 30, 2008, continue to be eligible for federal reimbursement under Title IV-E — but only to the extent that the services and assistance are provided to such a child under the same terms and conditions that applied during the demonstration project.
- *Authorizes states to use federal funds* under the Chafee Foster Care Independence Program *to provide independent living services and other supports to youth who — after reaching their 16th birthday —leave foster care for adoption or placement in kinship guardianship* and permit youth leaving foster care for kinship guardianship after reaching their 16th birthday to be eligible for Education and Training Vouchers. (Children who leave foster care for adoption after their 16th birthday continue to be eligible for Education and Training Vouchers under current law.)

Section 102. Family Connection Grants

- *Appropriates mandatory funding of $15 million* (for each of FY2009-FY2013) for Family Connection Grants (to be awarded on a competitive basis to public (state, local, or tribal) child welfare agencies or eligible private, non-profit organizations) for the support of one or more of the following: *kinship navigator programs, intensive family-finding efforts* that utilize search technology to find biological relatives, *family group decision-making meetings*, which, when appropriate, must safely address issues of domestic violence; and *residential family treatment centers that enable parents and children to live together in a safe environment* for no less than six months and that provide a full range of services to meet the family's needs (onsite or by referral), including substance abuse treatment services, children's early intervention services, family counseling, medical and mental health services, nursery and pre-school, and other services designed to support the family.
- *Requires HHS to annually award no less than $5 million* of the Family Connections Grants funds *to support of kinship navigator programs*, that, through information referral systems and other means, assist kinship caregivers in learning about, finding, and using programs and services to meet their own needs and those of the children they are raising, and promote effective partnerships among public and private agencies to ensure these kinship caregiver families are served.
- Requires HHS to set aside no less than 3% of the total annual funding for Family Connection grants for evaluation of grantee activities; and permits HHS to set-aside 2% of total funding for the grants for technical assistance to grantees.
- Provides that HHS may make no more than 30 new Family Connection grants each year; may not award these grants for less than one year nor more than three years; and that it must provide 75% of the funding for a grantee's approved program costs in the first and second year of the grant and 50% in the third year.
- Renames Title IV-B, Subpart 1 of the Social Security Act (which is now named "Child Welfare Services") as the "Stephanie Tubbs Jones Child Welfare Services Program."

Section 103. Notification of Relatives

- *Requires states (under Title IV-E), within 30 days of removing a child from the custody of his or her parent(s) to exercise due diligence to identify all adult grandparents and other adult relatives of the child and to provide them with* (1) *notice of the child's removal* from parental custody; (2) *an explanation of their options for participating in the care and placement of the child*; (3) a description of the requirements that must be met to be a licensed foster family home and the additional services and support for children placed in licensed homes; and (4) if state has opted to provide kinship guardianship assistance, a description of how the relative can enter into a kinship guardianship assistance agreement; this requirement is subject to exceptions due to family or domestic violence.

Section 104. Licensing Standards for Relatives

- *Codifies* (under Title IV-E) *existing federal guidance permitting states to waive "non-safety" licensing standards* (as determined by the state) *for relative foster family caregivers*, but only *on a case-by-case basis* and for a specific child in care.
- *Requires HHS to prepare and submit* to the Senate Finance Committee and the House Ways and Means Committee *a report on licensing of relative foster family homes, including* (1) the number and percentage of children living in licensed relative foster family homes and those living in unlicensed relative foster family homes; (2) the frequency with which states grant waivers of "non-safety" standards and the type of non-safety standards waived; (3) an assessment of how the use of such waivers have affected safety, permanence, and well-being outcomes for children in foster care; (4) a review of any reasons why relative foster family homes may remain unlicensed despite this waiver authority; and (5) recommendations for administrative or legislative actions to increase the share of relative foster family homes that are licensed while ensuring the safety of foster children and improving their permanence and well-being.

Section 105. Authority for Comparisons and Disclosures of Information in the Federal Parent Locator Service

- Permits state child welfare agencies more direct access to the Federal Parent Locator Service.

TITLE II. IMPROVING OUTCOMES FOR CHILDREN IN FOSTER CARE

Section 201. State Option for Children in Foster Care, and Certain Children in An Adoptive or Guardianship Placement, After Attaining Age 18

- *Permits states* (as of October 1, 2010) *to extend federal* (Title IV-E) *assistance to an eligible child after his or her 18th birthday if the child is in foster care under the responsibility of the state* or if the child left foster care for federal adoption or guardianship assistance after reaching his or her 16th birthday, *provided the child* has not yet reached his or her 21st birthday and *is in school*, employed (at least 80 hours a month), *in another activity designed to promote, or remove barriers to employment*, or is incapable of participating in any of those activities because of a documented medical condition.
- *Except in the case of the individuals described above, defines the term "child" as an individual under the age of 18 for all federal child welfare programs included in the Social Security Act* (i.e., Child Welfare Services, Promoting Safe and Stable Families, Foster Care and Adoption Assistance, and Chafee Foster Care Independence Program).

- Also permits children in foster care who are age 18 or older to retain eligibility for federal foster care maintenance payments while living independently in a supervised setting (as must be defined in regulations by HHS).
- Further permits states to continue federal kinship guardianship assistance up to age 21 for a child who has a mental or physical handicap that the state determines warrants this continued assistance (This was previously, and continues to be, the law with regard to provision of federal adoption assistance.)
- Prohibits payment of federal kinship guardianship assistance payments to a relative guardian if the relative guardian is no longer legally responsible for support of the child (who is under age 18) or if the state determines that the child is no longer receiving support from the relative guardian. (This was previously, and continues to be, the law with regard to adoptive parents and children receiving federal adoption assistance.)
- Makes October 1, 2010, the effective date for all the amendments made in this section (Section 201).

Section 202. Transition Plan for Children Aging Out of Foster Care

- *Requires states* (under Title IV-E) *to have procedures to ensure that 90 days before a child in foster care reaches his or her 18th birthday* (or 90 days before the later birthday up to which a state elects to provide Title IV-E foster care assistance), *the child's caseworker and other representatives* (as appropriate) *must work with the child to develop a personal transition plan* that includes specific options on housing, health insurance, education, local opportunities for mentors and continuing support services, and workforce supports and employment services.

Section 203. Short-term Training for Child Welfare Agencies, Relative Guardians, and Court Personnel

- *Allows states to claim federal reimbursement of the costs of providing short-term training* — related to carrying out the Title IV-E foster care, adoption and kinship guardianship assistance program — *to current or prospective relative guardians, staff of state-licensed or state-approved (private) child welfare agencies, and for certain court or court-related personnel handling abuse and neglect cases.*
- *Phases in a 75% federal reimbursement rate* for these relative guardian, private child welfare agency workers, and court or court-related personnel training claims beginning at 55% in FY2009 and rising by 5% annually (until the reimbursement rate reaches 75% for all Title IV-E eligible training costs in FY2013).

Section 204. Educational Stability

- Restates current requirement (under Title IV-E) that the state must assure that a child's foster care placement takes into account the appropriateness of the child's current educational setting and the proximity of that placement to the school in which the child is enrolled at the time.
- *Requires states to assure that they have coordinated with appropriate local educational agencies to ensure that the child remains in the school in which he or she is enrolled* at the time of the placement, *or*, if this is not in the child's best interests, to assure (with the local educational agencies) *that the child will be immediately and appropriately enrolled in a new school* with all of the education records of the child provided to the school.
- *Permits a state to claim federal reimbursement* at the state's Federal Medical Assistance Percentage or FMAP, which ranges from 50%-83% based on state per capita income) *for the cost of transporting a child to the school in which he or she was enrolled at the time of foster care placement.*
- *Requires a state to provide assurances that each school-age child who receives federal* (Title IV-E) *assistance* (whether in foster care, kinship guardianship or adoption) *is enrolled in school full-time*, or has already completed high school.

Section 205. Health Oversight and Coordination Plan

- *Requires each state* (under Title IV-B) — working through the state child welfare agency and the state agency that administers Medicaid and in consultation with pediatricians, other health care experts, and experts in, and recipients of, child welfare services — *to create a plan to ensure oversight and coordination of health care, for children in foster care; the plan must include a strategy to identify and respond to the health care needs of children in foster care, including their mental health and dental health needs*, and provide an outline of (1) the schedule for initial and follow-up health screens; (2) how health needs identified in these screens will be monitored and treated; (3) how medical information for children in care will be updated and appropriately shared, which may include development of an electronic health record; (4) steps to ensure continuity of health care services, which may include establishment of a medical home for every child in care; (5) oversight of prescription medicines; and (6) how the state actively consults with and involves physicians and other appropriate medical or non-medical professionals in assessing the health and well-being of children in foster care and in determining appropriate medical treatment for them.
- Stipulates that this requirement must not be understood to reduce or limit responsibility of the state Medicaid agency to administer and provide care and services to children served by the state child welfare agency under the Child Welfare Services program (Title IV-B, Subpart 1).

Section 206. Sibling Placement

- *Requires each state (under Title IV-E) to make reasonable efforts to place siblings removed from their home in the same foster care, kinship guardianship, or adoptive placement,* unless the state can document that joint placement is contrary to the safety or well-being of any of the siblings.
- *In the case of siblings who are not jointly placed, requires states to provide for "frequent visitation or other ongoing interaction between the siblings,"* unless the state documents that this would be contrary to the safety or well-being of any of the siblings.

TITLE III. TRIBAL FOSTER CARE AND ADOPTION ACCESS

Section 301. Equitable Access for Foster Care and Adoption Services for Indian Children in Tribal Areas

- *Permits* (as of October 1, 2009) *an Indian tribe, tribal organization, or tribal consortium with an approved Title IV-E plan to make claims for federal reimbursement of eligible foster care maintenance, adoption assistance, or kinship guardianship assistance payments* and for related child placement and administrative costs (including those for data collection and training) made on behalf of eligible children who are under tribal responsibility.
- For purposes of defining the tribal entities that may apply for direct federal Title IV-E funding, generally defines "Indian tribe" as any federally recognized tribe, a "tribal organization" as the recognized governing body of any such tribe, and describes a tribal consortium as any two or more Indian tribes or tribal organizations that together submit a single Title IV-E plan for approval.[42]
- With limited and specific exceptions, *requires tribes seeking direct federal support under Title IV-E to meet all the requirements of Title IV-E "in the same manner" as they must be met by a state* receiving these funds.
- *Provides for calculation of a tribe-specific federal matching rate for foster care maintenance payments, adoption assistance payments, and kinship guardianship assistance payments* (a "tribal FMAP"); provides that tribes with an approved Title IV-E plan receive this reimbursement rate directly from the federal government; also provides that if the tribe has a cooperative agreement or contract with a state to administer IV-E payments, the federal government must pay the state the tribal matching rate for the payments made under that agreement.
- Stipulates that any currently existing cooperative agreement or contract entered into between a tribe and state for the administration or payment of funds under Title IV-E must remain in effect after the enactment of this bill, subject to the right of either party to revoke or modify the terms of the agreement or contract, and, further, that states and tribes may continue to enter into agreements or contracts under Title IV-E.
- Permits tribal entities seeking to administer independent living services for eligible Indian children and youth to apply to HHS for an allotment of funds under the

Chafee Foster Care Independence Program (and/or for an allotment of Education and Training Voucher funds); and provides that successful tribal applicants are to receive an allotment amount(s) out of the state's allotment for the program(s) that is based on the share of all children in foster care in that state who are under the authority of that tribal entity.

- Stipulates specific parameters within which tribes with an approved Title IV-E plan may (for a limited time — unless extended by regulation or law) claim federal reimbursement, under that plan, for in-kind expenditures from third-party sources; requires HHS (no later than September 30, 2011) to issue regulations related to this kind of Title IV-E claiming by tribes.
- *Requires* (as of October 1, 2009) *a state*, under its Title IV-E state plan, *to negotiate in good faith with any tribal entity in the state that seeks an agreement with the state to administer all or part of the Title IV-E program on behalf of the Indian children* who are under the authority of the tribal entity; and similarly requires as of that date a state, under the Chafee Foster Care Independence Program, to negotiate in good faith with any tribal entity in the state that does not receive a direct federal allotment of Chafee funds if that tribal entity seeks an agreement or contract with the state to administer, supervise, or oversee the program on behalf of eligible Indian children under the tribal entity's authority.
- *Require HHS*, in consultation with tribal entities and affected states, *to issue interim final regulations no later than October 7, 2009,* to implement the tribal access provisions; provides further that these regulations must ensure that a transfer of responsibility for the placement and care of a child from a state child welfare agency to a tribal child welfare agency effects neither the child's eligibility for Title IV-E or Medicaid nor the services or payments provided to the child under those parts of the law; (adds that the regulations must ensure this is the case whether the child is transferred to a tribe that is operating its program under an approved Title IV-E plan or under a cooperative agreement with a state).
- Makes October 1,2009 (first day of FY2010) the effective date for most provisions in this section (Section 301). However, requirements in this section related to HHS regulations and certain "rules of construction" were effective with the date of enactment, October 7, 2008.

Section 302. Technical Assistance and Implementation

- *To improve services and permanency outcomes for Indian children and their families, requires HHS to provide technical assistance to tribes and states* regarding tribal administration of child welfare programs and required state-tribe interactions related to serving Indian children; *and implementation grants to tribes that are preparing a Title IV-E plan for approval*, which must not be valued at more than $300,000 and must be used to develop data collection systems, cost allocation plans, agency and tribal court procedures necessary to meet the case review requirements, or any other costs attributable to meeting any other requirement necessary for approval of a Title IV-E plan.

- Stipulates that an implementation grant must only be made to a tribal entity one-time and that as a condition of receiving the grant the tribal entity must agree to repay the total amount of the grant if it does not submit a Title IV-E plan to HHS for approval within 24 months of receiving the funds; (the repayment requirement must be waived by HHS if "circumstances beyond the control" of the tribe prevent its submission of a plan within 24 months).
- *Appropriates $3 million annually* (beginning with FY2009) for this technical assistance and implementation grants and permits HHS to provide this assistance and service either directly or through a grant or contract with a public or private organization knowledgeable in Indian tribal affairs and child welfare.

TITLE IV. IMPROVEMENT OF INCENTIVES FOR ADOPTION

Section 401. Adoption Incentives Program

- *Extends funding authority for Adoption Incentives for five years* (FY2009-FY2013) at $43 million annually; resets the base number of adoptions a state needs to finalize to earn an incentive award (in each of FY2008-FY2012) to the number it finalized in FY2007; raises the incentive amount available for an increase in the number of older child adoptions (from $4,000 to $8,000) and for special needs (younger than age nine) adoptions (from $2,000 to $4,000); continues prior law incentive payment amount of $4,000 for increase in overall number of children adopted from foster care; and ensures that states have 24 months to spend any Adoption Incentive awards earned.
- *Requires that any appropriated Adoption Incentive funds not needed to make awards for an increase in the number of adoptions finalized, must be paid as incentive awards for any state that increases the rate at which children are adopted from foster care;* to earn this award for adoptions finalized in any of FY2008 through FY2012 a state must achieve a "foster child adoption rate" that exceeds its previous "highest ever foster child adoption rate" (beginning with FY2002); the amount of the award is $1,000 times the increased number of adoptions achieved by the state that are attributed to the increased adoption rate.[43]

Section 402. Promotion of Adoption of Children with Special Needs

- Phases in (based on age, length of stay in care and membership in sibling group) *elimination of all income, resource, and family structure tests associated with eligibility for federal Title IV-E adoption assistance*, including such tests that were established as part of the prior law cash aid program, which was known as Aid to Families with Dependent Children (AFDC).
- *Begins the phase in of these revised adoption assistance eligibility criteria in FY2010 for any child who is age 16 or older* at the time his or her adoption assistance

agreement is finalized (in that or a later year) and *gradually lower this age, until FY2018, when the new eligibility rules will apply to a child of any age.*

- Provides that *as of FY2010* the revised adoption assistance eligibility criteria *also applies to any child who has been in care for 60, or more, consecutive months* at the time the adoption assistance agreement is finalized, without regard to the child's age at that time.
- Further stipulates that *as of FY2010* the revised adoption assistance eligibility criteria *also apply to any child who is a* sibling *of a child for whom the new eligibility rules are effective* (whether because of that child's age or length of stay in care), provided that the sibling will be placed in the same adoptive home as the child for whom the new eligibility rules apply.

Section 403. Information on Adoption Tax Credit

- Requires states to provide information to individuals who are adopting a child from foster care, and to those who the state learns are considering such an adoption, of their potential eligibility for the federal adoption tax credit.

Title V. Clarification of Uniform Definition of Child and Other Provisions

[The provisions of this Title are not a part of federal child welfare policy but are changes made to other parts of federal law, including the tax code, to offset costs of increased federal child welfare spending authorized in the previous titles of the enacted bill.]

Section 501. Clarification of Uniform Definition of Child

- Clarifies the uniform definition of qualifying child under the Internal Revenue Code (1) for purposes of the dependency exemption, the child credit, the earned income credit, the dependent care credit, and head of household filing status, to ensure that such an individual is unmarried and is younger than the taxpayer claiming the individual on his/her tax return; (2) for purposes of the child credit, provide that a qualifying child must be the dependent of the taxpayer claiming the credit; and (3) provide that if a taxpayer claiming a qualifying child is not the parent of the individual so claimed, he or she must have an adjusted gross income that is higher than either of the child's parents.

Section 502. Investment of Operating Cash

- In addition to the current investment options, permits the Treasury Department to invest excess operating cash for 90 days in repurchase agreements.

Section 503. No Federal Funding to Unlawfully Present Individuals

- Prohibits any interpretation of the bill that would "alter" any current "prohibitions on Federal payments to individuals who are unlawfully present in the United States."

TITLE VI. EFFECTIVE DATE

Unless a different date is stipulated in the Fostering Connections to Success and Increasing Adoptions Act of 2008, the effective date of the amendments made by the bill is October 7, 2008 (date of its enactment); for any state, permits a time-limited exception to the effective date of any requirement added by this bill (under Title IV-B or Title IV-E) if HHS determines that the state must enact legislation (other than legislation to appropriate funds) to comply with a new requirement.

End Notes

[1] For more information on the these earlier bills, see the subsection, "Origins of the Enacted Bill and Views" later this report.

[2] This report seeks to provide a "plain" language discussion of the bill. However, certain child welfare provisions may be subject to different interpretations. HHS has the authority to implement these provisions and, in doing this, will interpret their meaning.

[3] Section 475(7) of the Social Security Act.

[4] For programs implemented in place as of 2004, see Children's Defense Fund, *State's Subsidized Guardianship Laws at a Glance,* (October 2004).

[5] Congress initially granted child welfare "waiver" authority to HHS (P.L. 103-432, 1994) That authority is currently expired, although some states continued to operate assisted guardianship programs with Title IV-E dollars under previously approved waivers. As of September 30, 2008, the seven state believed to have ongoing demonstration projects (waivers) specifically addressing guardianship were IL, IA, MN, MT, OR, TN, and WI. See James Bell Associates, "Summary of the Title IV-E Child Welfare Waiver Demonstrations," June 2008.

[6] U.S. Department of Health and Human Services, *Synthesis of Findings, Assisted Guardianship: Child Welfare Waiver Demonstrations*, September 2005.

[7] Pew Commission on Children in Foster Care, *Fostering the Future: Safety, Permanence and Well-Being for Children in Foster Care,* May 2004, p. 16; U.S. Government Accountability Office (GAO), *African American Children in Foster Care: Additional HHS Assistance Needed to Hel States Reduce the Proportion in Care,* July 2007, p. 6.

[8] See S.Rept. 110-467 to accompany S. 3038, p. 5. These reasons are similar to those given for the creation of the adoption assistance program in 1980 (P.L. 96-272). See U.S. Congress, Senate, 96th Congress, 1st session, *Adoption Assistance and Child Welfare Amendments of 1979*, S.Rept. 96-336, p. 13 and U.S. Congress, House of Representatives, 96th Congress, 1st session, *Social Services and Child Welfare Amendments of 1979*, H.Rept. 96-136, p. 55-56.

[9] Regarding past legislative actions related to both kinship placement and guardianship under Title IV-E of the Social Security Act, see "Placement with Relatives and Guardianship," in U.S. Congress, Senate, 110th Congress, 2nd session, *Improved Adoption Incentives and Relative Guardianship Support Act of 2008,* S.Rept.

110-467, p. 2-3 [http://frwebgate.access.gpo.gov/cgi-bin/getdoc.cgi?dbname=110_cong_reports&docid=f:sr467.110.pdf].

[10] The enacted bill stipulates that this requirement is subject to exceptions due to family or domestic violence.

[11] The FPLS was created initially for child support enforcement purposes and only non-custodial parents of the child may be identified by name match. However, this information may also help to locate additional relatives. Under prior law states could seek information from the FPLS indirectly (through the state child support agency) rather than directly from HHS. For more information, see U.S. Department of Health and Human Services (HHS), Administration for Children and Families (ACF) Information Memorandum, "Appropriate Referrals, Requests for Location Services, Child Support Applications, and Electronic Interface between Child Welfare and Child Support Enforcement Agencies,"ACYF-CB-IM-07-06 (issued jointly with the Office of Child Support Enforcement), September 7, 2007 [http://www.acf.hhs.gov/programs/cb/laws_policies/policy/im/2007/im0706.htm].

[12] P.L. 110-351 does not specify how the state's "savings" are to be determined and it is not exactly clear how this requirement will be implemented.

[13] For purposes of the Title IV-E adoption assistance program, to qualify as a child with "special needs," the state must have determined that (1) the child cannot or should not be returned to the home of his/her parents; (2) that there is a factor or condition specific to the child (such as the child's age, membership in sibling group, race/ethnicity, medical condition, or a physical, emotional or mental disability) that makes it "reasonable to conclude" that the child will not be adopted without adoption assistance or Medicaid. Further, unless this is not in the child's best interest (e.g. because of significant bonding with foster parents), the state must determine that reasonable, but unsuccessful, efforts to place the child without such assistance have been made. See Section 473(c) of the Social Security Act.

[14] In certain instances, the home from which the child is removed might also be the home of another relative caretaker. Regarding the creation and evolution of the link between eligibility for federal cash welfare assistance, see "Title IV-E Foster Care and Adoption Assistance," in S.Rept. 110-467, p. 2, accompanying S. 3038.

[15] Many observers and stakeholders also believe this link is inappropriate for determining eligibility for federal foster care maintenance payments under Title IV-E. However, consensus on how to change this policy has not been reached. P.L. 110-351 leaves the link between federal foster care eligibility and the rules of the now repealed AFDC program in place, and, by making eligibility for federal foster care maintenance payments a precondition of eligibility for federal kinship guardianship assistance, it indirectly establishes this link with regard to the new kinship guardianship assistance program. For more information on the link, see CRS Report RL34388, *Child Welfare Issues in the 110th Congress*, especially the section "Delink Foster Care and Adoption Assistance from AFDC Rules" and Appendix A, by Emilie Stoltzfus.

[16] These FY2007 award amounts were determined in the last quarter of FY2008. However, available appropriated funds for Adoption Incentives (just over $9 million) were not sufficient to provide the full FY2007 award amounts at that time. HHS indicated its intent to pay a part of the FY2007 awards (roughly 84%) at the end of FY2008 and the remainder (roughly 16%) at the beginning of FY2009. See Adoption Incentive award history table at [http://www.acf.hhs.gov/programs/cb/programs_fund/adopt_incentive_history.htm].

[17] In its FY2009 Budget, the Bush Administration proposed fixing the Adoption Incentive baseline year as FY2007 and increasing award amounts for older and special needs adoptions. The enacted bill (H.R. 6893) adopted these proposals (although it increased the award amounts differently), added others (e.g., incentive for increase in rate) but did not adopt another Administration proposal to limit state use of any earned incentive award funds for finalizing adoption or other permanency options. For more information see CRS Report RL34388, "Adoption Incentives" in *Child Welfare Issues in the 110th Congress*, by Emilie Stoltzfus.

[18] For a description of how to calculate this award see the footnote on this question that is included under "Section: 401: Adoption Incentives Program," near the end of the report.

[19] For more information on the adoption tax credit, see CRS Report RL33633, *Tax Benefits for Families: Adoption,* by Christine Scott.

[20] For more legislative history on this issue see S.Rept. 110-467, p. 4, accompanying S. 3038 and for a comprehensive look at the issue of youth aging out of foster care see CRS Report RL34499, *Youth Transitioning from Foster Care: Background, Federal Programs, and Issues for Congress,* by Adrienne Fernandes.

[21] For additional information regarding living arrangements for older youth, see CRS Report RL34499, *Youth Transitioning from Foster Care: Background, Federal Programs, and Issues for Congress,* by Adrienne Fernandes.

[22] The assertion of safety, permanency, and well-being as primary federal child welfare policy goals was first introduced by the Clinton Administration as part of implementing new funding for family preservation and family support services (authorized in 1993 by P.L. 103-66). Before 2006 then, the sole *statutory* use of the term "well-being" in Title IV-B and Title IV-E — and as distinct from safety, permanence or child "welfare" — was a reference added by that 1993 law as part of the definition of "family support." (Although it is commonly cited as establishing safety, permanency, and *well-being,* as the primary federal child welfare goals,

the Adoption and Safe Families Act (P.L. 105-89, 1997) focused on safety and permanence and did not add the term "well-being" to the statute.) The 109th Congress, however, added "well-being" to Title IV-B and Title IV-E in several places. Notably, P.L. 109-288 (2006) restated the purposes of Title IV-B, subpart 1 to include "promoting the safety, permanence, and well-being of children in foster care and adoptive families." (For early discussion of "well-being" of children and families as a primary federal child welfare policy goal see U.S. Department of Health and Human Services, Administration for Children and Families, ACYF-PI-94-01, January 18, 1994; *Federal Register*, October 4, 1994, p. 50646-50673 and *Federal Register,* November 18, 1996, p. 58657.)

23 This means states are now *statutorily* entitled to, in most cases, a higher federal reimbursement rate for these transportation costs than was permitted by federal guidance issued on this topic in December 2007. That *guidance* clarified that states could claim reimbursement of 50% for these transportation costs. (See U.S. Department of Health and Human Services, Administration for Children and Families, Children's Bureau, *Child Welfare Policy Manual*, Section 8.1B, Question 27.)

24 For many years states have been required to collect "to the extent available and accessible" the health and education record of each child in foster care (as part of each child's case plan) and to take into account the proximity of the school in which a child was enrolled when placing a child in foster care. The 109th Congress enacted two changes that moved Congress in the direction of the 2008 requirements: (1) it removed the modifying phrase "to the extent available and accessible," leaving simply the requirement that states collect the health and education records of children in foster care (P.L.109-239), and (2) it added a new requirement that states must consult with physicians on appropriate care for children in foster care (P.L. 109-288).

25 S.Rept. 110-467, accompanying S. 3038, p. 5.

26 The definitions of "Indian tribe" and "tribal organization" included in P.L. 110-351 are the same as those included in Section 4 of the Indian Self Determination and Education Assistance Act and generally extend the authority to apply for these funds to all federally recognized tribes, as well as, the recognized governing body of those tribes. In addition, a "tribal consortium," including two or more tribes or tribal organizations acting together, may apply for direct federal funding under Title IV-E.

27 Projections in this section are from Congressional Budget Office (CBO), *Preliminary Estimates of Foster Care/Adoption Assistance Draft,* September 15, 2008.

28 In the event of a federal surplus, the bill projects an *increase in that* surplus of $15 million.

29 Over the first five years (FY2009-FY2013), CBO projects that the bill will reduce federal spending by $326 million, plus increase revenues by $123 million, for a reduction in the budget deficit of $449 million (or an increase in any budget surplus by that amount).

30 CBO included any expected effect of the policy permitting states to extend federal eligibility for kinship guardianship assistance to age 21 (for otherwise eligible children leaving foster care for kinship guardianship at age 16 or older) in this estimate.

31 As introduced in May 2008, S. 3038 included provisions primarily related to reauthorizing the Adoption Incentives program, delinking federal adoption assistance from income and related eligibility criteria, and supporting guardianship assistance under Title IV-E. The bill approved by the Senate Finance Committee on September 10, 2008, was the Chairman's Mark version of S. 3038 (brought by Senator Max Baucus), which was offered as a complete substitute to the original bill. The Chairman's Mark largely maintained the provisions included in the introduced bill while adding provisions related to direct tribal access to Title IV-E funding, continued Title IV-E eligibility for youth after age 18, transition planning for youth leaving foster care, a licensing demonstration project, and others . (See S.Rept. 110-467.)

32 H.R. 6307 was based in large part on the provision of Title IV of an earlier bill introduced by Representative McDermott in February 2008, the Invest in KIDS Act (H.R. 5466). The Subcommittee on Income Security and Family Support of the House Ways and Means Committee (Chaired by Representative McDermott) held a hearing in late February 2008 at which it received testimony on the provisions of H.R. 5466. In his prepared opening remarks, Representative Weller noted certain areas of agreement and disagreement with H.R. 5466 and asserted that "we should work together to identify provisions that have bipartisan support so we can get something done this year."

33 *Congressional Record,* September 17, 2008, p. H8317.

34 See CRS Report RL34388, *Child Welfare Issues in the 110th Congress*, by Emilie Stoltzfus.

35 See Statement of Representative McDermott, *Congressional Record*, September 17, 2008, p. H8317 and Senate Finance Committee, News Release, Statement of Senator Max Baucus, Chairman, Finance Committee, "Executive Session to Consider Adoption Incentive, Elder Justice, and Patient Safety Proposals," September 10, 2008.

36 Letter to Honorable Max Baucus, Chairman, Committee on Finance, U.S. Senate, (including the Department's views on the Chairman's amendment in the nature of a substitute for S. 3038, the Improved Adoption Incentives and Relative Guardianship Support Act of 2008), from Mike Leavitt, Secretary, U.S. Department of Health and Human Services (HHS), September 9, 2008; and Letter to Honorable Charles B. Rangel, Chairman, Committee on Ways and Means, U.S. House of Representatives, (including the Department's views on H.R. 6307, the Fostering Connections to Success Act) from Mike Leavitt, Secretary, U.S. Department of

Health and Human Services (HHS), June 24, 2008. Both letters were provided to the Congressional Research Services (CRS) by the U.S. Department of Health and Human Services (HHS).

[37] Ibid. Identical language in both letters.

[38] Beginning with its FY2003 budget the Bush Administration has annually proposed the Child Welfare Program Option. However, no legislative language has been publicly offered to implement the proposal. According to Budget documents, under this option states could elect to receive Title IV-E foster care funds as a lump sum (capped) and, further, to use those funds for the full range of child welfare purposes and in support of any child. For more information see CRS Report RL34388, *Child Welfare Issues in the 110th Congress,* "Appendix A," by Emilie Stoltzfus.

[39] Language quoted is identical in both letters (see cite above). However, the letter regarding H.R. 6307 provides examples of specific provisions HHS believes would weaken provisions for Indian children (alternative background checks for tribes, and broad permission for HHS to waive Title IV-E requirements if requested by the tribe). Those specific provisions were not included in the Chairman's Mark of S. 3038 and, subsequently, were not included in H.R. 6893, as enacted.

[40] Family Connection Grants were not authorized in the Chairman's Mark of S. 3038 and are not discussed in this letter.

[41] See letters of support inserted in the *Congressional Record,* September 17, 2008, H8316-H8317.

[42] The specific definitions of "Indian tribe" and "tribal organization" are as those terms are defined in Section 4 of the Indian Self-Determination and Education Assistance Act.

[43] To calculate the number of adoptions that are attributed to an increase in the adoption rate you must know the state's "foster child adoption rate" in the award year, the number of children in the state's foster care caseload on the last day of the fiscal year just prior to the award year, and the state's "highest ever foster child adoption rate." A state's foster child adoption rate must be determined by dividing the number of foster child adoptions finalized in the state in a given fiscal year by the number of children in that state's foster care caseload on the last day of the previous year. For example, if a state finalizes 150 adoption during FY2008 and on the last day of the previous fiscal year (September 30, 2007) it had 1,500 children in foster care then the state's foster child adoption rate for FY2008 is equal to 10%. That state earns an award for adoptions in FY2008 if this foster child adoption rate (10%) is above its "highest ever foster child adoption rate" — meaning the best foster child adoption rate the state has ever previously achieved beginning with FY2002. For example, if the highest ever foster child adoption rate the state in the example above had achieved before FY2008 was 9%, then for FY2008, the state's adoption incentive award amount based on the rate increase would be calculated as follows: Multiplying that highest ever rate (9%) by the 1,500 children in care on the last day of the fiscal year prior to the award year (September 30, 2007), subtracting this number 135 from the actual foster child adoptions achieved by the state in FY2008 (150) and multiplying the difference (15) by $1,000 for the award amount ($15,000). (The state's "highest ever foster child adoption rate" for FY2009 would be increased to 10%.)

INDEX

T

U

V

W

Y